Armor

DIVINE PROTECTION
IN A DARKENING WORLD

Armor

Divine protection
in a darkening world

KIM B. CLARK

**DESERET
BOOK**

Library of Congress Cataloging-in-Publication Data

Clark, Kim B. (Kim Bryce), 1949-
    Armor : divine protection in a darkening world / Kim B. Clark.
        p. cm.
    Includes bibliographical references and index.
    ISBN-13: 978-1-59038-756-6 (hardback : alk. paper)
    1. Bible. N.T. Ephesians VI, 10–17—Criticism, interpretation, etc.
2. Church of Jesus Christ of Latter-day Saints—Doctrines. 3. Mormon Church—Doctrines. I. Title.
    BS2695.52.C43 2007
    234'.13—dc22   2007010598

Printed in the United States of America
Sheridan Books, Chelsea, MI

10   9   8   7   6   5   4   3   2   1

CONTENTS

INTRODUCTION

This book began with an answer to prayer in the fall of 2002. It was a time of stress and anxiety in my life. Some of that stress came from work, and some came from my trying to be more diligent and faithful in living the gospel. At work, I was beginning my eighth year as dean of the Harvard Business School. I had been at the school as a member of its faculty since 1978. The school, founded in 1908, had long pursued a mission of educating leaders through its MBA program and its work in executive education. When I became dean in 1995, my colleagues and I felt strongly that the school was at an inflection point in its history. The pressures of globalization, new technologies, new forms of enterprise, and shifts in the geopolitical landscape meant that our students would face a world more turbulent, more uncertain, more fraught with risk than ever before.

But it was also a world of more opportunity, where business had become one of the most dynamic forces in society, and where leadership was in great need. If we were to prepare our students for that world, we felt the school needed to change. There was, of course, much about the school—its commitment to leadership, to excellence in teaching, to the creation of deep knowledge with power in practice, to the development of a faculty close to practice, and much more—that should endure. But the school needed to become far more global in its orientation and perspective, and far more skilled and capable in using technology in education. We needed to make entrepreneurship a central part of the school, and we needed to make the critical connection between leadership and values more explicit in our community and in our curriculum.

All of that meant that in 1995 we embarked on a period of substantial change. As the years wore on, it became ever clearer that to accomplish all that we wanted to, we would not only need to hire new faculty members, open up research centers outside the United States, develop greater capabilities in educational technology, and introduce many other changes, but we would need to raise a lot of money. I came to this conclusion reluctantly because I knew what it would mean: a lot of travel, a lot of time away from the work of building the institution day-to-day. But it was clear that we needed to do it, and so we launched the very first capital campaign in the history of the Harvard Business School. Our goal was to raise five hundred million dollars.

What is called in the parlance of the fund-raising world the "quiet phase" of the campaign began in early 2001. My colleagues and I traveled across the country and the world meeting with many of our most successful alumni, trying to find those who wanted to invest in creating the future of the school. Fortunately we found them. By September 2002 we had made enough progress to launch the campaign formally and publicly. Adding the campaign on top of everything else I had to do in the school made my work life complicated, hectic, and intense.

At the same time that the stress and intensity of my work life was ratcheting up, I was very actively involved in the Church, especially in missionary work. In 2000 I had been called to be a member of the stake mission presidency. When stake missions were disbanded in early 2002, I joined the high council and was given responsibility for missionary work in the stake. In fact, it was in the process of working with the missionaries and teaching people about the gospel of Jesus Christ that I had realized I needed to deepen my faith, strengthen my testimony, and be much more spiritually in tune. I had been active in the Church all my life, had served a mission, been married in the temple to the love of my life, raised seven wonderful children, had many great experiences in various callings in the Church, had many sweet spiritual experiences, and felt close to the Lord. But in the months leading up to the fall of 2002 I began to feel that I needed to do more and to do better.

And so I set out to try to live the gospel more fully, to be closer to the Spirit. Partly this involved eliminating things from my life— what I read, what I watched—that detracted from the Spirit. Partly it involved concentrating on things in my life—attending the temple, sharing the gospel—that brought me closer to the Lord.

By the fall of 2002 I felt I had made progress. But I also began to feel strong opposition. It seemed as if at the very moment when I began to feel that deeper faith and stronger testimony that I sought, I experienced feelings of darkness and doubt. At the same time that I experienced great spiritual blessings in sharing the gospel, I felt more barriers, more distractions in talking with people. Although I knew that I was doing what was right and was conscious of the Spirit in my life, there were times when I felt attacked by the forces of evil.

During this time of stress and anxiety I was impressed to seek a blessing at the hands of my home teacher and my stake president.

This provided great comfort and support. I stayed the course I had set.

One night, I awoke from what must have been a nightmare. I felt very anxious, worried, beset with strange thoughts and feelings of dread and darkness. I felt intensely the need for the Lord's help. I rolled out of bed onto my knees and asked Heavenly Father to help me. I prayed for strength, for guidance, for relief. As I got up, a phrase of scripture came into my mind. It was just a fragment, but it was the key I needed: "For we wrestle not against flesh and blood, but against principalities, against powers, against the rulers of the darkness of this world . . ."

I knew the fragment was scripture, but I could not recall its location. Since it was the middle of the night I decided to go back to sleep, but when I got up in the morning the phrase was still in my mind. I went to my computer and searched on the phrase, and there it was: Ephesians 6:12. As I read I realized that this verse was embedded in a longer passage. I had not remembered that the discussion of principalities, powers, and rulers of the darkness of this world came in the context of putting on the whole armor of God. But as I read the whole passage (Ephesians 6:10–17) I knew that this was the answer to my prayers. This was the message the Lord had for me. It told me what was happening to me, and it also told me what I needed to do. As so often happens, the message was not only to comfort, enlighten, and inform but also to assign and command. At that moment, I knew that this was the voice of the Lord saying to me:

> Finally, my brethren, be strong in the Lord, and in the power of his might.
>
> Put on the whole armour of God, that ye may be able to stand against the wiles of the devil.
>
> For we wrestle not against flesh and blood, but against

principalities, against powers, against the rulers of the darkness of this world, against spiritual wickedness in high places.

Wherefore take unto you the whole armour of God, that ye may be able to withstand in the evil day, and having done all, to stand.

Stand therefore, having your loins girt about with truth, and having on the breastplate of righteousness;

And your feet shod with the preparation of the gospel of peace;

Above all, taking the shield of faith, wherewith ye shall be able to quench all the fiery darts of the wicked.

And take the helmet of salvation, and the sword of the Spirit, which is the word of God. (Ephesians 6:10–17)

For me the answer was to go even deeper than I had gone, to do even more. It was to put on the *whole* armor of God.

The importance of that admonition has been driven home to me over the last few years as the prophet of the Lord has used the same scripture on several occasions. In the October 2003 general conference, President Gordon B. Hinckley said:

I believe and testify that it is the mission of this Church to stand as an ensign to the nations and a light to the world. We have had placed upon us a great, all-encompassing mandate from which we cannot shrink nor turn aside. We accept that mandate and are determined to fulfill it, and with the help of God we shall do it.

There are forces all around us that would deter us from that effort. The world is constantly crowding in on us. From all sides we feel the pressure to soften our stance, to give in here a little and there a little.

We must never lose sight of our objective. We must ever keep before us the goal which the Lord has set for us.

He then quoted Ephesians 6:10–12 and concluded: "We must stand firm. We must hold back the world. If we do so, the Almighty will be our strength and our protector, our guide and our revelator" ("An Ensign to the Nations, a Light to the World," *Ensign,* November 2003, 82).

President Hinckley used this scripture again in the First Presidency training session in January 2004. It was referred to again in general conference in April 2004. And so, in many ways, in many places, and at many times, this message has been made clear to me: Put on the whole armor of God.

As I sought to be true to that message, I realized that I needed to spend more time studying and searching the scriptures. And so I resolved to search and study this passage in Ephesians that had become so important to me. It has been a wonderful journey. Somewhere along the way I decided to share with my children what I was learning. Thus was born the idea of writing this book.

The structure of the book follows the structure of the scripture and the way I organized my study of it. Paul first gives the overall theme, then provides some context, and finally lays out specific detail of the armor of God. My study began with context and a search to connect Ephesians 6:10–17 to other scriptures related to it. I then focused on the "putting on" of armor in general, and finally worked on each of the elements of the armor of God as described by Paul. And so, chapter 1 of this book lays out background and provides context and perspective on this passage of scripture. Chapters 2 through 4 look at three examples in the gospel of ways in which we "put on" or "take unto" ourselves something that serves as a protection. Each of these examples involves making a covenant with God.

Covenants are central to understanding the armor of God and to "putting it on."

The rest of the chapters examine each of the elements of the armor of God Paul mentions: the girdle of truth, the breastplate of righteousness, the boots of the gospel of peace, the shield of faith, the helmet of salvation, and the sword of the Spirit—the word of God.

One last thought by way of introduction. A theme that recurs throughout this book is the atonement of Jesus Christ. At a deep and fundamental level, putting on the whole armor of God is about putting on Christ. It is about redemption and the power of the Atonement, about repentance and the baptism of water and of fire. It is about keeping the commandments of God and learning to do his will. It is about becoming new, changed in a mighty way in our hearts. It is about being filled with light—his light. It is about becoming like him. I make no apologies that this theme shows up so often in this book that it might seem repetitive. That is, in fact, the point. As Nephi said in his great farewell discourse long before the Savior walked the earth: "For we labor diligently to write, to persuade our children, and also our brethren, to believe in Christ. . . . And we talk of Christ, we rejoice in Christ, we preach of Christ, we prophesy of Christ, and we write according to our prophecies, that our children may know to what source they may look for a remission of their sins" (2 Nephi 25:23, 26).

My prayer is that we might know to look to him who has all power over all things for personal strength and protection and power in our wrestle "against principalities, against powers, against the rulers of the darkness of this world." I have come to know through my own experience over many years that Paul's introduction to the armor of God in verse 10 of Ephesians chapter 6 is not only an admonition but also a great and true promise: *Finally, my brethren, be strong in the Lord, and in the power of his might.*

CHAPTER 1

PUT ON THE WHOLE ARMOR OF GOD

The scriptures have the power to speak to us in ways that teach us and help us beyond our current understanding. Because they are the word of the Lord they can speak to us in new ways that are just what we need for the challenges that face us now. This is true even when the scriptures we read are familiar. We may have read them many times, but when guided by the Spirit we can find fresh insight that inspires and guides. Such was the case with Ephesians chapter 6 when I set out to search and study Paul's image of the armor of God.

The keyword here is *search*. When I began the process of understanding the Lord's message to me about putting on the armor of God, I decided to follow the counsel of the Lord and his prophets and really search the scriptures. As the Lord said to his disciples, "Search the scriptures; for in them ye think ye have eternal life: and they are they which testify of me" (John 5:39).

And so I searched and studied and prayed, and in the process I discovered the wonderful, inspired nature of Ephesians 6:10–17. I have come to love these words because they are exactly what the Lord promised: the words of eternal life. In the chapters that follow I have tried to capture what I have learned. Before we get there, however, some context and general observations about this scriptural passage may be helpful. In this chapter I want to look at three ideas that serve as a framework for Paul's message to the Ephesians (and to us): finding strength in the Lord, spiritual armor, and standing for truth and righteousness.

Finding Strength in the Lord

Paul's admonition to put on the armor of God comes at the end of his letter to the Ephesians. It is the culmination of his last exhortation and it begins with a verse that summarizes the whole point. Although putting on the armor of God is the dominant image of this scripture, that is not where Paul begins. This is what he says in verse 10: "Finally, my brethren, be strong in the Lord, and in the power of his might" (Ephesians 6:10). Paul signals here that what follows is about not trusting in the arm of flesh or our own understanding. Our trust is to be in the Lord, and in his power.

The Saints of Ephesus in Paul's day faced serious challenges, and so do we. They were building the kingdom of God in a difficult and dangerous world, and so are we. They were, in that sense, pioneers, and so are we. Indeed, building the kingdom takes pioneers in every time and every place. Consider, for example, the challenges facing my Great-Great-Grandfather Edward Bunker. Having joined the Church in 1842, Edward Bunker crossed the plains five times in the next thirteen years. He marched with the Mormon Battalion from Iowa to California. He returned from there to Iowa to bring his wife and child to Utah. Later Brigham Young called him on a mission to

Great Britain and, during his return, to lead a handcart company from Iowa to the Salt Lake Valley.

His work was just beginning. After all that walking and crossing, the prophet called again to send Edward Bunker and his family to southern Utah, where he became the second bishop of the Santa Clara ward. He and his loved ones experienced the floods and scorching sun of that region, along with the frustration of trying to grow cotton and other crops in that desert country. It was a hard, hard thing to do. But Edward Bunker and thousands like him had great faith in the Lord. They built wonderful communities in the face of daunting obstacles. And they did it because they were "strong in the Lord, and in the power of his might."

In an important sense, we are all pioneers. Or at least we have the chance to be pioneers, to labor on the very frontier of the Lord's work. Indeed, Paul's call to us to put on the armor of God is a call to work at the frontier, where the Lord works. No matter where we live, no matter what our circumstances, there is a frontier where the Lord and his servants are building out the kingdom of God.

In part, the frontier is within us and represents the parts of our lives that need changing and improving. In part, the frontier is in our families, where our spouses and children, our parents and siblings, need our love and example. In part, the frontier is in our wards and branches, where our brothers and sisters in the gospel need our help and support. In part, the frontier is in our communities, where together with the missionaries we proclaim the gospel and bring souls unto Christ. In all of these places we are pioneers, called to do the Lord's work at the frontier.

At the frontier we cannot do what must be done without the "power of his might." There are some parts of the kingdom that are by now fully settled where we can get by on our own understanding. Some of us have been shown or taught so well, or had so much experience, or been involved in so many activities that we can serve in callings and do what seems to others a perfectly acceptable job without diligently seeking help from the Lord. But just "getting by" in the settled parts of the kingdom is not what the Lord has in mind for us.

We have been called to *build* the kingdom by magnifying our callings in the Church. To do that, we must work at the frontier, where the Lord works. It is true that we may draw on examples of others and on our own talents and experience. But all of that is insufficient. The work is too hard, the challenges too great for us to succeed working alone. This is, after all, the Lord's work. And in that work we can join with him and receive the "power of his might." With that power, the Lord magnifies our capacity to do his work.

Spiritual Armor

The battle for which Paul seeks to prepare us in Ephesians 6 is not a battle with flesh and blood, but a spiritual battle with the forces of evil. We need therefore to don spiritual armor. What is the nature of that armor?

We can gain some general insight from Paul's use of the image of armor in several places in his writings. Perhaps the most evocative is in his letter to the Romans: "The night is far spent, the day is at hand: let us therefore cast off the works of darkness, and let us put on the armour of light. Let us walk honestly, as in the day; not in rioting and drunkenness, not in chambering and wantonness, not in strife and envying. But put ye on the Lord Jesus Christ" (Romans 13:12–14).

The battle with evil is about casting off the works of darkness and putting on the armor of light. Clearly, this armor is not about what is on the outside, but about what is inside of us, in our hearts. And what is there, if we put it on, is light. This immediately calls to mind the Savior's words in the Sermon on the Mount: "Ye are the light of the world. A city that is set on an hill cannot be hid. Neither do men light a candle, and put it under a bushel, but on a candlestick; and it giveth light unto all that are in the house. Let your light so shine before men, that they may see your good works, and glorify your Father which is in heaven" (Matthew 5:14–16).

There is a relationship here between what we do (our good works) and what we are (the light within). To the Romans Paul said that if we are to cast off the works of darkness we must walk honestly, as in the day. Here the Savior makes clear that we dispel darkness by the light that shines through our good works. This light, the light that is like armor, comes from the Savior himself. When he appeared to the Nephites following his resurrection, he said: "Therefore, hold up your light that it may shine unto the world. Behold I am the light which ye shall hold up—that which ye have seen me do" (3 Nephi 18:24).

If we are focused on doing the Lord's work, he promises us that we will be filled with light—his light: "And if your eye be single to my glory, your whole bodies shall be filled with light, and there shall be no darkness in you; and that body which is filled with light comprehendeth all things" (D&C 88:67; see also Matthew 6:22).

To put on the armor of light is to put on Christ. It is to take upon ourselves his name, to make what he taught and did a reality in our lives. It is to become like him.

Standing for Truth and Righteousness

The purpose of putting on the whole armor of God is, in Paul's words, "that ye may be able to stand against the wiles of the devil . . . that ye may be able to withstand in the evil day, and having done all, to stand" (Ephesians 6:11, 13). Paul's use of the word *stand* to describe success in the battle with evil evokes images of resistance and endurance in the face of attack. To stand is to not fall, to not succumb, to not flee. Certainly with the image of war in mind, this is a natural use of the word. But there is another sense of the word, a sense that carries with it an implication of active engagement in the spiritual battle.

In a court of law, for example, judges ask witnesses to "take the stand," where they will offer testimony. When someone "stands" for a cause, or a principle, it is in that sense—they are prepared to take the stand and be a witness for it. But this is not only in what they are prepared to say, but also in what they are prepared to do. To stand for truth and righteousness, for example, is to bear witness of the truth, to walk in the path of righteousness. Success in the battle against evil, therefore, requires that we *stand fast* (not fall, not run away) and that we *stand up* for what is right (bear witness, live according to true principles).

The idea that to "stand" is to be a witness, to offer testimony through word and action, connects the battle against evil to standards. The word *standard* has several meanings, but two are of particular interest here. The first comes from the Middle English word *estandard* (rallying place) and refers to a flag or banner or ensign of a nation, a chief of state, or an army. In the second meaning, a standard is an acknowledged measure of comparison for establishing value, or a recognized model of excellence (see http://dictionary.reference.com/ search?q=standard). Both meanings are salient in Paul's "wrestle . . . against the rulers of the darkness of this world."

The forces of darkness are often very subtle. They come in shades of grey and may even masquerade as something good and pleasant. Nephi described the works of darkness in the last days in just this way: "And there shall also be many which shall say: Eat, drink, and be merry; nevertheless, fear God—he will justify in committing a little sin; . . . And others will he pacify, and lull them away into carnal security, . . . [and] others he flattereth away, and telleth them there is no hell . . . and thus he whispereth in their ears, until he grasps them with his awful chains, from whence there is no deliverance" (2 Nephi 28:8, 21–22).

It is in just such a circumstance that we need standards, in both senses. We need a rallying point, an ensign to which we look for direction, and around which we can gather. And we need models of excellence, established benchmarks for righteous living, against which we can judge our course of action.

We need standards not only in principle but also in action. We need to be able to see the principles in action in the lives of the Lord's servants—in fact, in our lives. Thus, to "stand," in this sense, is to live according to the standards of the gospel. Having put on the whole armor of God, to stand is in fact to be a standard to which others may look and rally in the battle against evil.

Such standing is not to be done in isolation or without divine support. We are, of course, individually accountable for what we do. But this idea of being a light to the world, of standing for truth and righteousness, is about the Latter-day Saints standing together. Indeed, the commandment of the Lord is for those who would follow him to become members of the Lord's church and "stand in holy places." Consider the Lord's description of his disciples in the last days:

> And when the times of the Gentiles is come in, a light
> shall break forth among them that sit in darkness, and it
> shall be the fulness of my gospel; but they receive it not; for
> they perceive not the light, and they turn their hearts from
> me because of the precepts of men. . . . But my disciples shall
> stand in holy places, and shall not be moved; but among the

wicked, men shall lift up their voices and curse God and die. (D&C 45:28–29, 32)

Where are these holy places? And what does it mean to "stand" in them? From the very beginning the Lord has designated some locations on the earth as holy. For example, when Moses talked with the Lord on Mount Sinai, the Lord said to Moses, "put off thy shoes from off thy feet, for the place whereon thou standest is holy ground" (Exodus 3:5). Similar designations have been made in our era (see D&C 115:7, for example).

In addition to natural places designated by the Lord, some places we build become holy when the Lord's servants dedicate them to the Lord under the authority of the priesthood. A temple is a holy place where the space is dedicated to the Lord, and it becomes his house where he can dwell. Our chapels are dedicated to the Lord and set apart for worship services and for sacred ordinances. Thus, chapels, too, are holy places. But we can also make our homes holy places. We can dedicate them with the authority of the priesthood to be sacred places, and we can live in such a way that the Spirit of the Lord dwells there.

Righteous homes, chapels, and temples are holy places, and define where the Lord's disciples may "stand." In a sense, they also define milestones in the process of building the kingdom of God. The Lord's work is about pushing out the frontiers of righteousness, first in homes, then in chapels, and then in temples. And the command of the Lord is that the Latter-day Saints are to "Arise and shine forth, that thy light may be a standard for the nations; and that the gathering together upon the land of Zion, and upon her stakes, may be for a defense, and for a refuge from the storm, and from wrath when it shall be poured out without mixture upon the whole earth" (D&C 115:5–6).

This is the work of the Restoration, to establish the kingdom of God on the earth. We build the kingdom one soul, one home, one branch, one ward, and one stake at a time. In so doing, we gather the sheep of the Good Shepherd—the Saints of the latter days—in preparation for the day when he will come again. And when the Saints gather, the Lord creates holy places where the Saints may stand. The word *stand* has exactly the meaning here that Paul gives to it in Ephesians 6: to stand firm and fast, to not be moved, to not fall, to stand as a witness, and to be a standard to the world.

CHAPTER 2

TAKING ON THE NAME OF CHRIST

In Ephesians 6:10–17 Paul teaches us that to succeed in the battle against the forces of evil we must "be strong in the Lord, and in the power of his might." That is why he counsels us to arm ourselves and protect ourselves by "putting on" or "taking unto" ourselves the spiritual armor of God. When I began my study of this scripture, one of the first impressions I had was the deep connection between "putting on" the armor of God and the process of making covenants with the Lord.

As I reflected on the ordinances and covenants associated with baptism, the priesthood, and the temple, I realized that in making those covenants we "put on" or "take on" something heavenly to help us in our earthly journey. In the oath and covenant of the priesthood we take on the power and authority to act in the name of God. In the temple we take on the endowment. Each covenant we make in these ordinances is an essential part of the "whole armour of God."

But it all begins with baptism, in which we take on the name of Christ.

Paul himself made explicit the relationship between the armor of God and the name of Christ in his letter to the Romans when he said, "Let us . . . cast off the works of darkness, and let us put on the armour of light. . . . Put ye on the Lord Jesus Christ" (Romans 13:12, 14). Christ is the source of the light and power and strength we need to do battle with the forces of evil. How does one get access to that light and that power? The starting point is baptism.

When we enter the waters of baptism we make a covenant with the Lord to keep his commandments, to take upon ourselves the name of Christ, and to be a witness for him at all times, in all things, and in all places (see Mosiah 18:8–11). The symbolism of the ordinance—the old person buried in the water and the new person rising out of the water—is the outward, physical manifestation of an inner, spiritual reality.

That new inner reality begins before baptism with our commitment to make the covenant and live the gospel. Through the process of repentance we prepare ourselves to enter the waters of baptism and receive a remission of our sins, as the Lord made clear in Section 20 of the Doctrine and Covenants:

> *And again, by way of commandment to the church concerning the manner of baptism*—All those who humble themselves before God, and desire to be baptized, and come forth with broken hearts and contrite spirits, and witness before the church that they have truly repented of all their sins, and are willing to take upon them the name of Jesus Christ, having a determination to serve him to the end, and truly manifest by their works that they have received of the Spirit of

Christ unto the remission of their sins, shall be received by baptism into his church. (D&C 20:37)

The covenant we make at baptism is a living covenant. It has force and power in our lives every day. Each week we renew that covenant when we partake of the sacrament. Each Sunday, all over the world, members of the Church meet together in sacrament meeting. Amidst the hymns and the spoken word, the central part of the meeting is the administration of the sacrament. In the words of the sacramental prayer, members of the Church reaffirm their willingness to take upon themselves the name of Christ, keep his commandments, and always remember him (see D&C 20:77).

When I was a teenager I participated in this ordinance hundreds of times. On my mission in Germany I blessed the sacrament in German many, many times. Over the ensuing years I have blessed the sacrament with my sons and passed it on many occasions. But there is one experience with passing the sacrament that has a special place in my memory. It happened many years ago in the chapel in Weston, Massachusetts, in a special meeting called by the president of the Boston Stake. At the time I was serving on the high council. The president asked members of the high council to officiate in blessing and passing the sacrament to the members assembled.

Though I had passed the sacrament literally hundreds of times, this experience was different. From the beginning of the sacramental prayer I felt a powerful witness of the Spirit that I was engaged in an ordinance with a holy, sacred purpose. As we administered the emblems of the Lord's sacrifice and suffering to the members of the Church, a great sense of responsibility came over me. I knew deep in my heart and soul that we were acting on behalf of the Lord, doing what he would do if he were there. There was power in that chapel, the power of the atonement of Jesus Christ to redeem, to sanctify, to heal, to change the hearts of the children of God. I felt it that day, and I have felt it many, many times since then. As King Benjamin taught his people long ago, it is this power to change that is at the heart of what it means to take upon oneself the name of Jesus Christ.

We have in the record of Mosiah in the Book of Mormon one of the great sermons in all of scripture on the process of taking on the name of Christ. King Benjamin, a righteous prophet-king to the Nephites, gathered together his people to deliver to them a kind of valedictory address at the end of his reign and his life. After teaching the people about service to God and each other, and after announcing his son Mosiah as their new king, Benjamin focused on the Savior and His atonement. A good part of what he said about the Savior was given to him by an angel of the Lord who declared "glad tidings of great joy. . . . The time cometh, and is not far distant, that with power, the Lord Omnipotent . . . shall come down from heaven. . . . And he shall be called Jesus Christ, the Son of God" (Mosiah 3:3, 5, 8).

Those who gathered at the temple to hear King Benjamin received his words with great faith. Having been taught the doctrine of the Atonement, they sought mercy at the hands of the Lord, felt the Spirit of the Lord come upon them, and declared: "We believe all the words which thou has spoken . . . because of the Spirit of the Lord Omnipotent, which has wrought a mighty change in us, or in our hearts, that we have no more disposition to do evil, but to do good continually. . . . And we are willing to enter into a covenant with our God to do his will, and to be obedient to his commandments in all things" (Mosiah 5:2, 5).

Following this declaration of his people, Benjamin described to them the meaning and significance of what they had done. Because we make the same covenant at baptism, his words describe the meaning and significance of what we do as well: "And now, because of the covenant which ye have made ye shall be called the children of Christ, his sons and daughters; for behold this day he hath spiritually begotten you; for ye say that your hearts are changed through faith on his name; therefore, ye are born of him and have become his sons and daughters" (Mosiah 5:7).

The central message of this verse is found in the phrase: "your hearts are changed through faith on his name." This verse is a chiasm and that phrase is at its center. By rearranging the verse we can see this central role of the change of heart, and the name of Christ:

Ye shall be called the children of Christ, his sons and daughters (a)
  This day he hath spiritually begotten you (b)
    Ye say that your hearts are changed through faith on his name (c)
  Therefore, ye are born of him (b)
And have become his sons and daughters (a)

In this simple structure King Benjamin captures the meaning of taking upon us the name of Christ. That meaning has two parts. It is in the first instance a spiritual development process in which our hearts are changed. The people of King Benjamin described this as "a mighty change in us, or in our hearts," wrought by the Spirit. It is so profound and so powerful a change that the Lord and his prophets have likened it to being born anew. This change comes about through the second part of the central message: faith on the name of Christ.

It follows naturally that in taking upon ourselves the name of Christ we would exercise faith in the Savior. But King Benjamin wanted his people (and us) to see the full meaning behind this simple phrase. He goes on in his address to explain that the name of Christ is unique in all the world: "There is no other name given whereby salvation cometh." And then he connects the covenants we make at baptism and that we renew each week in sacrament meeting to our eternal salvation and exaltation:

> Therefore, I would that ye should take upon you the name of Christ. . . . And it shall come to pass that whosoever doeth this shall be found at the right hand of God, for he shall know the name by which he is called; for he shall be called by the name of Christ. . . . I say unto you, I would that ye should remember to retain the name written always in your hearts, that ye are not found on the left hand of God, but that ye hear and know the voice by which ye shall be called, and also, the name by which he shall call you. (Mosiah 5: 8–9, 12)

To take upon us the name of Christ is to hear the voice of the Lord in our lives today. It is to know that voice, and thus to know the name by which we shall be called, when the time comes for us to be called up to be at the right hand of God.

Here, then, are two interrelated aspects of taking on us the name of Christ: (1) the mighty change of heart, and (2) hearing the voice and knowing the name of the Lord.

A Mighty Change of Heart

When the prophets describe the change that occurs in those who take upon them the name of Christ, they use the image of the heart. This image captures something deep and profound in our very nature. Physically, the heart pumps blood throughout the body, bringing life-giving oxygen and nutrients to every part of us. That constant, rhythmic action sends the protection of our immune system to wherever it is needed and removes substances that would do us harm. When something happens to us that requires an active response from us—danger, love, misfortune, speaking in public—the heart beats faster, responding to the body's need for energy. It is there in the quiet times, even when we are asleep. It is there when we are active, giving us whatever we need. We can feel it, and we can sometimes hear it, beating away, giving us life.

For all of these reasons, man has used the image of the heart to capture what is at the very core of our emotional and spiritual life. When we speak of our heart in this way, we speak of the personal attributes that animate our lives—our innermost desires, our deepest drives, our courage, our empathy, our resilience, our attitudes, our deepest emotional commitments, our capacity for love. Like the physical heart that delivers life-giving blood to every part of us, the metaphorical heart delivers life-giving motivation and emotional energy and commitment to what we are and what we do. It is in this sense that the Lord and his prophets speak of the heart in the scriptures. And it is this heart that changes in a mighty way when we take upon us the name of Christ.

But why do our hearts need to change? And what is the nature of that change? King Benjamin gives us the answer:

> For the natural man is an enemy to God, and has been from the fall of Adam, and will be, forever and ever, unless he yields to the enticings of the Holy Spirit, and putteth off the natural man and becometh a saint through the atonement of Christ the Lord, and becometh as a child, submissive, meek, humble, patient, full of love, willing to submit to all things which the Lord seeth fit to inflict upon him, even as a child doth submit to his father. (Mosiah 3:19)

Our hearts need to change because, through the weakness of the flesh and our disobedience, we are far from God. Indeed, when we succumb to the "wiles of the devil" and follow the ways of sin and wickedness we become "carnal, sensual, and devilish" (Moses 5:13). Alma describes this state of affairs in plain language. Speaking to his wayward son, Corianton, he says: "And now, my son, all men that are in a state of nature, or I would say, in a carnal state, are in the gall of bitterness and in the bonds of iniquity; they are without God in the world, and they have gone contrary to the nature of God; therefore, they are in a state contrary to the nature of happiness" (Alma 41:11).

This is what King Benjamin meant when he said that the natural man, the man who lives "without God in the world," is an enemy to God. But we do not start out that way, and we do not have to be that way at all. In a revelation given to the Prophet Joseph Smith in 1833, the Lord said: "Every spirit of man was innocent in the beginning; and God having redeemed man from the fall, men became again, in their infant state, innocent before God. And that wicked one cometh and taketh away light and truth, through disobedience, from the children of men, and because of the tradition of their fathers" (D&C 93:38–39).

Though we begin life innocent before God and are "alive in Christ," as the prophets have taught, we are all subject to temptation, we are all taught the philosophies of men, and we all fall short. We are all sinners. The "natural man" within us affects us all. For some it is more, and for some it is less, but we all have to "put off the natural man" if we are to take upon us the name of Christ.

It seems logical that we have to take something off (the natural man) before we can put something on (the name of Christ). The first step in that process is to "yield to the enticings of the Holy Spirit" and repent of our sins. Repentance is the Lord's great personal development process. To begin the process of repentance is to begin to change our hearts. When we repent, we put ourselves—literally, our self, our soul—in the Lord's hands and make his atonement a reality in our lives.

– There are many wonderful discussions of the process of repentance available, and I will not attempt to do them all justice here. But I hope it will be helpful to summarize briefly what the process of repentance involves.

1. It begins with what Paul calls "godly sorrow" (2 Corinthians 7:9–11).

For us to change there has to be recognition that what we have done (or not done) is wrong. If we follow the "enticings of the Holy Spirit," that feeling of guilt, of knowing that we have violated the commandments of God, can lead to real remorse. While at the time the feelings of guilt and recognition of wrongdoing may not seem like "enticings," they surely are. Without the Spirit, the pain of guilt is just plain old pain and suffering. When the Spirit is involved, however, those feelings are tinged with hope. I do not mean that the gravity of the situation is in any way diminished. Nor do I mean that the pain is any less. I mean only that as the pains of guilt and recognition lead to remorse, the Spirit kindles within us a desire to change, to put things right. In this way, what is painful and full of sorrow becomes godly.

2. One who feels godly sorrow and desires to repent must "confess and forsake" (see D&C 58:43).

Confession is, indeed, good for the soul. And so is forsaking the sin. Admission of guilt must come first to oneself. This is a natural part of godly sorrow and the pain of recognition. The tinge of hope in that pain and sorrow is the Spirit teaching us that there is forgiveness down the path if we will abandon the sin and seek mercy at the Lord's hand. To walk that path we must act on that hope and forsake the sin. And we must confess, first and always to the Lord, and then in very serious cases to the bishop if the sin is such that

Church discipline may be required. We may also need to confess to others if we have injured them in some way in committing sin. Confession involves a full and total recounting of the sin, without excuse or rationalization. But it also involves asking for forgiveness. In this way we acknowledge our dependence on the Savior's power to redeem us, and we commit to do what is necessary to receive his forgiveness.

3. *The path of repentance requires, where possible, restitution.*

The repentant soul who desires to change must put things right. Confessing and forsaking the sin are part of that. But there also must be efforts to restore that which was taken or destroyed in committing sin. In this we follow the example of the sons of Mosiah, who were called to repentance by an angel of the Lord, and afterward traveled the country "zealously striving to repair all the injuries which they had done to the church, confessing all their sins" (Mosiah 27:35).

Sometimes restitution is straightforward. If we lie, we can set the record straight. If we steal something, we can return it. But sometimes restitution is not straightforward, and sometimes full restitution is not possible. Even in these cases, repentant souls will "strive to repair all the injuries" they have caused, perhaps with what Elder Neal A. Maxwell has called "compensatory restitution" through subsequent righteousness ("Repentance," *Ensign,* November 1991, 31).

4. *Obedience to the commandments is an essential part of repentance.*

The prophets have counseled us to "bring forth . . . fruits meet for repentance" (Matthew 3:8; Alma 13:13), and the Savior has said, "By their fruits ye shall know them" (Matthew 7:20). We cannot repent of our sins if we are not willing to keep the commandments of the Lord. President Spencer W. Kimball made this clear when he described this last element of the repentance process: "This step requires no holding back. If one neglects his tithing, misses his meetings, breaks the Sabbath, or fails in his prayers and other responsibilities, he is not completely repentant. The Lord knows, as do we, the degree of full and sufficient compliance we make with these fundamental aspects of the law of repentance, which is really God's law of progress and fulfillment" ("The Gospel of Repentance," *Ensign,* October 1982, 5).

Those are the central elements of the process of repentance. Those who pursue them with "full purpose of heart" will find pain and sorrow giving way to a growing sense of peace and joy (see 2 Nephi 31:13; 3 Nephi 10:6). It is not an easy road to walk, but the Lord's promises are real. In the preface to the Doctrine and Covenants, the Lord said: "For I the Lord cannot look upon sin with the least degree of allowance; Nevertheless, he that repents and does the commandments of the Lord shall be forgiven" (D&C 1:31–32). When we repent, the Lord blesses us with the sweet, healing power of forgiveness. We feel once again the companionship of the Holy Ghost and have the blessings of the Spirit in our lives.

I know this is true because of my own experience. Not long ago in a temple recommend interview my stake president asked me, "How do you know that you have been forgiven of your sins?" After a moment of reflection, I responded, "Because I have felt the power of the Spirit in my life and have a witness of the Holy Ghost that it is true."

But this is not the end of the road, only the beginning. Repentance is not a transaction—I do this, the Lord does that—but rather a development process. Though the elements of repentance laid out above may apply to a specific sin, what the Lord wants is our heart, all of us. Thus, the process of repentance can work further to help change our innermost desires, what we love most, that for which we yearn. The Lord's objective is a spiritual birth, the creation of a new person, through the power of the Atonement.

As we repent, we complete the process of putting off the natural man by losing "the disposition to do evil." Here again the experience of those who listened to King Benjamin's great discourse is instructive: "And they all cried with one voice, saying: Yea, we believe all the words which thou hast spoken unto us; and also, we know of their surety and truth, because of the Spirit of the Lord Omnipotent, which has wrought a mighty change in us, or in our hearts, that we have no more disposition to do evil, but to do good continually" (Mosiah 5:2).

Losing the disposition to do evil is a gift of the Spirit. It comes after much work on our part. It comes after fasting and prayer, after full repentance of sin and sustained obedience to the commandments of the Lord. It comes as we keep the covenants we make. Sometimes it comes with great speed and power (think of Alma the Younger and his miraculous conversion); sometimes it comes only after a long search. But it comes. If we are repentant, humble disciples of Christ, the Spirit of the Lord will work a mighty change in our hearts and we will lose the disposition to do evil.

But the Lord is not finished with us, even then. Though we have put off the natural man, we must still become "saint[s] through the atonement of Christ the Lord" (Mosiah 3:19). We must not only lose the disposition to do evil but develop the attributes of a true follower of Jesus Christ. And we must learn to do the will of the Father in all things. This truly requires a change of heart. And it is a mighty change indeed. But it is a change the Savior can help us make.

Through the Atonement, the Savior has power over all things. He will not force us to change, but he has the power to change us if we choose that path. We do that when we repent of our sins and plead for his mercy and forgiveness. We do that when we seek to become like him. And we do that when we commit to subject our own will to the will of the Father.

In this, Christ is the great exemplar. He who said, "I came down from heaven, not to do mine own will, but the will of him that sent me" (John 6:38), who in the hour of supreme agony and suffering said, "not my will, but thine, be done" (Luke 22:42)—he showed us the way. We, too, must sacrifice our own will, and come to God prepared to "submit to all things which the Lord seeth fit to inflict upon [us], even as a child doth submit to his father." When we bring that sacrifice to the Lord, the sacrifice of a broken heart and a contrite spirit, he blesses us with many opportunities to experience the great refining fire of the Holy Ghost. And through the power of the Atonement, we begin to develop the attributes that King Benjamin describes: meekness, humility, charity, and patience. In short, we become Latter-day Saints.

Knowing the Name and Hearing the Voice of the Lord

To take on the name of Christ is to experience a mighty change of heart—a change in our innermost desires, our deepest drives, and our emotional commitments. In this change our motivation becomes to seek after every good thing and to do the will of the Lord. Doing the will of the Lord comes in many forms, but its hallmark is a commitment to follow Jesus Christ wherever he may call us to go. Which brings us to the second dimension of taking on the name of Christ: hearing the Lord's voice in our lives.

What does it mean to hear the voice of the Lord? The Savior used the parable of the sheep and the shepherd to help us answer that question:

He that entereth not by the door into the sheepfold, but climbeth up some other way, the same is a thief and a robber.

But he that entereth in by the door is the shepherd of the sheep. To him the porter openeth; and the sheep hear his voice: and he calleth his own sheep by name, and leadeth them out. And when he putteth forth his own sheep, he goeth before them, and the sheep follow him: for they know his voice. . . . I am the door: by me if any man enter in, he shall be saved, and shall go in and out, and find pasture. (John 10:1–4, 9)

The words of the parable underscore the importance of hearing the voice of the Lord. When he calls and we hear him, we receive guidance and direction so that we can follow him. The Lord's invitation to "come follow me," or to "come unto me," requires that we hear his voice and heed his guidance and direction. There is more here than the working of the auditory nerve. We must not only perceive the voice of the Lord but act on it. To hear the voice of the Lord is to follow him. I believe one of the great unfolding dramas in our lives is the process of recognizing the Lord's voice and acting on it to follow him.

His voice is a voice we know. We heard it before we came to this earth, when we lived with our Heavenly Father. We were all there when our Heavenly Father laid out his great plan of happiness for us. We were there when Heavenly Father explained the need for a Savior and asked, "Whom shall I send?" And we heard Jesus say, "Here am I, send me." Not only did we hear his voice, we chose to follow him. Now, here on earth, we must also hear his voice and follow him.

The Lord speaks to us in many, many ways. We may hear his voice through prayer and personal revelation. Heavenly Father gave us our agency to choose right from wrong, but he also blesses us with the capacity to talk to him and to receive answers to our prayers. We can learn through the Spirit what the Lord wants us to do, and we can receive the guidance and direction we need to follow him. To hear the Lord's voice, we must only ask and listen.

I learned this principle one day on my mission. I had been in Germany for a few weeks and had found the work very challenging. Though I had experienced opposition before, this was the first time in my life that I had been thrown out of houses and scorned and ridiculed for what I believed. I was feeling discouraged and confused. One morning I knelt by the side of my bed and asked my Heavenly Father for help. As I prayed, three words came into my mind so clearly and distinctly that I thought someone had spoken them: "Believe in God." I immediately looked up and saw my companion standing by the counter fixing breakfast. I asked him, "Is there a scripture that says, 'Believe in God'?" He replied in a very offhand way, "Oh yeah, Mosiah 4:9." I opened the Book of Mormon and read Mosiah 4:9 and many other verses, and then I knew the message the Lord had for me: Believe in God, trust in him, he has all power and all wisdom, and he is in charge. I heard the Lord's voice that day and I have never forgotten the experience, or the message.

This experience shows that we may also hear the Lord's voice through reading the scriptures. In the Bible, the Book of Mormon, and the Doctrine and Covenants we have a record of the Lord's voice in history. We have it in the revelations and prophecies in the Old Testament. We have his words as heard by those who walked with him in his mortal ministry. We have his words in the Book of Mormon when he appeared to the ancient people in the Americas. We have his words in modern times when he spoke to the Prophet Joseph Smith. But there is more than this. If we read the scriptures with the Spirit, we can hear the Lord's voice today. That is what happened to me in Germany; it is what happened that morning when I read Ephesians 6:10–17 about the armor of God; and it is what the Lord had in mind when he said:

These words are not of men nor of man, but of me; wherefore, you shall testify they are of me and not of man; For it is my voice which speaketh them unto you; for they are given by my Spirit unto you, and by my power you can read them one to another; and save it were by my power you could not have them; Wherefore, you can testify that you have heard my voice, and know my words. (D&C 18:34–36)

I know this promise is true. When we read the scriptures with the Spirit, we can hear the voice of the Lord. The effect on us will be as though the Lord himself were standing next to us speaking to us with his own voice. And we will know what it is the Lord would have us hear. We will, in very fact, hear the voice of the Lord.

The words of the scriptures are often the words of the Lord's prophets in times past. But the Lord also speaks to us through living prophets. In The Church of Jesus Christ of Latter-day Saints we proclaim to the entire world that the fulness of the gospel of Jesus Christ, once lost from the earth, has been restored. And one of the great blessings of the Restoration is the presence on the earth of living prophets. When Joseph Smith, a young boy of fourteen, walked into the sacred grove in 1820, the heavens opened, and God the Father and his Son Jesus Christ ushered in this last dispensation. The heavens have remained open to this day, and will remain open. I know that the Lord speaks to us through the prophets who walk the earth today. The Lord has told us that they speak for him. Speaking of the Prophet Joseph Smith, the Lord said: "Thou shalt give heed unto all his words and commandments which he shall give unto you as he receiveth them, walking in all holiness before me; for his word ye shall receive, as if from mine own mouth, in all patience and faith" (D&C 21:4–5).

When the prophet of God counsels us to avoid unnecessary debt, when he advises us to be better neighbors, when he asks us to give up some of our leisure activities and spend more time in the temple, when he encourages us to share the gospel, when he warns us to avoid pornography or body tattoos, when he calls mature adults to serve as missionaries, in all of this he is giving us the word of the Lord. This is the Lord's voice, and we can hear it, if we will listen.

And then there are the ministering angels. They too make known the voice of the Lord. This much is clear from many, many scriptures that teach us about the work of the angels of God. When we read of angels bringing the word of the Lord to men and women on the earth, we are almost always reading about heavenly beings charged with the responsibility to minister.

But the scriptures make clear that sometimes *we* are the angels. In 1831 the Lord said, "And ye shall go forth in the power of my Spirit, preaching my gospel, two by two, in my name, lifting up your voices as with the sound of a trump, declaring my word like unto angels of God" (D&C 42:6). The Lord makes his voice known through us. It is part of the great plan of happiness here on earth that all of God's children can hear the voice of the Savior through their brothers and sisters who are called of God to proclaim his word. Those called to serve as missionaries are set apart to teach the truth to any who will listen. They speak the words of truth, and through the Spirit, those who listen can hear the voice of the Lord through his trusted servants.

But it is not just missionaries who are called to sound the words of truth in the Lord's plan. Indeed, all who enter the waters of baptism enter into a covenant with the Lord that they will speak the words of invitation and truth to their brothers and sisters. And in that way, their brothers and sisters, if they so choose, may hear the voice of the Lord in their lives. We are all called to declare the word of the Lord, "like unto angels of God."

Through our brothers and sisters, through prophets, through the scriptures, and through personal revelation we may hear the voice of the Lord. The Lord also speaks to us through the actions that he takes in our lives. To the Prophet Joseph he said that he speaks to us "by the voice of judgment, and by the voice of mercy all the day long" (D&C 43:25). If we are in tune with the Spirit, these actions by the Lord speak to us. They teach us, inspire us, and guide us. The Savior taught this principle when he gave us the parable of the fig tree: "When his branch is yet tender, and putteth forth leaves, ye know that summer is nigh: so likewise ye, when ye shall see all these things, know that it is near, even at the doors" (Matthew 24:32–33).

In all these ways the Lord makes known to us his voice. But to hear it we must act on it. Alma taught the importance of "hearkening" to the Lord's voice this way:

> Behold, I say unto you, that the good shepherd doth call you; yea, and in his own name he doth call you, which is the name of Christ; and if ye will not hearken unto the voice of the good shepherd, to the name by which ye are called, behold, ye are not the sheep of the good shepherd. . . . Therefore, if a man bringeth forth good works he hearkeneth unto the voice of the good shepherd, and he doth follow him. (Alma 5:38, 41)

To know the name by which we shall be called, we must "hearken" to the Lord's voice and follow him. This kind of knowing, hearkening, and following defines an active, sustained relationship between the Lord and us. The Lord does not call us only once but many, many times, all through our lives, indeed, "all the day long."

Sometimes he calls us to repent, to change our ways, and to keep the commandments; sometimes he calls us to serve in the Church; sometimes he calls us to take some action that will bless one of his children. And someday he will call us to come and receive the blessings of eternity. Thus, to know the Lord's voice is to hear it often, to hearken to it often, to have it as a constant guide. When the Savior says, "my sheep hear my voice," he means the sheep know his voice because they have responded to it, time after time, until they come to recognize it deep within them. In this way, the voice of the Lord becomes familiar. We come to know the voice, and the name, by which we shall be called.

King Benjamin taught this principle at the conclusion of his great address. After his people had made a covenant to take upon them the name of Christ, King Benjamin gave them this advice:

> I would that ye should remember to retain the name written always in your hearts . . . that ye hear and know the voice by which ye shall be called, and also, the name by which he shall call you. For how knoweth a man the master whom he has not served, and who is a stranger unto him, and is far from the thoughts and intents of his heart? (Mosiah 5:12–13)

⁓The great key is in our hearts, in our commitments, our desires. Taking on ourselves the name of Jesus Christ means that we desire to become like him, to experience a mighty change of heart. Through repentance and the power of the Atonement, we put off the natural man, lose the disposition to do evil, and, through the refining fire of the Spirit become latter-day Saints. By hearkening to the voice of the Lord, by responding to whatever he calls us to do, we learn to do the will of the Father. By serving him through serving our brothers and sisters, we come to know the Master. The voice of the Lord becomes familiar to us; his purposes and his work become "the thoughts and intents" of our hearts. The name of Jesus Christ, the only name given "whereby salvation cometh," is thus written in our hearts.

This great covenant that we take upon ourselves at baptism can be a great protection to us in the battle against evil. It is an important part of the "whole armour of God." When we take upon ourselves through covenant the name of Jesus Christ, we take the name of him who suffered and died for us. It is the name of him who is the Creator, the Redeemer, and the Savior of the world. He has all power over all things, and in him we will find strength and power and salvation.

CHAPTER 3

RECEIVING THE POWER, AUTHORITY, AND BLESSINGS OF THE PRIESTHOOD

When I was eighteen years old, my father gave me a priesthood blessing at a crucial point in my life. It was the last semester of my senior year in high school. Up to that point my high school experience had been the story of two people. One was the young man my parents (and the Lord) wanted me to be—active in the Church, Eagle Scout, varsity athlete in two sports, a good student, a leader in my ward and stake. The other person was the bass guitarist in a rock-and-roll band. About the middle of my senior year, one of my friends pointed out to me that I really was becoming these two different people. I acted and talked and treated other people one way when I was at church, and quite another way when performing with or hanging around the band.

Fortunately, I took that insight to heart and decided to quit the band. That began a long period of soul searching and repentance. It was not easy. One night during this period, when I felt especially confused, discouraged, and scared (could I really become the person

I should become?), I talked about all this—for the first time—with my parents. That was a hard conversation. I felt that I had let them and the Lord down, and I was so discouraged, I was not sure I could do what had to be done.

The conversation went on pretty long into the night, and the next morning my father gave me a blessing. Many years have passed since that morning, but I remember still what I felt as my father invoked the powers of heaven in my behalf through the authority and power of the priesthood he held. Fear and discouragement and despair gave way to the beginnings of hope and peace and confidence. I was by no means finished with the process I had to go through. There were many hard things in front of me, but from that day I knew I could work through them and become the person I ought to become.

I am now a little older than my father was when he gave me that blessing. Over the years the Lord has blessed me with wonderful children, and I have had many sweet experiences giving them priesthood blessings. And, like my father before me, and like many other Latter-day Saint fathers across the world, I have baptized my children, given them the gift of the Holy Ghost, and ordained my sons to the priesthood. My father also set the pattern for me in his callings in the Church: In many different ways he used the authority and power of the priesthood conferred on him to carry out his responsibilities. I have learned to do the same. In all of this, my father and I have followed the Lord's plan for using the powers of heaven to accomplish his work.

Surely this great priesthood power is an essential part of the armor of God, a critical part of our protection and defense against the forces of evil. It is also something we put on. When Paul says, "Be strong in the Lord, and in the power of his might" (Ephesians 6:10), one type of power he may be referring to is priesthood power.

One of the great blessings of the restoration of the fulness of the gospel is that the priesthood is once again on the earth, and its power, blessings, and protection are available to all who are prepared and worthy to receive them.

To understand the power of the priesthood we must begin with our Father in Heaven. God, our Father, established the great plan of salvation in order to "bring to pass the immortality and eternal life" of us, his children (Moses 1:39). This is his work and his glory. The power of God, the power through which our Father in Heaven brings to pass all that he does, is the power of the priesthood. As Elder Bruce R. McConkie said: "Priesthood is power like none other on earth or in heaven. It is the very power of God himself, the power by which the worlds were made, the power by which all things are regulated, upheld, and preserved" ("The Doctrine of the Priesthood," *Ensign,* May 1982, 32).

This is the power given to Jesus Christ through which he created the earth, wrought the Atonement, and brought to pass the resurrection. It is the power through which the Savior leads and guides his Church today. It is the power through which he will rule and reign when he comes again. Jesus taught this principle to his Apostles shortly before he ascended into heaven:

> And Jesus came and spake unto them, saying, All power is given unto me in heaven and in earth. Go ye therefore, and teach all nations, baptizing them in the name of the Father, and of the Son and of the Holy Ghost: Teaching them to observe all things whatsoever I have commanded you: and lo, I am with you alway, even unto the end of the world. (Matthew 28:18–20)

Each person who holds the priesthood of God on the earth today traces that authority back to Jesus Christ. In ancient times, this priesthood was called "the Holy Priesthood, after the Order of the Son of God" (D&C 107:3). Although we do not use this name today, the use of the word *order* here captures important dimensions of priesthood power. Two dictionary definitions of the word *order* are particularly appropriate in this context: (1) an organization of people united by a common fraternal bond or social aim; and (2) a group of people upon whom a government or sovereign has formally conferred honor for unusual service or merit. Both definitions are instructive.

The "Order of the Son of God" describes those who, through covenants they make with God, take upon themselves the name of Jesus Christ with all that that entails and receive priesthood power and authority in its fulness, including the ordinances of the temple and the new and everlasting covenant of marriage. (On this topic of the order of the priesthood, see especially Bruce R. McConkie, "The Ten Blessings of the Priesthood," *Ensign,* November 1977, 33–35; and Ezra Taft Benson, "What I Hope You Will Teach Your Children about the Temple," *Ensign,* August 1985, 6–10.)

The bonds here are the bonds of eternal covenant. And the aim is nothing less than our "immortality and eternal life," along with that of our families and indeed of all mankind.

We receive the priesthood through covenant—the oath and covenant of the priesthood. The Lord taught this principle in the 84th section of the Doctrine and Covenants:

> For whoso is faithful unto the obtaining these two priesthoods of which I have spoken [Aaronic and Melchizedek], and the magnifying their calling, are sanctified by the Spirit unto the renewing of their bodies. They become the

sons of Moses and of Aaron and the seed of Abraham, and the church and kingdom, and the elect of God. And also all they who receive this priesthood receive me, saith the Lord; for he that receiveth my servants receiveth me; and he that receiveth me receiveth my Father; and he that receiveth my Father receiveth my Father's kingdom; therefore all that my Father hath shall be given unto him. And this is according to the oath and covenant which belongeth to the priesthood. Therefore, all those who receive the priesthood, receive this oath and covenant of my Father, which he cannot break, neither can it be moved. (D&C 84:33–40)

The covenant we make when we receive the priesthood is eternal in its significance and majestic in its scope. On our side, we promise to be faithful, to be worthy to obtain both the Aaronic and the Melchizedek Priesthoods, and to magnify our priesthood callings. Our Father in Heaven on his side promises us that we will be sanctified by the Spirit, that we will receive physical strength and renewal, and that we will become heirs to the promises made to Abraham, and chosen servants of God. But that is not all. We also become, as Paul taught, joint-heirs with Jesus Christ of all that our Father has (see Romans 8:17). Here, as in all else that matters in the eternities, Jesus shows us the way. If we are faithful, if we receive the priesthood and magnify our callings, we will receive the Savior and the Father—and the Father's kingdom.

Thus, to receive the "Holy Priesthood" is to follow the pattern and example of the Lord Jesus Christ—the "Order of the Son of God." It is to do what the Savior has done, to receive the power and authority from the Father to do the will of the Father in all things. This is the "honor" conferred on us by God, but it is not because of special merit or unusual service we have already done. Although to receive these blessings we must be worthy of them, God gives us the priesthood so that we can become his servants, so that we might serve him in righteousness. And the service he would have us do is to become true followers of his Son, Jesus Christ, and to assist in carrying out the great work of salvation on the earth. It is a great honor to receive the priesthood, but that honor is given in expectation of great service. It is a call to serve, not only with heavenly authorization, but also with heavenly power. It is a call to do the work of the Lord.

The Lord's plan is, thus, very simple: He calls us to do his work and gives us, through the priesthood, the power and authority to act in his name. We are on the Lord's errand, to do what he would do if he were here. This power and authority of the priesthood is intimately connected to the atonement of Jesus Christ. It is power and authority that comes through him. Our ability to exercise the priesthood depends on the extent to which the redemptive power of the Atonement works in our lives. After all, if we are to act in his name, we must be worthy of that name. If we are to represent him, we must have that name "written in our hearts." If we are to do what he would do if he were here, we must be like him.

The Power of the Priesthood and Priesthood Keys

The revelations of the Restoration teach us that there are two priesthoods in the Church—the Melchizedek and the Aaronic:

> The Melchizedek Priesthood holds the right of presidency, and has power and authority over all the offices in the church in all ages of the world, to administer in spiritual things. . . . The power and authority of the higher, or Melchizedek Priesthood, is to hold the keys of all the spiritual blessings of the church. . . . The power and authority of

the lesser, or Aaronic Priesthood, is to hold the keys of the ministering of angels, and to administer in outward ordinances, the letter of the gospel, the baptism of repentance for the remission of sins, agreeable to the covenants and commandments. (D&C 107:8, 18, 20)

Because one who holds the Melchizedek Priesthood may also officiate in any of the offices of the Aaronic Priesthood, I will focus on the Melchizedek Priesthood in what follows.

The priesthood is the power and authority to *administer* in the Church, to preside, to direct the activities of all its organizations, and to carry out the mission the Lord has given his Church—to bring souls to Christ by proclaiming the gospel, redeeming the dead, and perfecting the Saints. It is also all the power and authority to *minister* in matters of the Spirit, including performance of all the ordinances of the gospel, from the blessing and naming of babies to baptism and confirmation; from giving the gift of the Holy Ghost to administering the sacrament; from blessings of healing and comfort to all the ordinances of the temple.

In these responsibilities to minister and administer, the priesthood connects the work of the Lord here on earth to the powers of heaven. This connection is explicit in the revelations. This is how the Lord describes the power of the priesthood to bring spiritual blessings to the Latter-day Saints:

The power and authority of the higher, or Melchizedek Priesthood, is to hold the keys of all the spiritual blessings of the church—to have the privilege of receiving the mysteries of the kingdom of heaven, to have the heavens opened unto them, to commune with the general assembly and church of the Firstborn, and to enjoy the communion and presence of God the Father, and Jesus the mediator of the new covenant. The power and authority of the lesser, or Aaronic Priesthood, is to hold the keys of the ministering of angels. (D&C 107:18–20)

In order to understand how the priesthood of God is the power of God, it is important to see this connection with heaven. The priesthood not only confers the authority to officiate in ordinances and to act in the various offices of the Church, but it opens to us the heavens. It grants us access to all the knowledge and understanding, all the power, support, help, and comfort possessed by angels, by the celestial members of the church of the Firstborn who are "just and true," even by the Lord Jesus Christ, and by our Father in Heaven. The priesthood is, in very fact, the power of God.

All of these blessings of power, of strength, of comfort, and of support operate in the Church through the priesthood, under the direction of those who hold the keys of these blessings. The distinction between the priesthood and priesthood keys is crucial to the order of the Church and to the operation of the priesthood in our lives. The keys of the priesthood are the rights to use priesthood power and authority in specific ways, to accomplish specific purposes in the kingdom of God. Some of the keys pertain to presiding authority in quorums, in wards, and in stakes. In a ward, for example, the bishop is the president of the Aaronic Priesthood and holds the keys of that office for that ward. Some keys pertain to missionary work and some to the great work of redeeming the dead through the ordinances of the temple.

In 1836 Moses appeared to Joseph Smith in the Kirtland Temple and committed to him the keys of the gathering of Israel. Other keys—including the sealing powers held by Elijah—were committed to the Prophet at the same time. Thus could Elijah say, after completing the restoration of these keys to the earth: "Therefore, the keys of this dispensation are committed into your hands; and by this ye may know that the great and dreadful day of the Lord is near, even at the doors" (D&C 110:16).

Today, the President of the Church, the members of the First Presidency, and the Quorum of the Twelve hold the keys of this dispensation, the dispensation of the fulness of times. At any one time, only the President of the Church actively directs the use of those keys in the Church. Through delegation, those in authority confer priesthood keys on those who must use them in the work of the Lord. Each bishop, every stake president, every mission president, everyone who holds priesthood keys, traces that authority back to the President of the Church. For example, in 1988 when I was called to serve as the bishop of the Cambridge Ward in the Boston Massachusetts Stake, my stake president received authorization from the First Presidency to ordain me to the office of bishop and to give me the keys of the priesthood that I would need to fulfill that calling. When I was released from that calling, I retained my ordination as a bishop, but those keys—the keys required to be the bishop of the Cambridge Ward—were given to the new bishop. Though I retained the ordination, and could serve as a bishop again without a new ordination, I would need to be called, set apart, and given priesthood keys to serve in that office in the Church.

This distinction between the priesthood and its keys helps us to understand the fact that the newest elder in the Church receives the very same priesthood—the Melchizedek Priesthood—held by the prophet of the Lord. The President of the Church holds a different office in the priesthood and in the Church, and holds the keys of the kingdom. But the priesthood is the same. This fact does not diminish the authority and power held by the President. Rather, it underscores the real power and authority available to that brand-new elder.

Whether that new elder puts to work all the power and authority available to him will depend on whether or not he magnifies his calling and is sanctified by the Spirit.

Magnifying Our Callings and the Powers of Heaven

Our Heavenly Father gives to his children the power and authority of the priesthood to bless their lives, as well as to accomplish his purposes in heaven and on earth. This heavenly power and authority can serve as a critical part of the armor of God in the battle against evil. But to realize all of those blessings we must magnify our callings and make the atonement of the Savior a reality in our lives. Alma taught this critical relationship between the power of the priesthood and the Atonement to the people of Ammonihah. His remarkable discourse on the priesthood is recorded in the thirteenth chapter of Alma. Alma establishes many important principles of the priesthood, but for our purposes these are the most salient:

1. Ordination to the Melchizedek Priesthood is a holy calling, prepared before the foundation of the world.

We are called to the priesthood before we come to earth. Once here, we realize that calling because of our faith and our choice to do what is right. The calling is holy because it is after the "order of the Son."

2. The calling to the priesthood is prepared with a "preparatory redemption." The calling is in and through the atonement of the Only Begotten Son.

We can be called to this holy calling only if we are redeemed through the atonement of the Savior. The Atonement prepares the way for the calling because it makes it possible for us to repent and receive a remission of our sins. In this way we become worthy to receive the holy calling of the priesthood.

3. Those who were called to the priesthood in the time of

Melchizedek brought forth works of righteousness, with exceeding faith and repentance. They were called to the priesthood and through their diligence were sanctified by the Holy Ghost.

To be called to the holy priesthood is a call to be sanctified by the Holy Ghost. It is a call to become pure and spotless before God. In Alma's language, it is a call to have our "garments . . . washed white through the blood of the Lamb" (Alma 13:11).

Alma emphasized the connection between the priesthood, personal righteousness, and sanctification by the Spirit to motivate the people of Ammonihah (and us) to be worthy to receive the priesthood and to be able to use it to do the Lord's work. The Prophet Joseph Smith taught this same principle:

> Behold, there are many called, but few are chosen. And why are they not chosen? Because their hearts are set so much upon the things of this world, and aspire to the honors of men, that they do not learn this one lesson—that the rights of the priesthood are inseparably connected with the powers of heaven, and that the powers of heaven cannot be controlled or handled only upon the principles of righteousness. (D&C 121:34–36)

The Prophet teaches us here that when we receive the priesthood of God we receive the right to deploy the powers of heaven in doing the Lord's work. We can see this by restating the "one lesson" in this passage: If we are called to the holy priesthood and act according to the principles of righteousness, we can handle or control the powers of heaven, because the powers of heaven are inseparably connected to the rights of the priesthood. The power of the priesthood is by its nature heavenly power. All exercise of that power, whether to minister, to preach, to ordain, to heal, to baptize, to bless, to serve, to preside, whatever it may be, all such exercise involves handling or controlling the powers of heaven. Thus, the Lord gives us the requirement that those who act with priesthood power and authority must do so in righteousness and according to righteous principles.

They must also act with the Spirit of the Lord. This, too, the Prophet makes clear:

> That they [rights of the priesthood] may be conferred upon us, it is true; but when we undertake to cover our sins, or to gratify our pride, our vain ambition, or to exercise control or dominion or compulsion upon the souls of the children of men, in any degree of unrighteousness, behold, the heavens withdraw themselves; the Spirit of the Lord is grieved; and when it is withdrawn, Amen to the priesthood or authority of that man. (D&C 121:37)

This passage lays out the consequences of unrighteousness behavior in regard to priesthood power. But in so doing it also shows us that the powers of heaven are here, present, carried by the Spirit of the Lord, when we exercise the priesthood in righteousness. This requires that we *act* according to true and righteous principles (e.g., with love, in service on the Lord's errand), and that we *be* righteous. We must not only use the priesthood in the right way, but we ourselves must strive to become true followers of the Lord Jesus Christ— repentant, receiving a remission of our sins, obedient to the Lord's commandments, striving to learn and do the will of the Father in all things. We will then have the Spirit of the Lord with us and will be able to exercise priesthood power, and thus the powers of heaven, in the Lord's work.

If we act on that promise, we will magnify our callings and so be true to the oath and covenant of the priesthood we hold. Magnifying our callings means that we go beyond the minimum requirement. It means that we serve with all our hearts. It means that we are fully and anxiously engaged in the work to which we have been called, led in everything we do by the Spirit of the Lord. These are the words of the Lord:

> For behold, it is not meet that I should command in all things; for he that is compelled in all things, the same is a slothful and not a wise servant; wherefore he receiveth no reward. Verily I say, men should be anxiously engaged in a good cause, and do many things of their own free will, and bring to pass much righteousness; for the power is in them, wherein they are agents unto themselves. And inasmuch as men do good they shall in nowise lose their reward. (D&C 58:26–28)

Here again is the strong connection between how we should act ("anxiously engaged") and what we should be ("the power is in them"). The Lord gives us a calling, but does not define for us in commandments or detailed instructions every specific step we should take in magnifying that calling. Take, for example, Jon Wood's call to be a ward mission leader. (This example is based on a true story, but the names have been changed.) The call meant that Jon was in charge of missionary work in his ward. Under the direction of the bishop he was to find, teach, and fellowship investigators, sit in council with the leaders of the ward, coordinate the work of the ward with that of the full-time missionaries, support and encourage members to do missionary work, teach and support new members, and plan missionary activities. Jon could have met the minimum requirements for this calling by going on exchanges with the missionaries, holding a correlation meeting with the full-time missionaries, reporting to the ward council once a month, setting up a sign-up sheet for members to have missionaries over for dinner, teaching the new member discussions to new members, and holding an occasional missionary fireside.

Jon decided, however, that there was much more that he could do. He decided to make a covenant with the Lord that if the Lord would put people in his path, he would speak to them and invite them to learn about the Church. Soon, he began to have many opportunities to talk with people about the Church, and some of those people accepted his invitation to come to church and to meet with the missionaries in his home. Jon bore testimony of these experiences in fast and testimony meeting, and he carried that spirit into the ward council, where he challenged the leaders of the ward to share the gospel and invite people to church. They accepted that challenge and were inspired by Jon's testimony. Jon worked with the bishop to focus ward council meeting on engaging all the ward's organizations in missionary work. The ward council began to identify several part-member and less-active families for the missionaries to visit.

There was more. Jon organized a workshop to teach members how to share the gospel and invite their friends and neighbors to come to church. He set up a meal program in which one of the ward missionaries arranged for the full-time missionaries to have dinner with less-active families. Jon organized a regular temple night where new members of the Church could attend the temple to do baptisms for the dead. He made sure that all new members were taught how to do family history and to prepare family names for temple work, that they all had a calling, were assigned home teachers (and visiting teachers where appropriate), and were assigned to be home or visiting teachers. Jon arranged for his ward to have a booth focused on family history at the local Town Day. Many ward members participated in demonstrating how to use the family history library and the resources on the Internet to do family history.

Jon Wood magnified his calling. He became the ward mission *leader*, and through his efforts the members of his ward caught the spirit of the work. His ward became a missionary-minded ward, and many people joined the Church as a result. Jon's experience shows that if we are righteous, and are led by the Spirit, the power is in us to be anxiously and effectively engaged. And, so engaged, we can bring to pass much righteousness by using the powers of heaven in doing the Lord's work. We come to see and pursue our callings as the Lord would see and do them if he were here. As we follow that vision of what is possible, the Lord blesses us with capacity and power far beyond our own. He works through us to extend and deepen the impact of our efforts. Thus, we are magnified, and we magnify our callings.

The Priesthood and the Whole Armor of God

When we receive the priesthood, we take upon ourselves the oath and covenant of the priesthood. When we are true to the promises we make, and magnify our callings in the priesthood, the Lord blesses us with the powers of heaven. We enjoy the great power and protection of the priesthood in the battle against evil. The priesthood, therefore, is indeed a critical foundation of the whole armor of God. And those blessings and that power are available to all of God's children who are worthy to receive them. Though in the Lord's plan only the brethren in the Church hold the priesthood, the blessings and power of the priesthood are available to all Latter-day Saints—men, women, and children—who qualify to receive them.

To understand how this works, we must first put behind us the "philosophies of men" that can, if we are not careful, influence how we think about the priesthood and its blessings. Perhaps the most important of those philosophies is the world's practice of equating personal value and worth with hierarchical position. "Moving up in the world," or getting promoted, confers on one increased stature, honor, recognition, and value in the eyes of the world. This is not the way of the Lord. Neither the power nor the authority of the priesthood, nor certainly its blessings, come from position or rank in a hierarchy. Nor does the place of an individual in the kingdom of God depend on such worldly notions. Though there is in the kingdom a hierarchy defined by the order of the Church, our current place in it does not determine our access to the powers of heaven, the blessings we receive, or our prospects for eternal life. Though members of the Church have different callings with authority of different scope, the Lord's calculus of eternal value, and the peace and joy of the gospel, do not depend on that scope. All of those blessings depend on personal righteousness, on obedience to the commandments, and on fidelity to the covenants we make with God.

The Lord's ways are very different from the ways of the world. For example, one day a member of the admissions board at Harvard Business School asked me about positions in the Church. A member of the Church had applied to the school and had described his leadership experiences in the Church as part of the application. The question I got was: "If someone becomes a Sunday School teacher after being an elders quorum president, is that a demotion?"

In answer, I said: "No, that is not the way it works. Let me give you an example. A few years ago Mitt Romney, who later served as governor of Massachusetts, was the president of the Boston Stake. He was responsible for the Church in much of the Greater Boston area. One Sunday, he was released from that position after serving for many years. The very next Sunday he was called to be the Gospel Doctrine teacher in Sunday School." In the ways of the world, such a move certainly would be a demotion. But in the kingdom of God it is simply a change of assignment.

Thus, part of our understanding of the universal availability of the blessings of the priesthood is to see that all the blessings of the Lord are predicated on personal righteousness and not on position or office. That is the first point.

The second point is the distinction between holding the priesthood and receiving the blessings and power of the priesthood. Elder Robert Hales underscored this distinction in an address in general conference in 1995:

> The priesthood of God gives light to his children in this dark and troubled world. Through priesthood power we can receive the gift of the Holy Ghost to lead us to truth, testimony, and revelation. This gift is available on an equal basis to men, women, and children. Through the blessings of the priesthood, we can be equipped with "the whole armour of God, that [we] may be able to stand against the wiles of the devil" (see Eph. 6:11–18). This protection is available to every one of us.
>
> Through the priesthood many other blessings are also available to all of the sons and daughters of God, making it possible for us to make sacred covenants and receive holy ordinances that enable us to travel that strait and narrow way back to our Father in Heaven (see Matt. 7:13–14). . . .
>
> And the blessings of the priesthood are available to *everyone*. ("Blessings of the Priesthood," *Ensign*, November 1995, 32; emphasis in original.)

Let me illustrate this distinction between holding the priesthood and receiving the blessings and power of the priesthood by describing the role the priesthood has played (and plays) in the lives of our children.

When our seven children—three girls, four boys—entered the world as brand-new babies, they were "born in the covenant." They became part of an eternal family, sealed forever by the power of the priesthood to my wife, Sue, and to me. When the children were a few days old, I took them in my arms and by the power of the Melchizedek Priesthood gave them a name and a blessing. Since that time I have laid my hands on their heads many times and by the power and authority of the priesthood and under the guidance of the Spirit blessed them with things to help them in their lives: guidance, comfort, health, strength, faith, peace, knowledge. Every day and every night, Sue and I kneel together as equal partners in the leadership of our family and plead with the Lord for the welfare of our children. We know that the Lord hears and answers prayers. Each of our sons and each of our daughters has *received* the blessings of the priesthood.

But there is much more. When the children were eight years old I baptized them and gave them the gift of the Holy Ghost. Through the power of the priesthood, which I held, I officiated in sacred ordinances through which the children made covenants with God, took upon themselves the name of Jesus Christ, and received the right to the constant companionship of the Holy Ghost. This is a gift of heavenly power: the power to receive revelation from God; the power to comfort; the power to bear testimony; the power of the gifts of the Spirit—to love, to have faith, to administer, to discern, to gain knowledge, to prophesy, to speak with the tongue of angels (see D&C 46:8–26). These gifts and that power are available to our daughters and to our sons in equal measure according to their faithfulness. Neither our sons nor our daughters had the priesthood conferred on them when they were baptized and received the gift of the

Holy Ghost, but through the power of the priesthood they received a gift that entitles them to great heavenly power.

From the time they were three years old until they turned twelve, our children participated in the Primary organization of the Church. Here they were taught by wonderful teachers who had been set apart by the authority of the priesthood under the direction of the bishop of our ward. These men and women taught the principles of the gospel and received guidance from the Lord about the needs of the children (including ours) in their classes. In addition to family home evening and other gospel discussions at home, our children were taught true principles and received the blessings of love and example from teachers who were authorized to serve in that capacity. This too was a blessing of the priesthood.

When the children turned twelve, the distinction between holding the priesthood and receiving its blessings became clearer. When our daughters turned twelve they became part of the Young Women organization. Over the next six years they were taught eternal principles of love and service and they prepared themselves to enter the temple and make eternal covenants with their Heavenly Father. They had wonderful teachers and advisors, women who had been set apart under the direction of the bishop of our ward and given authority to teach and lead our daughters in the paths of righteousness. During these years our daughters each received a patriarchal blessing under the hands of our stake patriarch, who was ordained to give blessings of guidance and great significance. As our daughters learned and developed, they received recognition of their personal progress. When they turned eighteen they joined the Relief Society, the women's organization in the Church, led by a president and her counselors who had been set apart and given authority under the direction of the priesthood. Throughout their teenage years, therefore, our daughters *received* the blessings of the priesthood.

When our sons turned twelve, I conferred on them the Aaronic Priesthood and ordained them deacons in the Church. With that authority they passed the sacrament and completed other assignments given them by the bishop. As with our daughters, our sons had wonderful teachers and advisors, set apart by the bishop to lead them and teach them true principles. Like their sisters, they received patriarchal blessings and learned important things about the Lord's plan for them. Throughout their teenage years they grew and progressed under the guidance of their priesthood leaders. Later, when they were nineteen years old, I conferred on them the Melchizedek Priesthood and ordained them elders in the Church. As elders, they have the authority to officiate in priesthood ordinances. The experience of our son Andrew is representative. He has served as a missionary, taught the gospel, blessed the sick, baptized new members of the Church, and given the gift of the Holy Ghost. His stake president called him to preside over a quorum of elders and gave him the appropriate priesthood keys to serve in that position. If authorized by the appropriate authority (a bishop or stake president), Andrew could confer the priesthood on someone else.

Once our sons received the Melchizedek Priesthood, they entered into the oath and covenant of the priesthood and took upon themselves all of the obligations and responsibilities we have discussed in this chapter. Although our daughters do not hold the priesthood, they too have made covenants with the Lord, and they too have responsibilities to magnify their callings. Take, for example, our daughter Erin. When Erin was called to be a member of the Primary presidency in her ward, she was set apart under the direction of the bishop. The bishop (or one of his counselors) laid his hands on her head and gave her authority to act in the office to which she had been called. That authority is based on the authority of the priesthood. It gave Erin the right to receive revelation for her assignments, to direct the activities within her jurisdiction, and to do the work given to her by the bishop, the Primary president, and the Lord. The act of setting apart a daughter of God does not confer on her the priesthood, nor does it give her priesthood keys. But it does give her authority derived from the priesthood. Coupled with the gift of the Holy Ghost, the setting apart gave Erin all the power and authority she needed to magnify her calling in the kingdom of God.

Should Erin someday be called, as her mother has been called, to serve as an ordinance worker in the temple, she would be set apart and given authority to officiate in temple ordinances. In the temple, sisters administer temple ordinances to sisters, and brethren administer them to brethren. These are priesthood ordinances, and the authority the sisters have is derived from priesthood authority.

Through their callings in the Church, through the covenants they have made, through the gift of the Holy Ghost, and through their mother and father, Erin and her brothers and sisters have received the blessings and power of the priesthood in their lives. The boys and girls in our family have different callings and assignments in the kingdom, but they all experience the blessings of the priesthood and share the same glorious promises of the gospel of Jesus Christ. Some of those blessings and promises they experience individually, but some—indeed, the highest blessings of the priesthood—come to them only if they forge an eternal partnership with an eternal companion.

Erin was the first of our children to experience these higher blessings. She was married in the Salt Lake Temple in 1995. Shortly before the marriage she was endowed in the temple with "power from on high" (D&C 95:8). She then was prepared to enter into the new and everlasting covenant of marriage with her husband, Brian, and with her Heavenly Father. In that simple but profound sealing in the temple, Erin and Brian were married for time and for all eternity and received together the highest blessings of the priesthood. Since that time five of Erin's siblings have been married in the temple and, with their eternal companions, received those blessings.

These eternal marriages underscore not only the universal availability of the blessings and power of the priesthood but the interdependence of men and women in receiving the highest blessings of the priesthood. Brian, for example, holds the Melchizedek Priesthood, but he cannot enjoy the fulness of the priesthood, cannot enjoy its highest blessings, without Erin. But with Erin, and with her faithfulness, he can.

Erin does not hold the priesthood, but Brian does, and through the covenants she has made with Brian and with God, and through her righteousness, she has received the highest blessings and power of the priesthood. These blessings and that power, the power to create an eternal family, to enjoy eternal life with our Heavenly Father, to be joint-heirs with Jesus Christ of all that the Father has—all of this Erin and Brian share jointly and equally before God.

That eternal family begins here on earth. On July 27, 1997, Erin gave birth to Kira Elise Bradford, and thus became a mother. This, too, is a calling in the kingdom of God. It is a calling that is different from the callings her brothers or her husband receive (they hold the priesthood and become fathers). As a mother, Erin worked in partnership with Heavenly Father to prepare a physical body for one of his special spirit children. She gave physical birth and brought Kira into the world. Because of her temple covenants, she also brought Kira into an eternal family. This, too, is a great blessing of priesthood power that Erin and Brian share as eternal partners. Erin thus has not only received the blessings of the priesthood in her life but also has been blessed to be a mother in Zion.

Like Erin and her brothers and sisters, we all have different assignments in the kingdom, but we all have access to the blessings and power of the priesthood. We all have different callings but are under the same obligation to magnify them. We all make eternal covenants with our Heavenly Father, and we must be true and faithful to those covenants in order to receive the fulness of the blessings he has prepared for us. And we must all use the blessings and power of the priesthood available to us to put on the whole armor of God. No matter our assignment, no matter our callings, we must learn to use whatever authority and power we are given to do the Lord's work in the Lord's way. But if we do that, oh what power, what heavenly influence we can enjoy!

CHAPTER 4

THE HOUSE OF THE LORD

On May 8, 2004, I sat in one of the sealing rooms in the Salt Lake Temple and witnessed the marriage of my son Michael to Hannah Tanner. It was a sweet, wonderful, powerful experience. As the ceremony that sealed Michael and Hannah to each other for time and for all eternity came to an end, I caught the eye of my wife, Sue. I believe we both had the same thought, and we smiled at each other as we remembered the day thirty-three years before when we had been married in that very same temple. Like Michael and Hannah, we had taken upon ourselves sacred covenants and obligations to each other and to the Lord. Under the authority of the holy priesthood, we had been sealed together forever, and that ordinance and the covenants we had made created an eternal family. Since that time seven children had been born to us in that covenant.

Four of those children (in addition to Michael) were sitting with us in the sealing room that day. Three of them had also been married in the Salt Lake Temple, and one would be married in a few months in the temple in Mesa, Arizona. (Our son Jonathan was married to Hannah's sister Deborah.) Sue's mother was there, and so were several of Sue's brothers and sisters. Although her dad had passed away in 2001, I am sure that he was there in spirit, watching over his grandson. My sister and her husband were also there, and I believe my mom and dad (who also had been married in the Salt Lake Temple fifty-eight years before) were there in spirit as well. Thus, there were at least three generations of eternal covenants represented in that room. Michael and Hannah entered into the bonds of eternal marriage surrounded not only by people who loved them but also by people to whom they were eternally connected. There was in that sealing room a chain of eternal covenants extending back through the generations. Michael and Hannah forged a new link in that chain, and drew strength and power from their own and their extended eternal family.

That experience in May 2004 reinforced another sense of connection I had felt in my very first temple experience in 1968. I had been called on a mission to southern Germany and was in the mission home in Salt Lake City for a few days before heading to Provo for language training. Very early one morning (3:00 A.M.!) we got up and went to the Salt Lake Temple to receive our endowments. That first temple session was a profound experience. I received a powerful impression of immediate connection to the ancient ones—to Adam, Enoch, Abraham, Moses, Elijah, Isaiah, and Jeremiah; to John the Baptist; to Peter, James, and John; and, of course, to the Lord Jesus Christ. Here I was in a sacred place, removed from the day-to-day bustle of the world, learning about the great plan of salvation, and engaged in sacred ordinances prepared by God, administered anciently and restored in our day. In the temple I felt the ancient, eternal powers of heaven at work.

Though I have been to the temple many, many times since that first time, that sense of powerful connection with the eternities is something I experience every time I go. That connection comes both in the ordinances of the endowment and in the application of the sealing power to create eternal families. Together with taking on us the name of Christ through baptism, and receiving the powers of heaven through the oath and covenant of the priesthood, these sacred temple covenants and ordinances are a vital part of the whole armor of God. Our Father in Heaven has prepared them to bless us and to protect and defend us against the powers of evil in our mortal journey. Indeed, the fulness of the Lord's blessings for us is in the ordinances of the temple. If we are to follow the admonition of Paul and "put on the whole armour of God," we must go to the temple.

Endowed with Power from on High

The temple and temple ordinances have been an important theme of the restoration of the gospel of Jesus Christ from the very beginning. Step by step and line upon line the Lord revealed to the Prophet Joseph Smith the central role of temples in redeeming the dead, in blessing the Saints with the fulness of the priesthood, and in preparing the servants of the Lord to proclaim the gospel of Jesus Christ in all the world. Shortly after the Church was organized, the Lord commanded the prophet to go to Ohio where the Saints would be "endowed with power from on high" (D&C 38:32).

Temple building has quickened in our day as the prophet of the Lord has sought to make the blessings of the temple much more accessible to the members of the Church. The commandment and the promise today are the same as they were in 1833: Come to the temple and be endowed with power from on high.

What is the nature of the endowment and this "power from on high" that we receive in the temple? To understand this, we need to understand the temple itself and the role it should play in our lives.

Power from the Presence of the Lord

In order to receive the endowment, we must enter into the temple, which is the house of the Lord. This designation is not only symbolic. It is in very fact his house, a sacred place, dedicated to him, where he may come and dwell: "And inasmuch as my people build a house unto me in the name of the Lord, and do not suffer any unclean thing to come into it, that it be not defiled, my glory shall rest upon it; yea, and my presence shall be there, for I will come into it" (D&C 97:15–16).

When we say that the temple is the house of the Lord we certainly mean that it is a special place, a holy place set apart for the Lord to visit. But the Prophet Joseph Smith taught something more. At the dedication of the Kirtland Temple he prayed that the temple would be a place of holiness, that "thy holy presence may be continually in this house" (D&C 109:12). Though the Lord is not always there physically, his presence, his glory, his spirit and influence, and his power are always there. If we are worthy to enter the temple, we may, therefore, feel the power of the Lord in his house. When we enter the temple, we enter into the presence of the Lord.

In the fall of 2000 I felt that power and presence in a special way during the dedication of the Boston Temple. Sue and I attended the last of four dedicatory sessions on Sunday afternoon. We sat in the celestial room, where we listened to wonderful talks and heard the prophet of the Lord, Gordon B. Hinckley, deliver the dedicatory prayer.

The Spirit was very, very strong in that celestial room as the congregation sang the closing song, "The Spirit of God like a fire is burning." Indeed it was. As we began to sing I looked at Sue, and both of us were so overcome with the power of that moment that we could hardly get a word out. We were not alone. I do not think there were many in that room who were able to sing with much effect. But the music was joyous and beautiful and powerful. As tears filled our eyes we sang these words:

> *The knowledge and power of God are expanding;*
> *The veil o'er the earth is beginning to burst.*
> *We'll sing and we'll shout with the armies of heaven,*
> *Hosanna, hosanna to God and the Lamb!*
> *Let glory to them in the highest be given,*
> *Henceforth and forever,*
> *Amen and amen.* (*Hymns,* no. 2)

In those sacred moments I knew that the words we sang were true, and I knew that the Boston Temple was in very fact the house of the Lord.

We receive strength and feel the power of God when we enter his presence in his house. We enter once to receive our own endowments, but we may return often to stand as proxies for those who have died without receiving these sacred ordinances. There is a divine plan at work here. We must be worthy to enter the temple if we are to receive our own endowments. But we must *remain* worthy if we are to serve in the temple throughout our lives as the Lord has commanded. Thus, if we live close enough to go often, temple service becomes an integral part of our lives if we follow the Lord's plan. How often is evident in this passage from a talk given by President Heber J. Grant in 1922:

> A little over a year ago I made up my mind that by planning my affairs . . . I could go to the temple at least once every week and have ordinances performed in behalf of some of my loved ones who had passed away. By making up my

mind that I could do this I had no difficulty whatever in going through the temple once a week during the entire year. . . .

I believe that if I can find the time to go to the temple and to do temple work once a week, there is hardly a man [or woman] in the entire Church of Jesus Christ of Latter-day Saints but that can find the time if he [or she] wishes to plan his [or her] work accordingly. (*Teachings of the Presidents of the Church: Heber J. Grant*, 54–55)

If we attend the temple regularly, if we enter into the presence of the Lord frequently, feeling the power of heaven will become a regular part of our lives. There is great power here in the pattern of worthiness that must be present in our lives, and great power in the temple itself. In this way, we receive what the Lord promised: power from on high.

Power through Knowledge

The endowment in the temple confers upon us knowledge. Because the temple is a place of holiness where the Spirit of the Lord is present in a direct and powerful way, it is a place of revelation. If we are worthy to enter, and if we are in tune and listening, the Spirit will give us insights into the plan of salvation, deepen our understanding of the gospel, and teach us what is of most worth to us in dealing with the challenges we face. The temple is a house of learning, and in that learning there is great power.

I believe there are three kinds of knowledge in the temple, and three ways in which we learn. The first includes specific facts about the plan of salvation, and specific information we need to know in order to progress eternally. The endowment takes revealed truth, often directly from the scriptures, and organizes it in ways that help us to remember what we hear. We learn about our Heavenly Father, about his Son, Jesus Christ, and about their purposes. We learn about the central role of the Savior in the plan of salvation, and the great redeeming power of the Atonement. We learn about the purpose of the earth and its creation, and about our place in it. We learn about our responsibilities, about the purpose of commandments, the importance of obedience, and the availability of heavenly support and comfort in our journey here on earth.

In all of this we learn essential, eternal truths about the plan of salvation. But the endowment also includes very specific information that we will need in order to complete our journey successfully and return home to our Father in Heaven. Brigham Young's definition of the endowment captures this idea quite clearly:

> Let me give you a definition in brief. Your endowment is, to receive all those ordinances in the house of the Lord, which are necessary for you, after you have departed this life, to enable you to walk back to the presence of the Father, passing the angels who stand as sentinels, being able to give them the key words, the signs and tokens, pertaining to the holy Priesthood, and gain your eternal exaltation. (*Discourses of Brigham Young* [Deseret Book, 1941], 416)

This aspect of the temple, the learning of specific facts and information pertaining to the plan of salvation, is much like going to school. We go there to learn.

The second kind of knowledge—symbolic knowledge—is different. We also learn when we encounter the rich symbolism of the temple, but what we learn depends very much on us—what we need, our preparation, our sensitivity to the Spirit, our attention and focus. The difference is a bit like the difference between learning about the history of poetry—the different styles and techniques, the poets, who wrote what, when—and learning from the greatest of all poems. The temple itself is, as President Howard W. Hunter taught us, the great symbol of our membership in the Church (see *Ensign,* October 1994, 2–5).

In the temple's physical structure, in the presentation of the endowment, in the procedures, in the ordinances, in every aspect of the work of salvation in the house of the Lord, there is symbolism, and thus much to learn. Here is a simple example. When we enter the temple, we come dressed in ways that would be appropriate in sacrament meeting. Out of respect for the Lord, we dress up to go to the temple. This means that we come to the temple wearing many different styles, many different colors, and many different qualities of fabric. But we then change out of our street clothes and put on temple clothing. Everything we put on is white: dresses, slippers, stockings, pants, belts, shirts, ties, socks, shoes. Symbolically, we leave behind the things of the world and take upon us the pure and simple things of God. We clothe ourselves in white to represent the purity of heart, the worthiness that should prevail in the house of the Lord. Moreover, the way we are dressed is a symbol of our equality before God. The distinctions and divisions of the world have no place in the temple. We are in fact all brothers and sisters, beloved of our Heavenly Father, and the way we dress in the temple reinforces that eternal truth.

That truth is not taught explicitly in the temple, but through symbols. There is nothing in the endowment ceremony, or in the sealing ordinances, or in the ordinances of baptism for the dead that explains the wearing of white clothing. That we learn through seeing the symbols and coming to understand what they represent. That understanding may come as an answer to a question we pose in the temple to one who has greater experience. Or it may come as an insight as we ponder what we see in the temple. In this kind of learning and this kind of knowledge, the Spirit is very important. And since there are many, many such symbols in the temple, there is always something new and important to learn.

This, too, is one of the blessings of attending the temple often. When we do so, and when we pay attention and seek the guidance of the Spirit, we may notice something we had never noticed before. This may bring new insights and new understanding. If we are prepared, the Spirit will teach us things we need to know. Through the symbols of the temple we may develop new insights, new understanding valuable to our own situation and our own challenges. In this way, the temple can be for us a personal house of learning.

The third kind of knowledge we receive in the temple is an eternal perspective. This knowledge builds on and comes from the first two, but adds a broader vision, a divine framework, and a heavenly vantage point. Where the first two give us specific truths, key bits of information, and powerful insights, this third kind of knowledge helps us see and understand the whole. It gives us a new lens through which to see our lives. In this kind of knowledge we begin to see ourselves as the Lord sees us. We begin to understand the grand sweep of history the way the Lord understands it. We see ourselves, our relationships, our families, and our personal challenges in their eternal context.

Elder John A. Widtsoe described this kind of knowledge and its potential impact on us this way:

> Temple work . . . gives a wonderful opportunity for keeping alive our spiritual knowledge and strength. . . . The mighty perspective of eternity is unraveled before us in the holy temples; we see time from its infinite beginning to its endless end; and the drama of eternal life is unfolded before

us. Then I see more clearly my place amidst the things of the universe, my place among the purposes of God; I am better able to place myself where I belong, and I am better able to value and to weigh, to separate and to organize the common, ordinary duties of my life, so that the little things shall not oppress me or take away my vision of the greater things that God has given us. (In Conference Report, April 1922, 97–98)

We may gain some insight into this kind of knowledge by drawing parallels to the grand vision Moses received as recorded in the Pearl of Great Price. In this vision Moses "saw God face to face, and he talked with him, and the glory of God was upon Moses," and God said to Moses: "And now, behold, this one thing I show unto thee, Moses, my son, for thou art in the world, and now I show it unto thee. And it came to pass that Moses looked, and beheld the world upon which he was created; and Moses beheld the world and the ends thereof, and all the children of men which are, and which were created; of the same he greatly marveled and wondered" (Moses 1:2, 7–8).

Moses later saw more of the earth and its inhabitants, and God taught Moses about the Creation, about the Savior, the Only Begotten of the Father, about his grand purposes, about his work and glory—"the immortality and eternal life of man" (Moses 1:39). Moses was astonished at the grand sweep of the great plan of salvation. His perspective was changed. He could not look upon himself or upon anyone else and see them in the same way. He could not pray to God in quite the same way. He had been blessed with a new framework for understanding his purpose on earth and his relationship to God.

That is precisely the eternal perspective available to us in the house of the Lord. And in that perspective, as in the symbolism of the temple, and in the specific instructions we receive, there is great power.

Power through Covenants

In the house of the Lord we make covenants with God. These are sacred obligations we enter into with our Father in Heaven. Elder James E. Talmage described temple covenants in this way:

> The ordinances of the endowment embody certain obligations on the part of the individual, such as covenant and promise to observe the law of strict virtue and chastity, to be charitable, benevolent, tolerant and pure; to devote both talent and material means to the spread of truth . . . ; to maintain devotion to the cause of truth; and to seek in every way to contribute to the great preparation that the earth may be made ready to receive her King,—the Lord Jesus Christ. (*The House of the Lord* [Deseret Book, 1976], 84)

Covenants help to establish the Lord's purposes in our lives. They teach us about his plans for us personally and for his children as a whole. Covenants bind us to the Lord and to our families, and they teach us about our responsibilities to him and to each other. Covenants we make with the Lord give focus and direction to our lives. President Boyd K. Packer explained the power of temple covenants to bring a focus on, and a commitment to, the work of the Lord, in these words:

> Church members will do for nothing what they could not be persuaded nor compelled to do for pay. Why? The answer is dedication and testimony. The answer is *covenant.*

We are a covenant people. We covenant to give of our resources in time and money and talent—all we are and all we possess—to the interest of the kingdom of God upon the earth. In simple terms, we covenant to do good. We are a covenant people, and the temple is the center of our covenants. It is the source of the covenant. (*The Holy Temple* [Bookcraft, 1980], 170)

When we go to the temple often and participate in the ordinances of the endowment on behalf of those who have passed away, we not only allow them the opportunity to make these sacred covenants with God but we renew our own commitments to him. In the commitment and discipline and focus these covenants require of us, there is great power. Furthermore, if we keep them, the covenants of the temple open to us the powers of heaven. The blessings the Lord promises us are remarkable. Speaking of the temple, the Lord said, "I have kept in store a blessing such as is not known among the children of men, and it shall be poured forth upon their heads" (D&C 39:15). Those who enter into and keep temple covenants shall know "the wonders of eternity. . . . And their wisdom shall be great, and their understanding reach to heaven" (D&C 76:8–9). These passages refer to those "who serve me in righteousness and in truth unto the end" (D&C 76:5)—in other words, those who enter into the new and everlasting covenant of the fulness of the gospel and keep the promises they make to serve the Lord in righteousness.

The revelation given to the Prophet Joseph Smith in the dedicatory prayer at the Kirtland Temple adds these wonderful promises: "And we ask thee, Holy Father, that thy servants may go forth from this house armed with thy power, and that thy name may be upon them, and thy glory be round about them, and thine angels have charge over them" (D&C 109:22).

Going forth from the house of the Lord armed with the power of God clearly involves the spiritual power we derive from being in the presence of the Lord, the knowledge we receive, and the covenants we make in the endowment. But the Lord's plan also allows us to take a part of the temple with us when we return to our homes. After we have received our own endowment we wear the temple garment morning and night throughout our lives. The temple garment, also called the garment of the holy priesthood, represents the covenants we make in the temple. Elder Carlos Asay described the way in which the garment allows us to take the temple with us:

> I like to think of the garment as the Lord's way of letting us take part of the temple with us when we leave. It is true that we carry from the Lord's house inspired teachings and sacred covenants written in our minds and hearts. However, the one tangible remembrance we carry with us back into the world is the garment. And though we cannot always be in the temple, a part of it can always be with us to bless our lives. ("The Temple Garment: 'An Outward Expression of an Inward Commitment,'" *Ensign,* August 1997, 23)

As an immediate, present remembrance, the garment helps us to be true to the covenants we make in the temple. But it also protects us against temptation and evil. The garment is white and is a symbol of purity. When we put it on, it calls to mind the divine standards of chastity, virtue, and righteousness. When we wear it as the Lord intends, we cultivate those habits of modesty and cleanliness so essential to keeping us free of immorality and wickedness. When we wear and care for the temple garment with respect and reverence, we invoke upon us the promises of divine protection against evil that are inherent in the covenant we make when we receive the garment in the temple.

The Apostle Paul taught that our bodies are the temple of God. How appropriate that we should clothe that bodily temple in the white, sacred garment of the temple, that we might remember our promises of devotion and commitment to our Heavenly Father, and that we might enjoy the protection of heaven against the powers of evil. Here, indeed, is the armor of God! Here is a symbol we take with us day and night, a symbol of the Lord's presence, of eternal truth, of sacred covenants. Here is a constant reminder of heavenly power, a reminder that we have been endowed with power from on high.

The Sealing Power and Eternal Families

In the great latter-day "wrestle . . . against principalities, against powers, against the rulers of the darkness of this world, against spiritual wickedness in high places," the family has become a focal point of the conflict. Both the family as an institution and specific individual families are under attack by the forces of evil. The assault on the family and on families is one of the great challenges of our time. In that battle, the creation of an eternal family through the sealing powers in the temple is a critical part of the armor of God and a tremendous source of divine strength and protection. I want to highlight three dimensions of the power of an eternal family: the family as a sanctuary, as a legacy of faith, and as a crucible of spiritual growth.

1. The Family as a Sanctuary

When a man and a woman marry in the temple, they make an eternal covenant with each other and with their Heavenly Father. They are sealed together forever in the bonds of a holy and sacred covenant of eternal marriage. That application of the sealing power of the holy priesthood creates an eternal family and brings with it sublime promises of a glorious future in which they will "inherit thrones, kingdoms, principalities, and powers, dominions, all heights and depths, . . . to their exaltation and glory in all things" (D&C 132:19).

This eternal covenant of marriage is different from all other covenants we make. In all the other covenants our partner in the covenant is our Heavenly Father. When we have completed those covenants, we take with us in our lives the promises we have made and received in our minds and in our hearts. Heavenly Father is surely our partner in the marriage covenant as well, but there is also another partner. In temple marriage, we make and receive eternal promises with our eternal companion. That companion, and those promises, are not just in our hearts and minds. They come home with us and live with us. In this sense, we literally take the temple home with us. The covenant we have made, the evidence of sealing power, the eternal promises and blessings we received in the temple are right there, next to us, every day.

If we are true to the covenant we have made, the presence of one who will be with us forever gives those eternal promises an immediacy that can be a source of inspiration and power. The divine power of that covenant, so evident in the temple and in the promises we receive, can live in our relationship with our spouse. It has force and power in our lives to the extent that it motivates and animates how we love, serve, and treat each other. Many of the promises and blessings associated with the marriage covenant we make in the temple pertain to our lives beyond the resurrection. But if we are true and faithful to that covenant we can bring the blessings of heaven into our homes now.

The day of your temple marriage is the first day of your eternal family. That day and all the days that follow are part of eternity, and you can begin now to live worthy of the influence and power of heaven in your family.

The covenant of marriage in the temple brings to husband and wife the highest blessings of the priesthood. The power and protection of heaven, which begins in the sacred relationship between husband and wife, may spread out and grow in influence and presence in their home and in their family. As children come, they are born in that eternal covenant and thus partake of its blessings and power. As the couple deepen their relationship, love and serve one another and their children, and keep all the covenants they make in the temple, the bond forged in the sealing room of the temple grows in strength and significance and influence in their lives. Their home and their eternal family become a sanctuary, a place of refuge and protection.

2. The Family as a Legacy of Faith

From 1995 to 2005 one of my responsibilities at Harvard Business School was to speak to graduating students on Commencement Day. In my talks I always shared with them something my mother taught me:

> As I have thought about the impact you can have and about this passage in your life, my thoughts turned to passages in my own life and something my mother taught me long ago. Every day, every time I walked out the door, she would look me in the eye, and she would say: "Kim, you remember who you are. Every day. Remember all those people who worked and sacrificed to make it possible for you to be where you are. Remember that when you walk out this door you carry that mantle of responsibility, the good name of this family, the hopes and dreams of your mom and dad. Remember the promise that is yours, the wonderful opportunities in front of you, the hope that is in you for a better world."

My mother taught me that my family gave me a legacy of faith. This phrase she used over and over again, "Remember who you are," had then, and has now, deep significance for me. Part of that significance lies in my relationships with my parents and grandparents. From a very early age I have been aware of the great blessing of being born into a family where faith in the Lord Jesus Christ was a reality, where service in the Church was a central part of family life, and where the principles of the gospel were not only preached but practiced. I know, too, the great blessing of loving, devoted parents whose commitment to one another was eternal, and whose marriage was sealed in the house of the Lord. That great example, and all that flowed from it, has been an immediate, powerful force in my life.

I also have known the blessing of grandparents whose love of their grandchildren was wonderful to experience. And I have seen my parents and Sue's parents become grandparents to our children, blessing them with unconditional love. Here are two examples of the power of grandparents:

Grandma Hunt (Sue's mother) had forty-nine grandchildren, but she never missed a birthday. Every birthday her grandchildren got a present and a little note from Grandma filled with the love that only grandmas can give. Though she was far away, her love radiated in their hearts.

Grandpa Clark was blessed with great spiritual insight into the lives of his grandchildren. Once, when one of our children was in tremendous pain and suffering from severe injury, Grandpa Clark gave a powerful priesthood blessing in which he promised that "waves of faith" from Grandpa and Grandma Clark would wash over this child, bringing protection and comfort through the power of the Spirit. The blessing was fulfilled and continues to this day.

The legacy of my family has meant love and warmth and shining example. It has also meant responsibility. "Remember who you are" meant to me when I was young, and it means to me now, not only that I must be grateful for those who have gone before but that I have a responsibility to carry on, to forge ahead, on the path they began. I am responsible for the legacy of faith I have received, and I am responsible for passing it on to my children, adding my own example and contribution in my life. I know that I will be held accountable for this responsibility. All those folks my mother talked about are not just my long-departed relatives. I am eternally connected to them through the great sealing powers of the temple. The day will come when I will see once again my parents and grandparents and great-grandparents and great-great grandparents and so on. They will want to know what I have done with their good names, what I have built on the foundation they laid.

A strong sense of responsibility is part of the legacy of my family. Another is inspiration. Through many family stories I have learned about the faith of my forebears and their courage and strength. I heard the stories of my Great-Great-Grandfather Edward Bunker, who crossed the plains five times, once as part of the Mormon Battalion. After he had established a prosperous farm in Ogden, Utah, Brigham Young called him and his family to leave their farm and settle in the desert of southern Utah. There he became the second bishop of the Santa Clara Ward and helped to build that community.

In learning about Edward Bunker I also learned about his wife, my Great-Great-Grandmother Mary McQuarrie Bunker. The move to southern Utah, and a later move to establish Bunkerville, Nevada, were filled with hardship and sorrow. But she was a woman of extraordinary courage and faith. She not only raised ten of her own children but was midwife, aunt, friend, and mother to an entire community. She was a woman of great faith, a woman of God.

Southern Utah was also the home of my Great-Great-Grandfather John Wesley Clark and my Great-Great-Grandmother Mary Evaline Brown Clark. Called by Brigham Young to settle Utah's Dixie in 1860, John and Mary Clark were part of that first pioneer group who settled what is now the beautiful and thriving community in Washington County, Utah. But when John and Mary first saw that country, it was harsh and formidable. They endured great hardship, drought, terrible floods, burning heat, and alkali soil. But they endured it well, brought thirteen children into the world, and laid the foundation for the wonderful Latter-day Saint communities in that part of the Lord's vineyard.

John and Mary Clark passed down their faith and courage to their children and grandchildren. That much is clear in the life of one of their grandsons, Owen Wilford Clark, my grandfather. One story will suffice. Grandfather Clark was called on a mission to Germany in 1907. Preaching the gospel in the Germany of 1907 was fraught with risk. There were no guarantees of freedom of speech, no protection of religious activity. My grandfather held street meetings and taught those interested in the gospel. He had some success and drew the attention of the local police. Because of his missionary activity, he was arrested by the city police and thrown in jail. He stayed in jail for a few days until the mission president came and helped him escape! (How is not quite clear.) He slipped out of town on the next train and was able to finish his mission. When I left for my mission to Germany in 1968, my grandfather gave me his 1907 German scriptures—truly a legacy of faith.

Those stories of my various grandparents are inspiring and instructive. I am connected to those faithful Latter-day Saints through the temple covenants they have made and especially through the covenant my mother and father made. I am the fifth generation in the Church, and so can trace those eternal covenants back to my great-great-grandparents. But what of the generations beyond that? Here, too, the sealing power of the temple makes possible an eternal family for those who have passed away before entering into these sacred covenants. Whether you are the fifth or the sixth or the first generation in the Church, there is work to do to forge those eternal connections.

This work of extending the blessings of the temple back through the generations is so important and so essential that without it, the Lord has said, the whole world would be wasted at his coming. But it will not be wasted. The sealing power has been restored, and all across the earth the hearts of the children are turning to the fathers (see Malachi 4:6). The work in the house of the Lord goes forward, creating eternal families and building a legacy of faith.

3. The Family as a Crucible of Spiritual Growth

Part of the power of the eternal family lies in the spiritual growth we experience in making it a reality. The beginning of an eternal family in the sealing rooms of the house of the Lord is truly just the beginning. There follows from that sacred moment the day-to-day work of building an eternal family. In that process of building, the family becomes a crucible of spiritual growth. It is a crucible because the learning there is intense and focused. In the great plan of happiness, we live in families, and we learn to love and serve a few of our Heavenly Father's children with whom we live and work very, very closely. The Lord wants us to learn to love everyone, but the plan is that we start by learning how to love and serve those we know intimately. In this there is great opportunity for growth.

Families are by divine design the best place for children to grow in righteousness and to learn about things of the Spirit. The First Presidency and the Quorum of the Twelve made this clear in the Proclamation on the Family:

We, the First Presidency and the Council of the Twelve Apostles of The Church of Jesus Christ of Latter-day Saints, solemnly proclaim that marriage between a man and a woman is ordained of God and that the family is central to the Creator's plan for the eternal destiny of His children. . . . Parents have a sacred duty to rear their children in love and righteousness, to provide for their physical and spiritual needs, to teach them to love and serve one another, to observe the commandments of God and to be law-abiding citizens wherever they live. ("The Family: A Proclamation to the World," *Ensign,* November 1995, 102)

This sacred duty of the parents has wonderful, positive consequences for the children, but it also is a great source of strength and power for the parents as well. The great responsibility that parents carry cannot be accomplished without spiritual growth. When we become parents we do not come ready-made. The capacity to "rear . . . children in love and righteousness" and to "teach them to love and serve one another" must be developed. That development is spiritual, and how deep it needs to go is evident in this revelation given to Joseph Smith in 1833:

Every spirit of man was innocent in the beginning; and God having redeemed man from the fall, men became again, in their infant state, innocent before God. And that wicked one cometh and taketh away light and truth, through disobedience, from the children of men, and because of the tradition of their fathers. But I have commanded you to bring up your children in light and truth. (D&C 93:38–40)

To bring up our children in light and truth we must ourselves be sources of light and truth. We must not only teach our children true principles but "bring them up" surrounded by and immersed in light and truth. The way we live (our "traditions"), the example we set, and the values that guide our actions must lead our children to God. Indeed, our children learn who God is and what he is like by the way that we treat them. In this there is great responsibility, but also great power and protection.

It is in a deep commitment to the process of spiritually growing and learning that parents find protection against spiritual complacency, against selfishness, against pride, against laziness, against whatever stands in the way of the sacred duty to rear our children in love and righteousness. That protection comes through spiritual growth and change. And when that duty begins in a sacred, eternal covenant with an eternal companion and with God, there is a special significance to, and a special power that flows from, the building of an eternal family.

An experience from the early days of my own marriage illustrates these principles. The relationship between husband and wife begins in the temple, but it is forged in daily living. In our case that forging process required a lot of change on my part.

One evening, about three or four months after we had been married, I came home from school (I was a sophomore in college), greeted Sue (who had just come home from work and was fixing dinner in the kitchen), sat down in the living room, and pulled out some homework. At the time we lived in a very small, very ancient apartment in Cambridge, Massachusetts. After dinner, I could tell that something was bothering Sue. I said something perceptive like, "Sue, is something bothering you?" She said she was fine, but it sure did not feel that way. I persisted. "Did I do something wrong?" I said. This time she did not say anything, by which I knew I was in big trouble.

I had no idea what I had done, but I had clearly done something, or failed to do something, that had upset Sue. Finally, after some more back and forth, she told me what was wrong, but what she said was so unexpected that it surprised me. "When you came home tonight," she said, "you could see that the floor needed to be swept, but you ignored it." I thought to myself, "That's it? That is what this is all about?" I then explained to Sue that I was more than willing, even happy to sweep the floor, and that all she had to do was ask and I would do anything she wanted me to do. I suggested that every day she make a little list of things she wanted me to do around the apartment, and I would do them gladly and well. (I also, unwisely, indicated that my mother had used this method to great effect.) To my surprise, what I thought was a very reasonable solution made Sue even more upset. I was baffled.

Sue then said something to me that has had a profound influence in my life. Right there in the little kitchen of #3C Shaler Lane, in the middle of a discussion about something as mundane as sweeping the floor, my eternal companion taught me a true principle and, in that moment, changed my life. This is what she said: "I am not going to make you a list of things that need doing. When you come home you need to see what needs doing and just do it. This home is just as much your responsibility as it is mine."

In that moment I had a flash of insight not only that Sue was right but also that I had a lot of changing to do. Sweeping the floor when it needed to be swept, or doing the dishes when the dishes needed to be done, would become an outward manifestation of the character of my commitment to my family, and of my relationship with Sue. That experience is still with me thirty-six years, twelve apartments and houses, seven children, and nine grandchildren later. The principle I learned that night is stated powerfully in the Proclamation on the Family (the key passage is in italics):

By divine design, fathers are to preside over their families in love and righteousness and are responsible to provide the necessities of life and protection for their families. Mothers are primarily responsible for the nurture of their children. *In these sacred responsibilities, fathers and mothers are obligated to help one another as equal partners.* ("The Family: A Proclamation to the World"; emphasis added)

The change I needed to undergo to make that principle a governing reality of our marriage was more than just paying attention and pitching in. It was all of that, but much more. I needed to see (and feel) the work and the caring and the equal partnership as a "sacred responsibility" deeply connected to the temple and the covenant that I had made with Sue and with Heavenly Father. I needed to put my faith in the Savior and the hope I felt for my eternal family into practice in the daily work of creating a home and a marriage. That work extended not only to household responsibilities but to the way we taught, disciplined, and nurtured our children. Sue and I needed to be on the same page in every aspect of our lives together.

Learning to take responsibility at home, and setting and enforcing limits for children, are everyday dimensions of being married and raising children. Though common, and even mundane, they are the stuff and substance of building an eternal family. But for me they were also a challenge that required significant spiritual growth. In those experiences I turned to the Lord and sought his help and guidance. I came to know the power of the promise in Ether, chapter 12, and thus of the grace of the Lord Jesus Christ: "And if men come unto me I will show unto them their weakness. I give unto men weakness that they may be humble; and my grace is sufficient for all men that humble themselves before me; for if they humble themselves before me, and have faith in me, then will I make weak things become strong unto them" (Ether 12:27).

Families truly can be a crucible of spiritual growth. When that growth occurs in the Lord's way, through humility, meekness, and faith, when it is motivated by commitment to eternal covenants made in the temple, we receive great power and protection. This is the Lord's plan. The temple is a source of power for us and for our families—power in the presence of the Lord, power in the knowledge we gain, power in the sacred ordinances of the endowment, power in the covenants we make, power in the eternal families we create. Truly, when we go to the temple and serve the Lord in righteousness, we make real in our lives the great admonition of Paul: "Be strong in the Lord, and in the power of his might. Put on the whole armour of God" (Ephesians 6:10–11).

CHAPTER 5

THE FOUNDATION OF TRUTH

As a young boy I heard and sang the great latter-day hymn "Come, Come, Ye Saints" (*Hymns,* no. 30). Raised on stories of the pioneers, I was touched then by the words of that hymn, and they touch my heart now. I especially loved that strong, defiant phrase: "Gird up your loins; fresh courage take." I have to admit, however, that for many years I did not understand fully what the phrase meant. Later I learned that ancient warriors clothed themselves in a thick, leather girdle that served both as a protection and as a foundation. They attached to the girdle other parts of the armor and their weapons of war. "Gird up your loins" was thus a call to battle.

Paul uses this image in Ephesians 6:14 when he says, "Stand therefore, having your loins girt about with truth." Truth is the great foundation, the protection and support in the armor of God. In the Doctrine and Covenants the Lord defines truth clearly and succinctly: "And truth is knowledge of things as they are, and as they were, and as they are to come" (D&C 93:24).

The knowledge of which the Lord speaks is comprehensive. It encompasses all things. We have been commanded in the revelations of the Restoration to search after this truth, to expand our knowledge of things as they are, as they were, and as they are to come. We are commanded to learn and to gain knowledge because that is an important part of our purpose here on earth and in the eternities: "Whatever principle of intelligence we attain unto in this life, it will rise with us in the resurrection. And if a person gains more knowledge and intelligence in this life through his diligence and obedience than another, he will have so much the advantage in the world to come" (D&C 130:18–19).

In addition to their impact on our personal progression, knowledge and learning allow us to more effectively serve God and his children, including our families. Brigham Young taught the Latter-day Saints that seeking after truth—all truth—was important in building the kingdom of God, and had the power to improve the lives of people in the world. It should be sought for those purposes. Hugh Nibley makes clear this connection between education and service to the Church and God's children (the words in quotation marks come from Brigham Young):

> "The business of the Elders of this Church (Jesus, their elder brother, being at their head), [is] to gather up all the truths in the world pertaining to life and salvation, to the Gospel we preach, to mechanism[s] of every kind, to the sciences, and to philosophy, wherever [they] may be found in every nation, kindred, tongue, and people, and bring it to Zion." The "gathering" was to be a bringing together not only of people but of all the treasures surviving in the earth

from every age and culture; "every accomplishment, every polished grace, every useful attainment in mathematics, music, and in all science and art belong to the Saints," and they "rapidly collect the intelligence that is bestowed upon the nations, for all this intelligence belongs to Zion. All the knowledge, wisdom, power, and glory that have been bestowed upon the nations of the earth, from the days of Adam till now, must be gathered home to Zion." "What is this work? The improvement of the condition of the human family." (Hugh Nibley, *Brother Brigham Challenges the Saints* [Deseret Book and F.A.R.M.S., 1994], 316)

A deep commitment to seeking after truth has roots both in the doctrines of the Church and in its history. From the founding of the "School of the Prophets" by Joseph Smith in 1833, to the creation of the Church Educational System for high school and college students, to the ongoing support of the three campuses of Brigham Young University, the leaders of the Church have created an institutional history of commitment to learning and education. (For a brief review of this history, see David P. Gardner, "Education," in Daniel H. Ludlow, ed., *Encyclopedia of Mormonism* [Macmillan, 1992], 2:441–46.) Moreover, the prophets and Apostles have created in their personal lives a living witness of the importance of learning, knowledge, and education. We have, of course, the example of Joseph Smith and Brigham Young, both of whom were largely self-taught and invested in learning throughout their lives. Among the current First Presidency and Quorum of the Twelve Apostles, a college education is common, and many of these leaders possess advanced degrees in medicine, engineering, law, education, business, political science, and the humanities. Gordon B. Hinckley, President of the Church, framed his personal commitment this way:

I love to learn. I relish any opportunity to acquire knowledge. Indeed, I believe in and have vigorously supported, throughout my life, the pursuit of education—for myself and for others. I was able to obtain a university education during the Great Depression, and from that time forward I have never been satiated with the pursuit of knowledge. From my point of view, learning is both a practical matter and a spiritual one (*Standing for Something* [Times Books, 2000], 59).

Latter-day Saints are committed to learning and education. For us, it is a commandment to seek knowledge, to enlarge our understanding, to learn throughout our lives. That learning is all encompassing. As the prophet wrote, learning is both a practical matter and a spiritual one. We are to learn about "things . . . in the earth, and under the earth; things which have been, things which are, things which must shortly come to pass; things which are at home, things which are abroad; the wars and the perplexities of the nations." But we are also to "teach one another the doctrine of the kingdom," that we "may be instructed more perfectly in theory, in principle, in doctrine, in the law of the gospel, in all things that pertain unto the kingdom of God" (D&C 88:77–79). We are thus to learn about the things of the Spirit, and of heaven, and the things of the earth and the world around us. Both the substance of what we learn and the effects of what we learn are practical and spiritual.

The search for truth is an important dimension of our journey in this life and in the life to come. But this search is not easy, and the journey is fraught with danger. As with so many things in our lives, something that is good—in this case, knowledge and learning—can become, if we are not careful, the focus of temptation and sin. In this chapter I want to look closely at what it means to search for truth, how we can avoid the dangers of that journey, and thus how we put on the foundation of truth in the armor of God. Our Heavenly Father has not only given us commandments to seek truth but provided the way for us to find it. The starting point is the Savior.

The Savior Is the Truth

At the Last Supper, when he "knew that his hour was come" (John 13:1), Jesus prepared his disciples for his death and resurrection and his departure from them. In this marvelous discourse he said these remarkable words about truth:

> In my Father's house are many mansions: if it were not so, I would have told you. I go to prepare a place for you. And if I go and prepare a place for you, I will come again, and receive you unto myself; that where I am, there ye may be also. And whither I go ye know, and the way ye know. Thomas saith unto him, Lord we know not whither thou goest; and how can we know the way? Jesus saith unto him, I am the way, the truth, and the life: no man cometh unto the Father, but by me. (John 14:2–6)

Thomas asked the great question, "How can we know the way?" and Jesus gave this remarkable answer: "I am the way, the truth and the life." What does it mean to say that Jesus Christ is the truth? If truth is knowledge of things as they are, and as they were, and as they are to come, how can such knowledge be identified with the Savior? The answer to this question is found in the revelations of the Restoration. Consider these passages from the Doctrine and Covenants:

For the word of the Lord is truth, and whatsoever is truth is light, and whatsoever is light is Spirit, even the Spirit of Jesus Christ. (D&C 84:45)

He that ascended up on high, as also he descended below all things, in that he comprehended all things, that he might be in all and through all things, the light of truth; which truth shineth. This is the light of Christ. . . . And the light which shineth, which giveth you light, is through him who enlighteneth your eyes. (D&C 88:6–7, 11)

The light shineth in darkness, and the darkness comprehendeth it not; nevertheless, the day shall come when you shall comprehend even God, being quickened in him and by him. Then shall ye know that ye have seen me, that I am, and that I am the true light that is in you, and that you are in me, otherwise ye could not abound. (D&C 88:49–50)

In the beginning the Word was, for he was the Word, even the messenger of salvation—the light and the Redeemer of the world; the Spirit of truth, who came into the world, because the world was made by him, and in him was the life of men and the light of men. . . . And I, John, bear record that I beheld his glory, as the glory of the Only Begotten of the Father, full of grace and truth, even the Spirit of truth, which came and dwelt in the flesh, and dwelt among us. (D&C 93:8–9, 11)

These scriptures identify three roles that the Savior plays in our lives that give meaning to the phrase: "I am . . . the truth." They are: Creator, Light of the World, and Redeemer.

Creator

Under the direction of our Heavenly Father, Jesus created all things. Indeed, John wrote, "All things were made by him; and without him was not any thing made that was made" (John 1:3). His work extended—and extends—beyond this earth. The Prophet Joseph Smith bore testimony that Jesus is the "Only Begotten of the Father—that by him, and through him, and of him, the worlds are and were created" (D&C 76:23–24; see also Hebrews 1:2). Jesus created all life on these worlds—the plants, the animals, and us. Before he came to the earth he appeared to the brother of Jared and taught him that "man have I created after the body of my spirit" (Ether 3:16).

In this process of creation Jesus was the instrument through whom our Heavenly Father brought all things into existence. The knowledge—the truth—that is embodied in all things came from God through his Son. Just as the master craftsman puts all that he knows about his craft into the works of his hands, so Jesus has put all that he knows into everything there is. That means that he knows the nature of life, in all its beauty and complexity. He knows all there is to know about the earth and its elements, the rocks, the mountains, the rivers, and the sands of the sea. He knows about galaxies and stars, where they came from and where they are going.

And he knows us. He knows us in general, how our bodies work, what makes us sick, how we get along or do not get along with each other. But he also knows us personally, who each of us is, what we need, what we might become. More than all of this, he knows the grand purpose for which all things were created. He knows the Father, and the Father's work, and the Father's life. All of this knowledge, all of this truth, he put to work (and puts to work) in the Creation to achieve the great plan of salvation. As the Creator, he is the truth.

Light of the World

Jesus not only made all things, not only embodied all truth in the works of creation, but he gives life to all that he has made and makes it possible for us to gain knowledge and truth ourselves. The Lord teaches that the light of Christ operates in both the physical and the spiritual realms (see D&C 88:7–13). Elder Theodore M. Burton taught this principle in a general conference talk:

> God's light includes the physical light we see, which makes us feel so warm and comfortable. God's light is also the power to understand and comprehend all things. In other words, all kinds of light are related to intelligence and truth. . . .
>
> The light of Christ therefore includes not only spiritual light but also physical light, and is a key to understanding that form of energy which is represented by the light we see all around us. ("Light and Truth," *Ensign,* May 1981, 29)

Physical light, the light that radiates from the sun, which shines from the lamps in our homes, is a unique phenomenon in the universe. It is one of the great universal constants. Light travels at a constant speed of 300,000 kilometers per second, and nothing in the universe travels faster. Light travels at that speed literally to "fill the immensity of space" as the Lord revealed to the Prophet Joseph (D&C 88:12). Physical light we see every day, and its influence on us and our world is profound. It not only illuminates our world but brings life-giving warmth and energy. The same is true in the spiritual realm. Spiritual light—the light of truth—radiates from the presence of God to fill the universe with life-giving enlightenment, understanding, and intelligence. By the light of Christ, our Heavenly

Father not only "enlighteneth [our] eyes" with physical light but also "quickeneth [our] understandings" with spiritual light (D&C 88:11).

The possibility of spiritual enlightenment and understanding through the light of Christ is given to everyone born into this world. Each of us has the God-given gift of conscience by which we may know the difference between right and wrong. This gift of light is essential to our agency, and thus to the plan of salvation and God's eternal purposes. But the enlightenment that comes through the light of Christ applies to all truth. When the Lord speaks of the light of Christ quickening our understandings, he speaks of a critical part of the process through which man discovers truth of all kinds. This does not mean that we can discover truth without effort on our part. Truth does not come without study and investigation, without our using our minds in its discovery. It simply means that those insights that yield new understanding come from the light of Christ. In any search for truth, whether it is in the study of some scientific field or in the study of the gospel, there are moments when we connect previously unconnected facts, or see a new way to frame a problem, or see a relationship between two ideas we had not seen before. Such insights are critical moments in the discovery of truth.

The importance of such insights may seem straightforward when it comes to things of the Spirit. But they are important in the search for any kind of truth, including the discoveries of science. We live in a time when scientific knowledge is growing at an accelerated rate. It is growing so fast, and is so powerful and pervasive in its influence on our lives, that it is easy to attribute all of that growth and power to the methods and the brilliance of the scientists involved. Yet even (some would say especially) the most powerful and profound results in all of science rest on a "quickening" of understanding that comes from the light of Christ. In the case of the discovery of the special theory of relativity, for example, Einstein woke one morning in the spring of 1905 when a "storm broke loose in my mind." Based on conversations with Einstein about that morning, Banesh Hoffman said:

> His basic discovery came on waking up one morning, when he suddenly saw the idea. This had been going around and around at the back of his mind for years, and suddenly it wanted to thrust itself forward into his conscious mind. We know brilliant ideas come at crazy times. You may be walking, or lost in the forest, and suddenly the idea comes—almost as if it's coming from somewhere. Einstein once said . . . "Ideas come from God." Now he didn't believe in a personal God or anything like that. This was his metaphorical way of speaking. You cannot command the idea to come, it will come when it's good and ready. He put it in those terms: "Ideas come from God" (interview with Banesh Hoffman, cited in Denis Brian, *Einstein: A Life* [John Wiley and Sons, 1996], 61)

In this example, and in many others, the experience is something quite like turning on a light in a dark room. Such insight does not come without effort. After much preparation, after much study and work, after seeking for the truth in the right places, we may receive the insight, and we "see" where we had not "seen" before. This is why the image of a lightbulb going on is so often used to capture a moment of insight or inspiration. But the revelations of God teach us that there is something deep and true in that analogy. Such insights really are like physical light.

Moreover, the analogy works both ways. In the physical realm we are able to see when light reflects off an object, enters the eye, and is processed through the retina to the brain. But that physical process results in "seeing" only if we are ready and prepared to see what the light illuminates. I may walk by a beautiful garden every day on my way to work, for example, and never actually "see" the beauty that is there, nor understand the garden's design or the craft that produced it. Unless I pay attention, unless I am prepared to receive all that the light carries, I will not see the garden. But if I am prepared and if I pay attention, the light of the sun illuminates that garden, and I may see its beauty and perhaps even appreciate its design and the skill of the gardener. The same is true with things of the Spirit. Here, too, I may see that which I had not seen before. If I am prepared and if I am looking in the right places, I may see truth through insights produced by the light of Christ operating in the spiritual realm. In a beautiful and profound way, Jesus Christ is the light of the world. He is, indeed, the truth. (I am indebted to H. Kent Bowen, in a conversation on August 26, 2004, for the idea that we do not always "see" what is there to be seen, either physically or spiritually.)

Redeemer

The atonement of Jesus Christ is the central truth in all of God's creations. The facts of his life and ministry are connected to all that is true, and give meaning and purpose to our lives and the world around us. Jesus Christ was and is the Only Begotten of the Father. He was "born of Mary, . . . she being a virgin, a precious and chosen vessel, who shall be overshadowed and conceive by the power of the Holy Ghost, and bring forth a son, yea, even the Son of God" (Alma 7:10). He ministered for a short time among his people, and everywhere he went he healed them physically and spiritually. To all who walked with him then, and to all who walk with him now, he taught the truth to those with ears to hear. In his actions and behavior he lived the truth, so that all who saw him then, and all who learn of him now, could know how to live the truth in their lives.

In the garden of Gethsemane and on Calvary he descended

below all things, and suffered all things. When his work was finished he died, and his body was laid to rest in a sepulchre. While his body lay in the tomb he visited the world of spirits and there taught the truth and organized the work of bringing the truth to all who have lived on the earth without hearing it. On the third day he took up his body and rose again. He conquered sin and death, and rose triumphant over all things. He did all these things to bring about the great plan of salvation for all of God's children.

All that is true is connected to this great, unmatched act of love and sacrifice—the earth and everything on the earth, all the worlds that God has created, the heavens and all they contain, who God is and his purposes, who we are, where we came from, why we are here, where we are going, indeed, all that has happened and will happen in the unfolding drama of life on earth. All these things Jesus comprehended in his atonement. All these things have meaning because of his atonement. In fact, and in truth, Jesus Christ is the Savior and Redeemer.

The atonement of Jesus Christ is very personal and specific. Here, too, the Atonement is deeply connected to truth. In those hours in the Garden and on the cross Jesus came to know by his own experience what each one of us experiences. Alma taught:

> And he shall go forth, suffering pains and afflictions and temptations of every kind; and this that the word might be fulfilled which saith he will take upon him the pains and the sicknesses of his people. And he will take upon him death, that he may loose the bands of death which bind his people; and he will take upon him their infirmities, that his bowels may be filled with mercy, according to the flesh, that he may know according to the flesh how to succor his people according to their infirmities. Now the Spirit knoweth all things;

nevertheless the Son of God suffereth according to the flesh that he might take upon him the sins of his people, that he might blot out their transgressions according to the power of his deliverance; and now behold, this is the testimony which is in me. (Alma 7:11–13)

This scripture is literally true. Jesus took upon himself the pains and sicknesses, the infirmities, the sins and transgressions of each one of us. Elder Merrill J. Bateman taught that this was personal and specific:

The Savior, as a member of the Godhead, knows each of us personally. Isaiah and the prophet Abinadi said that when Christ would "make his soul an offering for sin, he shall see his seed" (Isa. 53:10; compare Mosiah 15:10). Abinadi explains that "his seed" are the righteous, those who follow the prophets (see Mosiah 15:11). In the garden and on the cross, Jesus saw each of us and not only bore our sins, but also experienced our deepest feelings so that he would know how to comfort and strengthen us. ("The Power to Heal from Within," *Ensign,* May 1995, 14)

If I apply these principles to myself, their meaning is clear: The Savior knows the truth of my life. He has experienced what I experience. My experiences are his. He knows the truth of my life because he has experienced my personal sins, grief, sadness, depression, sickness, weaknesses—whatever critical experiences define my life or block my eternal progress, he has experienced. He experienced them not because he experienced sin in general or grief in general, but because he suffered the consequences of my sins, and because he felt my grief. He knows the truth of my life because he comprehends the meaning and purpose of my experiences. He knows not only the "whats" of my life but the "whys." Moreover, in his atonement he has overcome them all. This means that he not only knows my past, but he knows what my future may become. He has the solution to everything that stands in the way of my personal happiness in this life and eternal life in the world to come.

Jesus is my Savior. He has paid for my sins. He has felt my grief and pain, and he has overcome it all. He not only knows the sins I commit but feels their effects infinitely. He has absorbed all that suffering in his suffering. But he also knows what I need to do to change and become who I really can become. He knows the problems I face and what to do about them. He has already overcome those things in his atonement. If I trust in him and have faith in him, I too can overcome through him whatever I face.

As the Creator, as the Light of the World, and as the Redeemer, Jesus Christ is the truth. When Paul admonishes us to "stand, . . . having your loins girt about with truth," the most important truth we need is the truth that is in Jesus Christ. If we put the Savior at the center of our search for truth, we will create the foundation and protection we need in the battle against the forces of evil.

CHAPTER 6

THE SEARCH FOR TRUTH

The Lord has commanded us to seek truth and he has given us the way to seek it. In the Lord's way we gain true knowledge and intelligence through diligence (digging, seeking, studying) and through obedience (exercising faith by keeping the commandments of the Lord). Obedience to the commandments of the Lord creates experiences that teach us true principles. Jesus taught this connection between obedience and truth: "Then said Jesus to those Jews which believed on him, If ye continue in my word, then are ye my disciples indeed; and ye shall know the truth, and the truth shall make you free" (John 8:31–32).

To obedience and faith the Lord would have us add the hard work of seeking and studying. Indeed, whenever the Lord talks to us about seeking truth he always connects study and faith. In a

This chapter is adapted from an essay I wrote on being educated and faithful, which appeared in *Why I Believe* (Deseret Book, 2002), 103–12.

revelation to Joseph Smith in 1835, for example, he said, "And as all have not faith, seek ye diligently and teach one another words of wisdom; yea, seek ye out of the best books words of wisdom; seek learning, even by study and also by faith" (D&C 88:118).

Such faithful seeking is motivated by eternal covenants and centered in the gospel of Jesus Christ. If we seek to learn in this way, the Lord has promised that we shall be blessed with light and truth: "And if your eye be single to my glory, your whole bodies shall be filled with light, and there shall be no darkness in you; and that body which is filled with light comprehendeth all things" (D&C 88:67).

In the Lord's plan, the search for truth involves the mind and the spirit. It is about building a life of faith and obedience, and a life of learning. The most important truth to be gained is a testimony of Jesus Christ and his atonement. But gaining knowledge of all kinds is important, and that knowledge—including the truth that is in Jesus Christ—is to be had through reason (study) and revelation (faith).

Why does the Lord connect study and faith in this way? Why this linking of reason and revelation, of the intellect and the spirit? Part of the answer is that inspiration from God is a powerful way to gain the kinds of knowledge and intelligence essential to our education here on earth. This includes the insights that come from the light of Christ and revelation through the Holy Ghost. Through obedience to the commandments we are worthy of the constant companionship of the Holy Ghost. A life of faith and obedience can, therefore, create habits of prayerful contemplation and quiet reflection that open our minds and our hearts to revelation and inspiration.

Early in my graduate training I had an experience with this principle. It remains a vivid reminder to me of the way the Lord blesses us with insight and understanding through the power of his Spirit. In the fall of 1974 I took a class on Labor Economics and Industrial

Relations Systems from a professor named John Dunlop. It was my first year in graduate school in the Economics department at Harvard University. Professor Dunlop was a major figure in the University (he had been dean of the Faculty of Arts and Sciences) and in the field of industrial relations. I enjoyed the class and wanted to do well in the final exam. I studied long hours in preparation. Just before the exam I knelt in prayer and asked the Lord to bless me with his Spirit, and to help me remember what I had learned.

The exam was held on a winter day in January of 1975 in Memorial Hall, a large, cavernous space with hundreds of students taking all sorts of exams. I opened up the exam to discover that Professor Dunlop had given us two recently published articles. We were to read and critique each one. I went to work. As I read and pondered the first article I had a remarkable experience. It was as though a window opened in the ceiling of Memorial Hall and a shaft of intelligence and knowledge poured into my mind. As I read I knew exactly what the problems and issues with the paper were and I knew exactly what to write. I was well prepared for that exam, but what happened to me was way beyond my normal experience. I did not labor over an outline, nor did I spend a lot of time pondering the argument. I just picked up my pen and began to write.

I finished the first essay and picked up the second paper. The same thing happened. As I read, my mind was flooded with ideas. I comprehended exactly what was going on in that paper, and exactly where the problems were. I once again picked up my pen and wrote. When I finished the second essay I knew in my heart that the Lord had blessed me with his Spirit beyond anything I had ever experienced before. It was powerful and humbling. I walked out of the exam knowing that my capacity had been magnified. I had experienced what the prophets have called "pure intelligence" flowing from the Holy Ghost.

Many years later the blessing of that day became clearer. Twenty years after the fact I learned that Professor Dunlop told colleagues that exam was why he called me up and asked me to work for him as a research assistant the next term. In May of 1975 when he was named Secretary of Labor in the Ford administration I went with him to Washington. When he returned to Harvard he left the economics department and joined the faculty of the Harvard Business School. I returned to the economics department and completed my doctoral studies in 1978. Professor Dunlop was instrumental in opening up doors for me at HBS. Following graduation I joined the faculty of HBS. There is no question in my mind that the blessing of inspiration I received on that day in January of 1975 was a crucial step on my path to HBS.

I have experienced the inspiration of the Spirit many times in my life. I know that through the light of Christ and through the Holy Ghost we can receive knowledge and understanding from the Lord. So, part of the purpose for connecting faith to study is the Lord's desire to help us learn through inspiration. But it is also true that using our minds to actively seek knowledge in the way that the Lord outlines helps prepare our minds to receive that inspiration. This principle is at the heart of the following reprimand received by Oliver Cowdery, who served as scribe to Joseph Smith during the translation of the Book of Mormon. Oliver had sought permission to try to translate, and had not had success:

> Behold, you have not understood; you have supposed that I would give it unto you, when you took no thought save it was to ask me. But, behold, I say unto you, that you must study it out in your mind; then you must ask me if it be right, and if it is right I will cause that your bosom shall

burn within you; therefore, you shall feel that it is right. (D&C 9:7–8)

The Lord promises confirmation, but only after hard thought and study. Joseph Smith taught the same principle and emphasized the connection between the intellect and the spirit: "We consider that God has created man with a mind capable of instruction, and a faculty which may be enlarged in proportion to the heed and diligence given to the light communicated from heaven to the intellect" (*Teachings of the Prophet Joseph Smith* [Deseret Book, 1976], 51).

And again: "The things of God are of deep import; and time, and experience, and careful and ponderous and solemn thoughts can only find them out. Thy mind, O man! if thou wilt lead a soul unto salvation, must stretch as high as the utmost heavens" (*Teachings*, 137).

The Prophet thus taught that our intellect receives "light from heaven"; that we can expand our capacity to learn from that light if we are diligent; and that our minds are essential to finding out the things of God, as we ponder and learn from our experience; but they must be connected to heaven if we are to achieve all that God has in store for us. There is no distinction here between secular and religious knowledge, or between the spirit and the intellect.

We may have separated the spirit and the intellect into different compartments of our lives, but according to the Prophet, that is not our true nature. In that sense, connecting study and faith is the Lord's plan for learning because it is precisely the best way to learn. The process he gives us for gaining knowledge—exercise faith, study, seek, ponder, pray, keep the commandments—is thus intended to help us integrate the intellect and the spirit.

Dangers in the Search for Knowledge

The Lord's plan does more than give us a powerful way to learn. It also serves as a protection against the dangers that lie in the path of our search for truth. And there are dangers. Jacob had this to say about knowledge and learning:

> O that cunning plan of the evil one! O the vainness, and the frailties, and the foolishness of men! When they are learned they think they are wise, and they hearken not unto the counsel of God, for they set it aside, supposing they know of themselves, wherefore, their wisdom is foolishness and it profiteth them not. And they shall perish. But to be learned is good if they hearken unto the counsels of God. (2 Nephi 9:28–29)

To be learned, to search for and attain truth, is good, but things can go terribly wrong if we are not careful. Some of the dangers we face are matters of the mind and some affect our hearts. I will discuss four here: shallow thinking, cynicism, pride, and greed. Each poses a serious challenge to being educated and faithful.

Shallow Thinking

Searching for truth the way the Lord has commanded us can be difficult work. Whether we are learning about organic chemistry or the doctrine of the Atonement, the search for truth takes time and energy and focus. Sometimes the search is uncomfortable. It may be hard. We may uncover things that are difficult to understand. We may encounter ideas that conflict with our beliefs or that point up some problem in our behavior. Searching for truth takes time, and we are busy; there are many claims on our time and our attention.

For those who would be educated and faithful, the danger here is to be satisfied with a surface understanding, or worse, to never search at all. We can live our lives without searching for truth and still do many things of importance, things we know we should do. It is possible to keep many of the commandments and be very active in the Church and never engage in the search for truth. It is possible to read the scriptures and not search them or study them. It is possible to go through many years of formal schooling and not cultivate habits of lifelong learning. We may be familiar with current theories in science and the humanities, but fail to probe them deeply or consider them carefully. Such theories may stand in opposition to revealed truth, or may be used in that way by those who actively seek to tear down our faith. If we do not probe deeply and see them clearly, we may lose our way and put our faith in the "wisdom of men."

The surface may be more comfortable (or more popular) than the depths, but shallow thinking does not fulfill the Lord's mandate. Unless we embark on the search for truth in the Lord's way and resolve to go beyond the surface, we may know something of the gospel, and something of the world we live in, but we are not fulfilling the Lord's admonition to seek wisdom and understanding.

Cynicism

If we forge ahead on the path of knowledge and learning, other dangers lurk on the journey. These dangers are perhaps more subtle, and potentially more difficult to see and overcome. The very process of education is one of them. Sometimes people learn in very passive ways. They read, or listen to someone else, or watch a teacher solve a worked-out problem. But active modes of learning—writing papers, formulating hypotheses, running experiments, developing evidence and argument, presenting ideas and discussing them, opening up oneself and one's ideas to critique—are far more effective and thus are widely used. This is especially true where teachers seek to impart a deeper understanding of fundamental principles, and to develop critical habits of mind, rather than simply to transmit certain facts. In that context, prevalent in colleges and universities, students and teachers treat each other's ideas with a practiced skepticism.

I have lived and taught and learned in such an environment for over thirty years. All of my experience has taught me the importance of carefully scrutinizing ideas, of attention to methodology, of asking hard questions about evidence and logic. Putting students through such educational experiences helps them become what William James called "tough minded." But early in my years as a student I saw the dark side of this process, a side that can have serious consequences for our spiritual welfare. I once participated in a seminar in which a doctoral student presented the results of his research to other students and to faculty. It did not take long to realize that the students in the seminar were primed to find the flaws in the work (and, as is often case, there were flaws to be found). But the comments from some were sharp and biting. They attacked the methods, as they should, but their sarcasm, even when tinged with humor, cut the person as well. I left that seminar with an uneasy feeling because I realized how easy it would be for me to fall into that pattern of behavior.

As the years passed I became a teacher and witnessed (and lived) the tension between the value of a rigorous examination of ideas, and the development of a climate of respect for each other in the learning process. This tension is common in our colleges and universities, but it sometimes occurs in the Church as well. I have been in Gospel Doctrine classes that had some of the hallmarks of an academic seminar, including skepticism and sharp critique. In such classes, the discussions may have intellectual interest, but they do not invite the Spirit of the Lord, nor build true understanding. Even in a college seminar, without a strong commitment to respect for each other, a misguided emphasis on rigorous scrutiny can turn healthy skepticism into cynicism and a mean-spiritedness that can, if not recognized and addressed, become a canker on the spirit, affecting one's behavior not only in the world of the classroom but in everything one does.

Such cynicism and meanness is not productive of real learning, and it stands in direct contradiction to the commandments of the Lord. The Lord said it clearly in these words: "Wherefore, be not weary in well-doing, for ye are laying the foundation of a great work. And out of small things proceedeth that which is great. Behold, the Lord requireth the heart and a willing mind; and the willing and obedient shall eat the good of the land of Zion in these last days" (D&C 64:33–34).

The challenge for all who would be educated and faithful, then, is to be tough-minded, but not hardhearted. I shall return to that challenge below.

Pride

Not only are there dangers in the search for truth, but the possession of knowledge carries dangers as well. Here, Jacob was most emphatic: a little learning goes a long way to make one proud and arrogant. If such were the case several hundred years before Christ's birth in the society depicted in the Book of Mormon, it is certainly true in the world of the early twenty-first century.

Knowledge is wonderful. When my son hurts his shoulder (as he did) and needs a difficult operation (also true), I want the very best surgeon with the most advanced knowledge to perform the operation. The difference between the best and the average is enormous, all the more so when the problem is challenging and difficult. For the individuals who have such knowledge, it is natural to feel an intrinsic sense of accomplishment; one has to work hard to acquire it, and having it expands one's perspective and sense of purpose and allows one to deliver real solutions.

The same is true with spiritual knowledge. Those who have great spiritual knowledge can be a powerful source of insight and support when we are faced with difficult questions in our lives. Like the surgeon, they too may feel a sense of accomplishment in what they know. But this sense of accomplishment may be a slippery slope; both in the world and in the Church we must deal with what the scriptures call the "honors of men." Learning brings recognition from society and from the communities of practice (engineers, lawyers, doctors, leaders, scientists, artists, officials, teachers, and so forth) one may aspire to join, or to which one already belongs. Moreover, within such communities there is often a hierarchy of status and influence based on knowledge and expertise.

Communities of practice with influence and status based on knowledge can have a very positive impact on society. Those with significant knowledge and learning can offer to society service of great value, and can help to establish high standards of practice that can lift up the quality of work everywhere when transferred to others. This is true in the world, and it is true in the Church. But such a position in a community and in society can breed in those who possess such knowledge a self-importance and conceit that may degenerate into willful pride and arrogance. The scriptures describe such people as "walking with stiff necks." In effect, those who receive great honor from their colleagues, who receive accolades from society, begin to believe that they are better than other people. And the "honors of men" may, in particular, lead them to place their own wisdom or understanding ahead of the words of the prophets and the counsels of God.

The challenge is to have high standards without being stiff-necked.

Greed

Society confers status and honor on those who are knowledgeable. It has ever been thus. But in our day, society goes even further.

We live in an economy that places increasing economic value on knowledge, at least on the kinds of knowledge that are critical to the creation of new technologies, new forms of entertainment, new products and services. And with a modern capital market that translates future value into current wealth, some have accumulated wealth on a truly remarkable scale. They have in turn become the models for many, many others. In a knowledge economy, Jacob's warning becomes even more salient because now, in addition to the "honors of men," learning and education could—and likely will—bring wealth as well.

This is dangerous ground. Here again Jacob cuts to the heart of the problem:

> But wo unto the rich, who are rich as to the things of the world. For because they are rich they despise the poor, and they persecute the meek, and their hearts are upon their treasures; wherefore, their treasure is their god. And behold, their treasure shall perish with them also. (2 Nephi 9:30)
>
> The hand of providence hath smiled upon you most pleasingly, that you have obtained many riches; . . . ye are lifted up in the pride of your hearts, and wear stiff necks and high heads because of the costliness of your apparel, and persecute your brethren because ye suppose that ye are better than they. . . . Before ye seek for riches, seek ye for the kingdom of God. And after ye have obtained a hope in Christ ye shall obtain riches, if ye seek them; and ye will seek them for the intent to do good—to clothe the naked, and to feed the hungry, and to liberate the captive, and administer relief to the sick and the afflicted. (Jacob 2:13, 18–19)

If education becomes the brass ring, if it becomes a ticket to wealth, and nothing more, then it becomes a way, albeit a socially acceptable way, to give expression to greed. If our search for knowledge and learning, however, has a higher purpose—to serve others and God—then we may use the wealth that comes along for good purposes. But the danger is clear. The challenge is always to do good, whether we do well or not.

Following the Lord's Plan for Learning

These are the dangers on our journey to acquire learning and knowledge. We may encounter hard work and uncomfortable ideas and stop searching altogether or fail to dig deep. We may lose our way, paradoxically placing too much faith in the wisdom of men. Moreover, the process of education and the possession of knowledge may breed within those who learn a cynicism, a pride and arrogance, a greed that can be destructive of the spirit and of faith. If your own voice, or the voice of your colleagues in your circle of practice, or the many voices of the world, are so loud that you cannot hear the Lord, you will fail to learn all you can, and will fall prey to the "cunning plan of the evil one" of which Jacob warned long ago.

The Lord's plan for the Latter-day Saints to "seek learning, even by study and also by faith" is designed to help us avoid the dangers and overcome the challenges, so that we can be both educated and faithful. The most important thing to do in our search is to ground it in the Savior. Faith in the Lord Jesus Christ, a testimony of the truth that is in his life and ministry and atonement, is a sure foundation on which to build. The Lord himself gave us the great key when he said, "But seek ye first the kingdom of God, and his righteousness; and all these things shall be added unto you" (Matthew 6:33). Though the Lord spoke of food and clothing in this passage, the principle applies also to our search for truth.

So, how should we put the Lord's plan into practice? Over the years I have observed a pattern of behavior in the lives of many of my LDS friends and colleagues that helps to make the Lord's plan a reality. There are four elements: an attitude of humility; focused prayer; deep, lifelong study of the scriptures; and service to the Lord on the frontier.

Humility

Early in my college years my uncle taught me what I will call "the sacrament meeting test." It was designed to help us maintain perspective and avoid both cynicism and pride. Many years ago my uncle (who at the time was a professor at the University of Southern California) was sitting in sacrament meeting listening to a talk given by a member of his ward. As the man talked, my uncle noticed several errors of grammar and sentence structure. The man's delivery was awkward, and the logic of his talk was at best incomplete. These problems attracted my uncle's attention. By the time the man finished his talk, my uncle had developed a devastating critique of the logical structure of the argument and the methods of presentation.

As he walked from the meeting, however, my uncle's conscience kicked into gear and he heard that "still small voice" telling him that something was wrong. On reflection, he realized that he had brought the tools and methods of his classroom into sacrament meeting and had failed to hear the man's message. Then he remembered that his father had taught him that the really important questions are always: What is the message of this talk? What is the speaker trying to teach me? What would the Lord have me learn? This is a far more productive approach to sacrament meeting in general. But it also helps to prevent cynicism and intellectual arrogance. For my uncle this was a defining moment.

For me, sacrament meeting has become a litmus test for my own heart. Whenever I find myself analyzing sacrament meeting talks rather than listening for the message in them, I know I am on dangerous ground and need to focus on what the Lord wants me to learn.

My uncle's story motivates the first element in the pattern I want to describe: Those Latter-day Saints who succeed in combining study and faith seek to develop humility. No matter the circumstance, they ask: What can I learn from this experience? What is the Lord trying to teach me? What does he want me to learn? They accept and embrace opportunities to serve others because they know that in doing so they serve God. And they attend the temple, not only because it is the Lord's house and a house of learning but because they leave behind the distinctions of the world and stand equal before God with all their brothers and sisters. An attitude of humility is important in helping us maintain high standards while avoiding stiff-neckedness.

Focused Prayer

Being teachable, serving others, making the temple a central part of one's life—these are activities that foster an attitude of humility. And humility helps us not to take ourselves too seriously and thus ignore the counsels of God. The second element in the pattern—prayer—also protects against intellectual arrogance and cynicism. Prayer is an essential part of a life of faith. But I have in mind here a particular kind of prayer, a prayer that brings to Heavenly Father the specific, practical, mundane issues and problems of our study. In this pattern, we lay before him the specific issues with which we are wrestling and seek his guidance. The wrestling and the seeking are important. We go before God without all the answers and acknowledge that God has them, all of them. It does not matter what the subject is or how big the issues are, the prophets tell us to take them to the Lord in prayer.

A specific prayer to God for help acknowledges our need before him. But it is incomplete. It is also very important to thank him for his mercy and blessings. Such specific, focused prayers of thanksgiving evoke in us a sense of gratitude. Gratitude is the foundation for treating others with respect and for approaching our journey of learning with a sense of optimism. And that respect and optimism help guard against cynicism and allow us to be tough-minded without being hardhearted.

Lifelong Learning

The third element of the pattern is a commitment to lifelong learning, especially to rigorous study of the scriptures. Where the first two elements focus on avoiding spiritual dangers, the last two address our need to keep our minds active and engaged in the kind of searching, seeking process that the Lord outlines in his plan. And this seeking must be lifelong.

A commitment to learning throughout our lives is not the traditional pattern we find in modern society. In society's typical pattern, education occurs early in life, followed by many years focused on applying that education to earning a living and raising a family, followed by years of retirement in which one may offer some service to church or community. This so-called "Learn-Earn-Serve" model of life is now obsolete. (There is some question whether it ever had much application to Latter-day Saints, who serve extensively throughout their lives.) One cannot possibly hope to sustain a productive life of work and service on the basis of a few years of education early in one's life. Knowledge simply is increasing so fast that one must plan on a lifetime of learning in order to be effective and productive in the world.

The world, therefore, has now caught up with the Lord. For it has never been the Lord's plan that we would learn a lot in school and then put our minds to rest, working only on applying what we had learned for the rest of our lives. A careful review of the scriptures about study and faith reveals absolutely no time limits, no deadlines, and no calendar constraints on learning. It is to be lifelong. And those Latter-day Saints who are educated and faithful learn throughout their lives in a variety of ways, including formal programs, continuing education, reading widely, and so forth. But a litmus test of this element of the pattern is their approach to the scriptures.

For us as Latter-day Saints, the scriptures include the Bible (both Old and New Testaments), the Book of Mormon, the Doctrine and Covenants, and the Pearl of Great Price. We also believe in continuing revelation and that when modern prophets speak under the direction of the Spirit of God, what they say is scripture. These records of God's dealings with his children and his revelations to his prophets can be read at many levels. But educated and faithful Latter-day Saints take seriously the Lord's plan for learning (which applies to all kinds of knowledge), and they study them rigorously. The Lord commands us not just to read the scriptures but to "search" them, to "feast" on them. This requires that we use our minds, indeed, every bit of our mental capacity, to study the scriptures deeply and rigorously. Doing so may reveal new patterns, new connections we had never seen before. It may give us new understanding of the context in which revelation has occurred, new insight into the purposes of the Lord's commandments, new ways to think about our responsibilities.

Of course, the Lord wants us to bring our hearts and our spirits with us on our search. Indeed, studying the scriptures this way helps us to integrate the spirit and the intellect. That is what makes our approach to the scriptures such a powerful litmus test of our adherence to the Lord's plan for learning. Of course, the scriptures are special and come with special promises from God. He provides extra help in teaching his children about his word. But, if Latter-day Saints study the scriptures this way, they develop a capacity for learning—using reason and revelation in an integrated way—that can be used in every context.

Serving the Lord on the Frontier

The final element of the pattern is about service to the Lord. It is connected to humility and to the emphasis on our purpose in the Lord's plan for learning: to prepare for service in the kingdom of God. The Lord makes clear that the purpose of his plan of learning is to prepare the laborers in his kingdom to go out and do his work (see D&C 88:78–80). As we discussed in chapter 1, it is in the nature of that work that the Lord is always at its frontier. In the early days of the Church, the frontier was always right at hand. There were few "laborers" and much to be done, and much of what had to be done had never been done before. The Latter-day Saints of that day were stretched and pushed and challenged almost every day of their lives. And the Lord was always there because they were at the frontier, where he always works.

Today the Lord's plan of learning and his focus on the frontier are the same, but we face a very different situation. We find ourselves part of a Church with 12 million members worldwide, with a large and capable organization, full of people who know how to do much of what needs to be done. Indeed, there are many, many Latter-day Saints who are so experienced and capable that they can accomplish what they are asked to do without the Lord's help. At least they can back in the more settled parts of the kingdom where things are familiar and comfortable.

There is a frontier today, perhaps not as obvious as the one in 1830, but it is there in the individual lives of God's children (including our own) and in the great work of the Lord occurring all across the world. It is at this frontier that we find the Lord at work. And at this frontier, Latter-day Saints can accomplish what must be done only with the Lord's help. That is why service at the frontier of the kingdom is a distinctive element in becoming educated and faithful. It is here, in the unfamiliar territory of the frontier, that our stock of knowledge and our intellect and our spiritual wisdom are inadequate. They are absolutely vital, necessary, but in the end, not enough. We have to turn to the Lord and rely on him for help. And thus, we have to grow, sometimes spiritually, sometimes intellectually, but always in ways that serve God's children and move his work forward. Thus, service at the frontier adds to our capacity in the Lord's way.

Taken together, these four practices—cultivating an attitude of humility, engaging in focused prayer, committing to lifelong study of the scriptures, and serving at the frontier—define a way of life that will help us to search for truth and avoid the dangers along the way. As we search in the Lord's way, the great promises in the scriptures will become a reality in our lives. We will come to know the Savior and develop a deep and abiding testimony of his atonement. We will keep his commandments and thus "find wisdom and great treasures of knowledge, even hidden treasures" (D&C 89:19); indeed, we will "[receive] truth and light, until [we are] glorified in truth and [know] all things" (D&C 93:28).

Our Father in Heaven will "give unto [us] knowledge by his Holy Spirit," and we will enjoy the blessings of the dispensation of the fulness of times, "a time to come in the which nothing shall be withheld" (D&C 121:26, 28). This dispensation is a day of revelation in which nothing will "hinder the Almighty from pouring down knowledge from heaven upon the heads of the Latter-day Saints" (D&C 121:33). Thus, as we search for truth in the Lord's way, our knowledge will grow and deepen and we will be "prepared in all things" to serve in the kingdom (D&C 88:80). Truth will be our sure foundation and we will be able to "stand . . . , having [our] loins girt about with truth" as we put on the whole armor of God (Ephesians 6:14).

CHAPTER 7

THE BREASTPLATE OF
RIGHTEOUSNESS

One of the great blessings of serving a mission is the opportunity to be close to people who experience the power of repentance in their lives. Working with people who give up their old way of life for a new and better one is inspiring. To be present as they experience a change of heart, qualify for and enter the waters of baptism, and receive the joy and happiness that comes from the gift of the Holy Ghost is to be taught a great lesson about the redeeming power of the atonement of Jesus Christ. As they continue in the strait and narrow path, as they become Latter-day Saints, they become a living example of what Paul meant when he counseled us to "stand . . . having on the breastplate of righteousness" (Ephesians 6:14).

When I served a mission in Germany in the late 1960s, I met a family who went through that change of heart and put on the "breastplate of righteousness." The story begins with a master sergeant in the U.S. Army stationed in Germany. This sergeant was in charge of the mess hall at one of the military bases in southern

Germany where I served. He was a very tough and demanding boss. He ruled that mess hall through fear and intimidation. The mess hall ran very well, but people who worked there had to endure a lot of yelling and swearing from the sergeant. He smoked and drank and was always angry. It was a difficult place to work.

One day, the sergeant's two clerks were transferred, and he received two new ones. The two new clerks did not know each other, but they quickly discovered that they were both members of The Church of Jesus Christ of Latter-day Saints. After they had been in the mess hall for a few days, they both received the same impression: Give the sergeant a copy of the Book of Mormon. They both were returned missionaries, and both recognized the true nature of the impression they had received, but they had a hard time putting it into practice. Frankly, they were scared to even talk to the sergeant, let alone offer him that book. But they encouraged and supported one another, and one day they went into his office together and offered him a copy of the Book of Mormon. They had feared a tirade, but he took the book and said he would read it.

The next step was to send the missionaries to visit the sergeant and his family. One Saturday evening the missionaries knocked on the sergeant's door. They could hear the sounds of a party in the apartment, and when the sergeant opened the door, they could tell that he had been drinking. They introduced themselves and offered to come back later. He waved them off but invited them back.

When the missionaries returned, they discovered that the gruff, mean, angry sergeant was a façade. Inside that public persona was a very troubled man who had been searching desperately for answers to the problems in his life. He had a serious problem with alcohol. He loved his family, but he and his wife were at odds over many things and he was afraid his marriage was going to break apart.

The missionaries taught that family the gospel of Jesus Christ.

Both the sergeant and his wife began to read the Book of Mormon and to pray. They met with the missionaries often. The gospel was a like a lifeline: once they got ahold of it, they held onto it and would not let it go. For them, the redeeming, saving power of the atonement of Jesus Christ became a reality. They attended the small branch of the Church on the base and found a welcome and a love they had not known before. They learned about the Word of Wisdom and committed to live it. They accepted the law of tithing. The missionaries taught them about family home evening and about the temple and building an eternal family.

I met the family shortly after they had joined the Church. My companion and I taught them and worked with them following their baptism. I had not known the old sergeant, but the new sergeant was a joy to know. He was warm and friendly. The old anger, the cynicism, the profanity, the meanness were gone. In their place were kindness, humor, joy, and love. The sergeant was not perfect, but he was a new man. From all accounts of the mess hall, after his baptism he still was demanding and still set high standards. But everyone who worked there marveled at the change in him. Because of that change, we had opportunities to teach other people, and missionary work in that branch flourished.

Those two LDS clerks assigned to the sergeant did not know what was behind the façade, but the Lord did. And the Lord reached out and touched the sergeant and his family. Together they saw the light and through baptism entered into the strait and narrow path that leads to eternal life. They changed their ways, received the commandments of the Lord with a glad heart, and kept them. The sergeant became a righteous man and his wife became a righteous woman. In the language of Paul, they put on the breastplate of righteousness.

The image of the breastplate is powerful. In ancient times of war, the breastplate protected the heart, the lungs, and other vital organs against attack. In our spiritual "wrestle . . . against principalities, against powers, against the rulers of the darkness of this world," the breastplate of righteousness is rooted in the mighty change of heart that the sergeant experienced, and thus in the atonement of Jesus Christ. In this chapter I want to explore the nature of righteousness, what it means to put on the breastplate, and how we keep it on once we have it.

The starting point is a phrase the Savior used in the Sermon on the Mount. This phrase captures an important set of ideas about the breastplate of righteousness. Speaking of the importance of devotion to the kingdom of God, he said:

> Therefore take no thought, saying, What shall we eat? or, What shall we drink? or, Wherewithal shall we be clothed? . . . for your heavenly Father knoweth that ye have need of all these things. But seek ye first the kingdom of God, and his righteousness; and all these things shall be added unto you (Matthew 6:31–33)

It is the phrase "seek . . . his righteousness" that packs such meaning for our study of the breastplate of righteousness. What does the Lord mean when he admonishes us to seek the righteousness of our Heavenly Father? I would like to mention three different ways of thinking about that passage, three different but interrelated principles, each taking us into a deeper understanding of ourselves and the breastplate of righteousness: obedience to the commandments, doing the will of the Lord, and becoming like the Savior.

Obedience to the Commandments of the Lord

Obedience is the foundation of the armor of God in general, and of the breastplate of righteousness in particular. The Lord gives us commandments to create a righteous structure and focus to our lives. Because they are his commandments, the behavior they entail is right. Those who receive them and obey them do what is right, and thus they experience righteousness, a state of being that Heavenly Father intends for his children.

Obedience to the commandments of God has been a hallmark of the righteous life from the beginning. Adam and Eve received commandments in the Garden, and later when they were driven out they received more commandments to guide their lives. The scriptures testify that God has commanded his children in all times, from Adam down to Noah; from Abraham, Isaac, and Jacob down to Moses; from the world of the Old Testament prophets and Lehi and Nephi down to Mormon and Moroni in the Book of Mormon; from the advent of the Savior on the earth to Peter, James, and John; and down to the Restoration through the Prophet Joseph Smith. In all these times and dispensations, obedience to the commandments of God defined the righteous life.

We live in the dispensation of the fulness of times when the fulness of the gospel of Jesus Christ is on the earth. Through the Restoration the Lord has reaffirmed commandments that have been part of the gospel from ancient times, including the law of chastity, tithing, and the Ten Commandments. Through revelation God has commanded us to put into practice the new and everlasting covenant of the gospel of Jesus Christ, to love and serve our neighbor, to seek out our departed ancestors and make the blessings of the temple available to them, to "succor the weak, lift up the hands which hang down, and strengthen the feeble knees" (D&C 81:5), and much else. We also are blessed to live at a time when there are prophets on the earth, and they have given us commandments from God quite specific to our day and our times. The Word of Wisdom is a good example, but through the prophets the Lord also has commanded us to hold family home evening, pay a generous fast offering, hold family prayers, and share the gospel of Jesus Christ with those around us who do not have it.

When we enter the waters of baptism, and when we receive the ordinances of the endowment in the temple, we make covenants with our Heavenly Father that we will keep the commandments of the Lord. Obedience is thus a sacred obligation, established through promises we make to God. If we are true and faithful to those promises, we will truly seek the righteousness of God. But that obedience must be much more than halfhearted, mechanical compliance. The Lord has said, "He that . . . receiveth a commandment with doubtful heart, and keepeth it with slothfulness, the same is damned" (D&C 58:29). What the Lord wants from us is a heart that is full of faith, and diligence in obedience.

Doing the Will of the Lord

Jesus taught that love of God and of our brothers and sisters ought to be the great motivating power behind obedience to all of God's commands:

> Then one of them, which was a lawyer, asked him a question, tempting him, and saying, Master, which is the great commandment in the law? Jesus said unto him, Thou shalt love the Lord thy God with all thy heart, and with all thy soul, and with all thy mind. This is the first and great commandment. And the second is like unto it, Thou shalt love thy neighbor as thyself. On these two commandments hang all the law and the prophets. (Matthew 22:35–40)

When we seek the righteousness of God motivated by this all-encompassing love of which Jesus speaks, we not only keep the commandments but seek to do the will of the Lord in all things. Certainly it is the Lord's will that we keep his commandments. But doing the will of the Lord in all things entails a more personal, a more specific, and a deeper commitment.

The commandments of the Lord that are revealed through the prophets, written down and established formally in the doctrines of the kingdom, are general and apply to all Latter-day Saints. The will of the Lord is something different. The Lord makes known his will to us through the Holy Ghost. It may come as a quiet impression through the Spirit directing us to take action or make a decision. It may come as we read the word of the Lord and receive an insight that guides us in his work. It may come in an hour of prayer as we seek the Lord's help. It may come through the ministering of angels who bring us specific messages from the Lord. It may come in many different ways. But when it comes, it is the will of the Lord. And if we would seek the righteousness of God, we must learn to do the will of the Lord.

These messages and impressions are personal and specific to the situations and circumstances we face. They are carried by the Spirit of the Lord and thus come when we are in tune with the Spirit. And they put us on the Lord's errand. The will of the Lord, therefore, is always about the Lord's work, and thus always about taking action to bring about righteousness in the kingdom. When we learn to do the will of the Lord in all things, we learn to do what the Lord would do if he were here. This principle was revealed to the Prophet Joseph Smith when the Lord said, "Wherefore, as ye are agents, ye are on the Lord's errand; and whatever ye do according to the will of the Lord is the Lord's business" (D&C 64:29).

An experience that my wife had many years ago illustrates in a powerful way what it means to do the will of the Lord. One day Sue got a strong impression that she should call a certain sister in our ward. This woman, her husband, and their three children had just moved into our ward a short time before. Sue wondered what to make of the impression she received, because she knew of no reason she should call the sister. But the impression was clear, and she acted on it. Not knowing why she was calling, she felt a little awkward for those first few minutes on the phone. Sue asked the sister how she was doing, and if there was anything that she could do to help her. The woman declined her help, but Sue persisted, offering to come over and just visit. She agreed, and Sue went to her house.

There Sue discovered a remarkable situation and an inspiring story. As they talked, the sister began to tell Sue about their little four-year-old son, who suffered from a disease in which tumors grow in the brain. Shortly before the family moved to Boston, their doctors in Salt Lake City had told them that their little boy had only a few months to live. With the move to Boston for a new job, they had to change health insurers, and they knew that the new insurance would not cover a pre-existing condition. They had been counseled not to seek medical care for their son.

This sister had said nothing to anyone in our ward about the situation. The move had been very hard. The anxiety and fear of losing her little boy and the challenge of caring for her other small children had begun to wear on her. The night before Sue called, she had been very, very discouraged. Through her tears she had pleaded with the Lord for help and guidance. During her prayer she heard the words, "Don't worry, Sue Clark will call in the morning." The Lord knew this sister, and he knew Sue Clark, and he sent Sue to help her. And Sue, doing the will of the Lord, called and went. Sue put the sister in touch with our bishop; with a professor at the Harvard Medical School, who advised her on the medical issues; and with a woman who worked at Massachusetts General Hospital, who helped get medical coverage for the child. All of these people lived in our ward.

The Lord guided this woman and her family to Boston, and he guided Sue to them. There followed a wonderful experience for our family. The little boy underwent surgery many times and on those occasions we had the other children in our home. On many occasions those children would come over to our house and entertain (and inspire) our teenagers.

Looking back on those days, I realize that the Lord was watching over that family and over that little boy. He is an amazing young man. Not only did he live beyond the few months the doctors in Salt Lake thought he had, he has lived for many years. He is now twenty years old and is an inspiration to all who know him. He is blind, and he has some difficulty walking, but inside his weakened body is a mighty, joyous spirit. I know the Lord has worked through him to bless the lives of many people. And I know that when Sue called that day she heeded the promptings of the Spirit and did the will of the Lord.

When we do what Sue did, we not only seek the righteousness of God, we establish it in that situation where the Lord directs. His will prevails through the actions we take. Thus, to seek the righteousness of God and to establish it, we must act on the impressions of the Spirit. Indeed, if we act immediately in some way, even if it is only to write down the impression for action later, we become more sensitive to the Spirit and thus more capable in the service of the Lord. (I am indebted to Elder Richard G. Scott's teachings to a group of LDS students in Boston for the idea of writing down impressions immediately if we cannot act until later.) Acting on impressions requires us to exercise faith. But when we act in this way, with faith, the Lord uses us in his work. And we are doubly blessed: We are blessed with the peace and confidence that comes from following the promptings of the Spirit, and the Spirit teaches us the true principles that underlie the Lord's work as we do it. We thus not only have the joy that comes from being on the Lord's errand, but we also grow in knowledge and understanding of heavenly things and in our capacity to do the Lord's work.

Becoming Like the Savior

The personal growth that comes from doing the will of the Lord leads to the third principle in the search for the righteousness of God: to become like him. To seek the righteousness of God is not only to obey and to do his will but also to become as he is. We are the sons and daughters of God and we can be "heirs; heirs of God, and joint-heirs with Christ" (Romans 8:17). There is within us the possibility of becoming like our Heavenly Father and like his Son, the Lord Jesus Christ. This is not a distant prospect, but rather a process that goes on here and now as we seek the righteousness of God. The Savior taught this principle plainly and clearly to the Nephites when he appeared to them following his resurrection. In his first visit to them he said, "Therefore I would that ye should be perfect even as I, or your Father who is in heaven is perfect" (3 Nephi 12:48). Later, speaking to his disciples, he said, "Therefore, what manner of men ought ye to be? Verily I say unto you, even as I am" (3 Nephi 27:27).

To become like Christ sounds, to say the least, daunting. But it is the very purpose of our Father in Heaven's work, and part of the threefold mission of the Church. This is precisely what Paul taught the Ephesians: "And he gave some, apostles; and some, prophets; and some, evangelists; and some, pastors and teachers; for the perfecting of the saints, for the work of the ministry, for the edifying of the body of Christ." Paul goes on to define what he means by perfecting the saints: "Till we all come in the unity of the faith, and of the knowledge of the Son of God, unto a perfect man, unto the measure of the stature of the fulness of Christ" (Ephesians 4:11–13).

Christ is the standard against which we measure our progress.

This is the purpose of our search, to be perfected in all things, that we might obtain the righteousness of God and become like Jesus Christ.

This means that our search for righteousness is a development process. Obeying the commandments and doing the will of the Father are not easy or convenient or without opposition. But as we obey despite obstacles, as we learn to do the will of the Lord in the face of temptations and weaknesses and even persecution, the Lord shapes us. He takes us and sends us on his errand, gives us assignments in the kingdom, and teaches us and trains us through our experience. In this way we begin to develop the "righteousness of God" within us.

The Apostle Paul gives us important insights into this process. He first admonishes us to persevere in our search despite problems and obstacles: "Let us lay aside every weight, and the sin which doth so easily beset us, and let us run with patience the race that is set before us, looking unto Jesus the author and finisher of our faith" (Hebrews 12:1–2).

The word *finisher* here means one who completes or perfects. Jesus is not only the standard or measure of our search, he is our great teacher and personal developer. He develops us by applying a divine program of discipline:

> For whom the Lord loveth he chasteneth. . . . Furthermore, we have had fathers of our flesh which corrected us, and we gave them reverence: Shall we not much rather be in subjection unto the Father of spirits, and live? For they verily for a few days chastened us after their own pleasure; but he for our profit, that we might be partakers of his holiness. Now no chastening for the present seemeth to be joyous, but grievous: nevertheless afterward it yieldeth the peaceable fruit

of righteousness unto them which are exercised thereby.
(Hebrews 12:6, 9–11)

The "peaceable fruit of righteousness" comes to those who obey
the commandments of God, who do the will of the Lord, and who
are shaped and developed ("exercised") by the hand of the Lord. Part
of that shaping comes through our experience on the Lord's errand
as we learn and grow. But part comes through confronting and overcoming our sins and our weaknesses. All of us have weaknesses or
personal problems, and all of us may confront situations where those
weaknesses and problems hinder our ability to do the Lord's work.
Such weaknesses need not lead to sinful behavior. They may be such
commonplace problems as fear of speaking in public, or disorgani-
zation, or depression, or poor writing ability, or a deep lack of confidence, or fear of what others may think of us. In such matters, the
promises of the Lord are clear: through the atonement of Jesus Christ
we may overcome every weakness, every affliction, every problem
that stands in the way of our obeying the Lord's commands, doing
his will, and becoming like him. Our search for the righteousness of
God, therefore, must take us through and beyond these obstacles.

We can learn much about this process from Moroni's interview
with the Lord recorded in the twelfth chapter of Ether. Worried about
his ability to accomplish the will of the Lord, Moroni lamented his
weakness in writing: "Thou hast also made our words powerful and
great, even that we cannot write them; wherefore, when we write we
behold our weakness, and stumble because of the placing of our words;
and I fear lest the Gentiles shall mock at our words" (Ether 12:25).

But the Lord said:

Fools mock, but they shall mourn; and my grace is sufficient for the meek, that they shall take no advantage of

your weakness; And if men come unto me I will show unto them their weakness. I give unto men weakness that they may be humble; and my grace is sufficient for all men that humble themselves before me; for if they humble themselves before me, and have faith in me, then will I make weak things become strong unto them. Behold, I will show unto the Gentiles their weakness, and I will show unto them that faith, hope and charity bringeth unto me—the fountain of all righteousness. (Ether 12:26–28)

The Lord does not promise that the weak things will go away. He promises, "Weak things [will] become strong unto them." The weaknesses may still be there, but with the Lord's help we can work through them to do his will and keep his commandments.

Thus, our search for the righteousness of God must lead us to Christ. He is the fountain of all righteousness. Through the Atonement he has received all power over all things, including whatever it is that stands in the way of our search. That certainly means our personal weaknesses, but it also means our sins. All of us fall short. We all commit sin; we all depart from the strait and narrow path. When we lose our way, the Lord's commandments help us to forsake our sins and return to the path of righteousness.

The Lord gives us the guideposts that mark the strait and narrow path, but when we stray, he commands us to repent. As with all of his commandments, this one comes with a promise: Through the atonement of Jesus Christ we may find forgiveness and remission of our sins. When the Lord says, "my grace is sufficient," he teaches us that the forgiveness and the strength we receive are gifts born of his love and his mercy.

Moreover, as we discussed in chapter 2, faithful, sustained repentance brings about a mighty change of heart. When we recognize our sins, put aside our pride, and come to the Lord seeking his forgiveness, he not only forgives but also heals and makes us new. The life of Alma the Younger, a great Book of Mormon prophet, illustrates the healing, transforming, redeeming power of the Atonement. His experience is a metaphor for our search for righteousness. Our wandering from the strait and narrow path may be quite different from Alma's, but no matter what our circumstance, we must go through what Alma went through if we are to experience the change of heart that is the key to putting on the breastplate of righteousness.

Alma, the son of Alma the prophet, was a rebellious, wicked man who sought to destroy the church of God. (The story is found in Mosiah 27 and Alma 36.) He had great success in his destructive venture until an angel of the Lord confronted him with great power, spoke with the voice of thunder, and commanded him, "Go thy way, and seek to destroy the church no more . . . even if thou wilt of thyself be cast off" (Mosiah 27:16). Alma was so overcome by the angel's visit that he lost consciousness. (In Alma 36:11 Alma says that he "fell to the earth and . . . did hear no more.") The sons of Mosiah carried him to his father's house where for three days and three nights Alma went through a dramatic conversion. He remembered, in his words, "all my sins and iniquities, for which I was tormented with the pains of hell," and thought for much of that time that it would be better to be "banished and become extinct both soul and body," rather than "stand in the presence of my God, to be judged of my deeds" (Alma 36:13, 15).

In those moments of great remorse he felt the full weight of what he had done. In his mind there was no prospect of redemption to soften the blow of guilt that fell like a hammer. He believed in God, but in these hours of pain he did not think about the Savior or the possibility of redemption until, in a moment of inspiration, he remembered something his father had taught. Here is Alma's description of what happened in that moment of light:

> I remembered also to have heard my father prophesy unto the people concerning the coming of one Jesus Christ, a Son of God, to atone for the sins of the world. Now, as my mind caught hold upon this thought, I cried within my heart: O Jesus, thou Son of God, have mercy on me, who am in the gall of bitterness, and am encircled about by the everlasting chains of death. And now, behold, when I thought this, I could remember my pains no more; yea, I was harrowed up by the memory of my sins no more. And oh, what joy, and what marvelous light I did behold; yea, my soul was filled with joy as exceeding as was my pain! (Alma 36:17–20)

There is much for us to learn from this passage about the search for the righteousness of God. Touched by the light of Christ and inspired by the Spirit of the Lord, Alma remembered the words of God as he heard them from his father. This was not a simple reflection. His mind "caught hold upon this thought" like a drowning man catches hold of a lifeline. In that moment there was recognition and faith and hope. The Lord had answered the prayers of Alma's father, and Alma had been brought to see the light. He realized that the guilt, shame, and despair of his sinful, wicked past were not his lot forever. He could be redeemed from that awful future he had imagined only moments before. And so, Alma cried "within my heart" to the Savior and threw himself on the mercy of the Lord Jesus Christ. There was in that cry for help and for mercy a complete and total commitment to forsake his sins and become a new person. And then he felt the healing, redeeming power of the Atonement through an outpouring of the Spirit of the Lord. When he had regained his strength, Alma explained to his father and all those who had gathered to pray for him, "I have repented of my sins, and have been redeemed of the Lord; behold I am born of the Spirit" (Mosiah 27:24).

Following Alma's plea for mercy, the Lord blessed him with forgiveness and the joy of redemption, and taught him what his experience meant:

> And the Lord said unto me: Marvel not that all mankind, yea, men and women, all nations, kindreds, tongues and people, must be born again; yea, born of God, changed from their carnal and fallen state, to a state of righteousness, being redeemed of God, becoming his sons and daughters; and thus they become new creatures; and unless they do this, they can in nowise inherit the kingdom of God. (Mosiah 27:25–26)

For Alma, the contrast between his "exquisite . . . bitter . . . pains" and his "exquisite and sweet . . . joy" was a measure of the mighty change of heart that all of us need to go through to be spiritually born of God, to be redeemed of God, to be changed to a state of righteousness. Alma marveled that all of us have to go through what he had just gone through. But we do. The Lord taught Alma then, and he teaches us every time we read this passage, that this change of heart is essential to obtaining the righteousness of God, to becoming like Jesus is, and to attaining eternal life as an heir of the Father in his kingdom.

Alma's experience is a wonderful metaphor for the search for righteousness. Alma himself taught that the mighty change of heart he experienced sustains us on what he calls the "paths of righteousness." There are challenges to overcome, weaknesses to face, and temptations to avoid on those paths so that we might do all the Lord would have us do and become all that he would have us become. Yet the mighty change of heart is mighty indeed. When we come unto Christ as Alma did, with a contrite spirit and a broken heart, the power of the Atonement can work in us through the Spirit of the Lord to change us and bless us with capacity far beyond our own. Walking in those paths is a new way of life in which we follow Alma's admonition to be "humble, and . . . submissive and gentle; easy to be entreated; full of patience and long-suffering; being temperate in all things; being diligent in keeping the commandments of God at all times; asking for whatsoever things ye stand in need, both spiritual and temporal; always returning thanks unto God for whatsoever things ye do receive" (Alma 7:23).

Moreover, when we walk in those paths, when we "hunger and thirst after righteousness," the Savior promises that we will be "filled with the Holy Ghost" (3 Nephi 12:6). The Spirit blesses those who truly seek the righteousness of God with "peace . . . which passeth all understanding" (Philippians 4:7), "exquisite . . . joy" (Alma 36:21), and "the pure love of Christ" (Moroni 7:47). Indeed, those who walk in what Peter called the "way of righteousness" (2 Peter 2:21) are blessed by the Spirit not only to feel the Savior's love but also to love as Christ loves. In the remarkable words of Mormon:

> The first fruits of repentance is baptism; and baptism cometh by faith unto the fulfilling the commandments; and the fulfilling the commandments bringeth remission of sins; and the remission of sins bringeth meekness, and lowliness of heart; and because of meekness and lowliness of heart cometh the visitation of the Holy Ghost, which Comforter filleth with hope and perfect love, which love endureth by

diligence unto prayer, until the end shall come, when all the saints shall dwell with God. (Moroni 8:25–26)

And so, we come full circle. The first and great commandment is to love God with all our heart, mind, and soul; when we obey his commandments and repent of our sins, the Lord blesses us through his atonement with forgiveness and a mighty change of heart; we experience the power of the Holy Ghost in our lives, especially the gift of the pure love of Christ; because of the mighty change in heart, and because of the love we feel, our desires are directed to God. We walk in his paths, the paths of righteousness. We keep the commandments and do the will of the Lord. We are in his hands, shaped and perfected through his work and through the refining power of the Spirit to become like him. This is what it means to "seek . . . his righteousness"; this is what it means to put on the breastplate of righteousness—to keep the commandments, to do the will of the Lord, to become like him. All along the way the atonement of Jesus Christ gives that search meaning and purpose and power. As with every other element of the armor of God, putting on the breastplate of righteousness is to "be strong in the Lord."

CHAPTER 8

THE PREPARATION OF THE GOSPEL OF PEACE

Not long ago two members of our family were diagnosed with cancer. The first was my twenty-one-year-old daughter, Julia. She called one day to ask for advice about a lump on her neck. The lump proved to be a lymph gland enlarged by Hodgkin's disease. Since that time Julia has experienced two operations and months of chemotherapy. Three months later, while Julia was living at home for treatment, my wife, Sue, was diagnosed with what turned out to be cancer of the colon. Shortly after the diagnosis she underwent major surgery. There followed difficult days of recovery in the hospital before she was able to return home.

In those months, we learned much about cancer and how it works. Cancer cells grow in an uncontrolled, haphazard way. They invade and destroy the tissues and organs around them, and they can spread the work of destruction far beyond where they start. If the cancer is not stopped, it will grow and spread until it causes death. It is, therefore, important to find cancer cells early and good to get rid of them before they wreak havoc in the body. But it is hard to find them early. When cancer first begins there are no outward signs it is there. It grows quietly at first, hidden away until it grows enough to disrupt. Sometimes there are blood tests or physical examinations that will reveal the presence of cancer in the body at an early stage of its development. But sometimes we find out about it only when its destruction becomes obvious.

Cancer can also disrupt lives. When it happens, or when the doctors suspect it has happened, there are lots of tests, including different kinds of imaging and often biopsies. The treatment options are difficult. Sometimes the treatment is to cut out the cancer (and surrounding tissue). In other cases the doctors prescribe toxic drugs that kill rapidly growing cells everywhere in the body. Yet another therapy is to bombard the cancerous cells with radiation. And in some cases the patient has to undergo all three.

Interlaced with all of this coming and going from doctors' offices and hospitals and laboratories is the worry, the fear associated with a disease that can bring an end to mortal life. Every case is different, but every case of cancer comes with that underlying apprehension and fear. We experienced all of this in a double dose over those several months. The tests and the operations and the treatments disrupted our lives. There was much pain and suffering (cancer is one of those diseases where to save your life the doctors have to do some pretty bad things to your body), and there was much anxiety, worry, and fear.

But the fear and the anxiety gave way to hope and to confidence. Through the faith and fasting and prayers of our family, our ward members, and many good friends, we felt the hand of the Lord in our lives. Through many priesthood blessings we experienced inspiration and hope. Those blessings did not promise an end to the pain and the suffering. But they did bring the strength and power of heaven. We have come to understand that Julia and Sue do not walk this path alone. The Savior of the world walks with them. We have seen the powers of heaven work on their behalf, and we felt a great outpouring of the Spirit of the Lord as we prayed for them and served them in this difficult hour. In all this, the love in our family has increased, we have been united in our faith, and we know that the will of the Lord will be done. Though they must endure things that are hard and painful, the Lord has blessed Sue and Julia, and he has blessed our family, with the peace of heaven.

The promise of peace through Jesus Christ was a dominant theme in the gospel preached by the Savior in his earthly ministry and by his prophets throughout the ages. This peace of which the prophets speak is not the peace of the world, but the peace of the Spirit born of the exercise of faith and obedience to the commandments of the Lord. As long as we are faithful and true to the covenants we have made, the promise of peace is a true promise no matter what may happen to us. The peace of the gospel stands in sharp contrast to the turmoil and tribulation in the world. And yet, the peace of the gospel does not mean that we experience no problems or tribulation, or that we see no temptation or darkness in the world. It means that the Lord Jesus Christ helps us confront them, withstand them, and overcome them. This principle is an important part of Paul's description of the armor of God. As he admonishes us to "put on the whole armour of God" in preparation for spiritual battle, he counsels us to "Stand therefore, having . . . your feet shod with the preparation of the gospel of peace" (Ephesians 6:14–15). The word *preparation* here implies not only that we are to be ready for spiritual battle through the gospel of peace but that the gospel of peace will be a foundation, a firm footing, for our "wrestle . . . against the rulers of the darkness of this world." In this chapter I examine the peace the gospel brings, and its role as a preparation and foundation for our battle against the forces of evil.

My starting point is one of my favorite parts of the Book of Mormon, the story of Helaman and his two thousand stripling warriors. I first heard this story as a little boy. I remember sitting in Primary gazing in awe at the Arnold Friberg painting of Helaman and the stripling warriors heading off to battle. I was fascinated by the account of their courage and faith in the face of overwhelming odds. These were the sons of Lamanites who had been converted to the gospel of Jesus Christ through the ministry of Ammon and the other sons of Mosiah. These people, called the people of Ammon in the Book of Mormon, had made a covenant with God never to take up arms again, even in defense of themselves or their families. Their sons, however, had not made that covenant, and were prepared to help defend their families and the people of Nephi from the Lamanite armies. Two thousand and sixty of them marched under the leadership of Helaman into the great fifteen-year war against the Lamanites described in chapters 48 through 62 of Alma.

These were young men of courage and ability, but also of great faith and righteousness. Under the inspired leadership of Helaman, these young Ammonite warriors fought with great strength. Though they fought in many battles, and though they all were wounded, none of them were killed. In many of these battles they provided the crucial margin of difference between victory and defeat.

In one particularly difficult episode Helaman and his warriors faced a much larger Lamanite force, with no reinforcements and with little food to sustain them. They had looked for many days for additional support from the governor of the land, but they had to wait many months, and what arrived was far from sufficient. In that moment of great peril, Helaman's account of the action they took teaches us an important lesson about the relationship between war and the peace of the gospel. Helaman first recounts his concern about the lack of support they had received:

> And now the cause of these our embarrassments, or the cause why they did not send more strength unto us, we knew not; therefore we were grieved and also filled with fear, lest by any means the judgments of God should come upon our land, to our overthrow and utter destruction. (Alma 58:9)

Under attack every day, and faced with few provisions and no prospect of material support, Helaman turned to God:

> Therefore we did pour out our souls in prayer unto God, that he would strengthen us and deliver us out of the hands of our enemies, yea, and also give us strength that we might retain our cities, and our lands, and our possessions, for the support of our people. Yea, and it came to pass that the Lord our God did visit us with assurances that he would deliver us; yea, insomuch that he did speak peace to our souls, and did grant unto us great faith, and did cause us that we should hope for our deliverance in him. (Alma 58:10–11)

Helaman and his warriors went on to defeat the armies of the Lamanites through an inspired strategy that resulted in no loss of life on either side. Though still without support and still in a precarious position, Helaman's concluding comment on this battle and their prospects is evidence of his faith and the peace of the gospel: "We trust God will deliver us" (Alma 58:37).

There is in this story a pattern for our lives. In a moment of great fear, when anger and despair easily could have taken hold of their hearts, Helaman and his warriors turned to God and found peace. In that moment of anguish, the Lord "spoke peace" to their souls.

They felt the sweet assurance that they were in the Lord's hands. That peace brought feelings of hope, hope that no matter what lay ahead, "we should hope for our deliverance in him." Out of that peace and that hope came a renewed confidence to move forward despite what seemed insurmountable odds. They moved, took action guided by the Spirit, and the Lord delivered them as he had promised he would. He did it in his way, on his timetable (they were in peril for many months), but he did it.

We, too, face difficulties in our lives and we, too, may turn to God and find peace. I know from my own experience that this is true. But the peace of the gospel that Paul speaks of in Ephesians, the peace that is part of the armor of God, is more than a feeling of comfort or solace, as important as those feelings are. It is something much deeper. Paul speaks of the "preparation of the gospel of peace," a preparation for spiritual battle. In his description of the armor, he puts the gospel of peace on our feet. It is, therefore, our support, our foundation in our wrestle with wickedness. The peace of the gospel is in Jesus Christ, in his commandments, in his example, in his atonement. He is the Prince of Peace. Speaking to his disciples, and knowing the turmoil they faced and the difficult battles they would have to fight, Jesus said: "Peace I leave with you, my peace I give unto you: not as the world giveth, give I unto you. Let not your heart be troubled, neither let it be afraid" (John 14:27). Later, he taught them the source of that peace: "These things I have spoken unto you, that in me ye might have peace. In the world ye shall have tribulation: but be of good cheer; I have overcome the world" (John 16:33).

These are the promises of the Savior, promises of that deeper peace of which Paul speaks. What is the nature of this peace? How does it work in our lives? In what sense is this peace a preparation, a foundation, for spiritual battle? The Savior taught his disciples that they should not look for peace in the world but rather in him. The peace of the gospel of Jesus Christ is an inner peace, a peace of the spirit and the soul. In order to understand what this peace is and how the gospel brings it, I have found it useful to ask a simple question: if we are not at peace, if we do not have this peace of which the Savior speaks, with whom or with what are we at war? Three possibilities come to mind: (1) with our Father in Heaven, (2) with other people, or (3) with ourselves. In this framing of the problem I follow President Marion G. Romney, who wrote: "Peace has been variously defined, but perhaps we might think of it as 'harmony within one's self, and with God and man.' This conception includes all elements in the dictionary definition.

"The condition opposite to peace and harmony, say the lexicographers, is characterized by conflict, contention, disputation, strife, and war" ("The Price of Peace," *Ensign*, October 1983, 3).

In what follows I use these three relationships as a framework for studying the peace of the gospel and its critical role in the armor of God. As we look at each of these relationships, we shall see from whence war comes and how the gospel establishes peace. Peace is not just the absence of war, but there can be no peace if we are at war. The beginning of peace is to recognize where the conflict is and to take action to stop it. We can then move forward to find the deep peace the gospel brings.

Peace with God

In his masterful address, King Benjamin taught his people that "the natural man is an enemy to God" (Mosiah 3:19). Though we are his children and have within us divine potential, in our natural state we are apart from him. Alma's words to his son Corianton lay out this doctrine clearly. Speaking of the fall of Adam and Eve, he said:

But behold, it was appointed unto man to die—therefore, as they were cut off from the tree of life they should be cut off from the face of the earth—and man became lost forever, yea, they became fallen man. And now, ye see by this that our first parents were cut off both temporally and spiritually from the presence of the Lord; and thus we see they became subjects to follow after their own will. . . . Therefore, as they had become carnal, sensual, and devilish, by nature, this probationary state became a state for them to prepare; it became a preparatory state. (Alma 42:6–7, 10)

In this probationary state we are physically separated from the presence of God and are subject to the temptations of Satan. We may remove ourselves even further from God and his influence if we follow our own will and give place to the "natural man" in our lives. The "natural man" is the man or woman who lives "without God in the world," who is carnally minded, and who yields to the temptations of the devil (Alma 41:11). To the extent that we follow Satan and give place in our lives for the "natural man," we become dead to the things of the Spirit and put ourselves in a state of war with God.

Whether we actively rage against God and sin against that which is good, or accept wickedness in our lives in a state of carnal security, or simply ignore God, it matters not. To the extent we do any of these things, we act contrary to the will of the Lord and to his eternal purposes. To that extent we bring spiritual death and darkness into our lives and are at war with our Heavenly Father.

The gospel of Jesus Christ—the good news of the Savior's advent in the world and his atonement and resurrection—opens the way for us to overcome the natural man, to be reconciled with our Father in Heaven, and to find the deep peace the Savior promised. Though we are separated from God through the fall of Adam and Eve, God does not leave us alone in the world to fend for ourselves. All of us have the light of Christ, which leads us toward that which is good. Through the light of Christ all of us may know the difference between good and evil. If we follow that light and choose good, it will lead us to the strait and narrow path of the gospel. Along the way we may feel what King Benjamin called the "enticings of the Holy Spirit," and thus begin to taste spiritually what it would be like to be in the presence of our Father in Heaven again. Because our spirit has lived with Heavenly Father we know in our souls what it feels like to be in his presence. Thus, the Spirit can touch our souls, call up that divine memory, and "entice" us to put off the natural man and come home to our Heavenly Father.

Each of us who seeks to find the peace of the gospel must enter the strait and narrow path through the gate of baptism by water and by the fire of the Spirit. We must follow what the scriptures call the doctrine of Christ: faith in Christ the Son of the living God, repentance, baptism, and the gift of the Holy Ghost (see 2 Nephi 32:6). These are the first principles and ordinances of the gospel of Jesus Christ. Jesus likened these ordinances to a rebirth. He taught Nicodemus, "Except a man be born of water and of the Spirit, he cannot enter into the kingdom of God" (John 3:5). There is both symbolism and reality in the rebirth of baptism and the gift of the Holy Ghost. There is the symbolic burial in the water and the coming forth of a new person out of the water, quickened by the Spirit through the gift of the Holy Ghost. But there is reality here as well. The power of the Atonement is real. The change of heart is real. The Lord really does forgive our sins. His mercy and grace are real. Through that power and through the ministry of the Holy Ghost we become new, spiritually born of Christ.

As we saw in chapter 7, Alma experienced this powerful change of heart and the rebirth through Christ in his conversion. He also found the peace of the gospel. He described this experience to his son Shiblon:

> Now, my son, I would not that ye should think that I know these things of myself, but it is the Spirit of God which is in me which maketh these things known unto me; for if I had not been born of God I should not have known these things. . . . I was three days and three nights in the most bitter pain and anguish of soul; and never, until I did cry out unto the Lord Jesus Christ for mercy, did I receive a remission of my sins. But behold, I did cry unto him and I did find peace to my soul. (Alma 38:6, 8)

In that moment of forgiveness, in the sweet joy that came as the Holy Ghost filled his soul and bore witness to him that the mercy of Christ was real, Alma experienced once again the presence of his Heavenly Father. Though he remained a mortal man, subject to all the experiences of mortality, he was a new person, spiritually "born of God." As Alma himself said of his experience: "I have repented of my sins, and have been redeemed of the Lord; behold I am born of the Spirit" (Mosiah 27:24). Through the atonement of Jesus Christ Alma was once again spiritually alive. By exercising faith in Christ, by repenting of his sins, by keeping the commandments of God, Alma overcame spiritual death.

Until his encounter with the angel, Alma literally had been at war with God, trying to destroy the Church and leading as many people away from God as he could. Because of his gross wickedness Alma suffered great pain and agony of soul as he realized that Heavenly Father was real and that he had been at war with him. His plea to the Savior for mercy brought redemption and feelings of joy. And it brought peace to his soul.

The peace Alma experienced was a gift of the Spirit that came through the power of the Atonement and on condition of repentance and obedience. The Spirit worked on Alma, and it works on us, in two ways to bring about this deep peace. In the first, the Spirit heals us. Sin and wickedness and all the emotions that flow from them—anger, guilt, pain, cynicism, cruelty, hatred, darkness, sorrow—are like a cancer in our spirit. Like the cancer that strikes us physically, this spiritual cancer poisons and disrupts the life of the spirit and our communion with the things of heaven, and thus with our Heavenly Father. If, as was the case with Alma, that cancer grows and spreads, we become dead to the things of the Spirit. We cut ourselves off from the presence of the Father, and we suffer spiritual death.

But the miracle of the Atonement means that we can be healed. We can be completely rid of the cancer of sin. We can be reborn of the Spirit and once again be spiritually alive, spiritually whole. This is what the Savior meant when he said to those who had survived the great destruction in the lands of the Book of Mormon following his death and resurrection, "O all ye that are spared because ye were more righteous than they, will ye not now return unto me, and repent of your sins, and be converted, that I may heal you?" (3 Nephi 9:13). This is what the prophet Malachi meant when he prophesied of the Savior: "But unto you that fear my name, shall the Son of Righteousness arise with healing in his wings" (3 Nephi 25:2).

Healing is the first way the Spirit works on us to bring about this deep peace with God. The second is love. The atonement of Jesus Christ makes possible the healing of our spirits and our redemption from spiritual death. Everything about the Atonement testifies of the divine love that our Father in Heaven and the Lord Jesus Christ have for us. The Father loved us so much that he was willing to send his

Only Begotten Son, his Firstborn, into the world to suffer the agony of Gethsemane, scourging and ridicule at the hands of evil men, and renewed agony and an awful death on the cross at Calvary. Jesus Christ suffered all of that because of his great love for the Father, and because of his pure and perfect love for us.

That bearing of our burden, that love, was specific and personal. Our Father and our Savior know our names. They know us better than I know my children. And they love us personally. When we reach out to the Savior, when we come unto him, as Alma did, we are blessed to feel that personal love of the Father and of the Son. As the Spirit heals us, we can feel that love through the Spirit in a deep and powerful way. As Alma knew, so we know and feel in the depth of our souls that God our Father and his Son Jesus Christ love us.

In the experience of that love there is great joy and great unity and harmony with God. Moreover, there is a sweet and powerful sense of confidence in knowing deep in your heart that the Father of us all, and the Savior and Redeemer of the world, love you with an unending and all-encompassing love. Their love is an active, powerful force. They have acted on that love to create you and to pay for your sins and to overcome the pain and sickness and turmoil in your life. When you feel that love, the Spirit bears witness that because of their love for you they will act time and time again for as long as it takes to save you and redeem you. This is the love that "never faileth." In that testimony, born of the Spirit to your soul, there is the confidence and assurance that brings deep peace. Paul taught this principle to the Romans:

> Who shall separate us from the love of Christ? shall tribulation, or distress, or persecution, or famine, or naked-ness, or peril, or sword? . . . Nay, in all these things we are more than conquerors through him that loved us. For I am

persuaded, that neither death, nor life, nor angels, nor principalities, nor powers, nor things present, nor things to come, nor height, nor depth, nor any other creature, shall be able to separate us from the love of God, which is in Christ Jesus our Lord. (Romans 8:35, 28–30)

The deep peace with God that the gospel brings is a gift of the Spirit. It comes through the healing power of the Atonement and through the love our Father and the Savior have for us. It is a result of the redemption from sin wrought by Jesus Christ and the restoration of the true relationship we had with our Heavenly Father before we came to the earth. It comes only when we walk the strait and narrow path of faith, repentance, and obedience to the commandments of the Lord.

Peace with Our Brothers and Sisters

The same principles that bring peace with God also bring peace to our relationships with other people. Indeed, we cannot obtain peace with our Heavenly Father and remain at war with someone else. If we are to live the gospel of Jesus Christ in its fulness, we must seek to establish relationships of peace in our families, in our neighborhoods, at school, at work, everywhere we go. Jesus underscored the importance of peace and harmony in his sermon to the Nephites following his resurrection:

> And there shall be no disputations among you, as there have hitherto been; neither shall there be disputations among you concerning the points of my doctrine, as there have hitherto been. For verily, verily I say unto you, he that hath the spirit of contention is not of me, but is of the devil, who is the father of contention, and he stirreth up the hearts of

men to contend with anger, one with another. Behold, this is not my doctrine, to stir up the hearts of men with anger, one against another; but this is my doctrine, that such things should be done away. (3 Nephi 11:28–30)

In order to establish relationships of peace and harmony, we must overcome the temptations of the devil to "contend with anger." If we give in to those temptations repeatedly, we may come to have the "spirit of contention" and thus remove ourselves from the Spirit of the Lord. The foundation for overcoming these temptations is the doctrine of Christ: faith in Jesus Christ, repentance, baptism of water and of the Spirit, and obedience to the commandments. The healing, redemptive power of the Atonement that flows from applying this doctrine in our lives will help us to establish peace with others just as it helps us establish peace with God. Here, too, the mighty change of heart that comes through the ministry of the Holy Ghost will lead to a new way of life, a new pattern of interactions with other people, a pattern characterized not only by the absence of contention but by service and love. And out of that service and that love comes the deep peace of the gospel of Jesus Christ.

Taken together, the imperatives of peace—eliminate anger, contention, and strife from our interactions, and establish relationships of service and love—are at the core of the gospel. They are what it means to live the gospel. We establish them as a pattern in our lives through the small and simple acts of love and service of everyday life. This pattern of living is a familiar theme in lessons and talks in church. When I was growing up, my mom and dad and my Primary and Sunday School teachers taught me this pattern in many different ways. I learned the Golden Rule and the principles of the Sermon on the Mount. Phrases like "turn the other cheek," "love thine enemies," and "pray for them that despitefully use you" became familiar to me. The words of the Savior are not abstractions or generalities about overcoming contention or serving in love. These are words about the real work of daily life.

I learned this principle in a powerful way one day in a Book of Mormon class at BYU—Provo. The teacher, Terry Warner, taught us about the "network of anger and contention" that we create if we do not put into practice what the Savior taught. To illustrate this network he used the following example: Suppose you are driving in your car and in a hurry. Perhaps you are late for an important meeting. You come to a red light and stop. The light turns green, but the driver in front of you fails to notice immediately. Impatient and anxious, you honk your horn. The car in front begins to move, but not very fast. You look for an opening and see your chance to pull into the parking lane and get around the slow car. You quickly move into the parking lane only to discover that another car coming from the side street is trying to nose its way into traffic. Fearing another delay, you accelerate and cut off the nosing car before it can take that open space in the line of traffic. You have gained a precious few minutes in your journey, but behind you is the network of anger. The person you honked at is angry at being honked at and a few minutes later takes out that anger by honking at someone else. The person you cut off is frustrated and angry with you for not letting them get into traffic. They get so frustrated that they jump into traffic in a very tight place, making the car behind them slam on the brakes. And the network continues. By the time the day is over your impatience and anger could have propagated in the network to many, many people.

When I first heard this example I realized that Brother Warner was talking about me. I had done exactly that more than once. I had never thought of the network before. But Brother Warner taught me that the network works for kindness and love as well. If you let someone into traffic, thus helping them to avoid a long delay, you may spread some kindness in the world. Moreover, if someone cuts you off, you can stop the network of anger by following the Savior's teachings. Indeed, the Savior himself is our best example. He endured ridicule, abuse, and unjust punishment and said, "Father, forgive them; for they know not what they do" (Luke 23:34). He did not return anger for anger, but rather absorbed his tormentors' anger in his love.

We can do the same in the face of contention and anger and even unjust actions on the part of others. This does not mean that we need condone bad behavior or look the other way when wrongdoing takes place. After all, the Savior cleansed the temple of moneychangers with swift and powerful action. It does mean that if we "[reprove] betimes with sharpness," we must do so only when "moved upon by the Holy Ghost" (D&C 121:43). And even then we are to show love to those so reproved, so that anger and resentment do not take root in them.

In order to stop the network of anger and contention, and to spread goodwill and kindness, we must confront and overcome deep-seated, hardwired drives and instincts that are part of the natural man. Each of us has a system governed by the brain that protects us when we feel threatened or when fear strikes. This is clear when the danger is physical. Think about what happens inside of you when the driver in front of you slams on the brakes and you have to stop very quickly. Your brain recognizes the danger before you become conscious of it, and it initiates several chemical pathways that are designed to help you respond effectively to the danger. You can feel the effects of increased adrenaline and other changes in body chemistry as blood vessels dilate, your heart pumps faster, and you take swift and (hopefully) effective action. Most of these changes in your body are not under your control. They are automatic, and they work more quickly than you can think.

These protective mechanisms also work when the threat we perceive is emotional or psychological. If the danger is to our pride, or to our sense of what rightfully belongs to us, or to any number of expectations we have about how the world should work or how we should be treated, these natural mechanisms of defense and protection spring into action. When someone cuts me off in traffic, even when I am not in physical danger, I can feel those drives at work prompting me to anger or resentment. And, of course, Satan is always at work tempting me to give full voice to those impulses. But, in contrast to the physical response system, I can learn to control my response to psychological and emotional threats so that I do not give in to temptation and propagate ill will. If I can overcome the natural man, I can stop the network of anger and contention.

I believe that overcoming these natural instincts is one of the great challenges we face in establishing a pattern of peace in our lives. It really does take a mighty change of heart. The change needed is mighty because the impulses and drives of the natural man are very powerful. They are so powerful that we cannot overcome them alone. But we are not alone. There is one who has overcome these things and stands ready to help us overcome them as well. The healing, redeeming power of the atonement of Jesus Christ is available to all who exercise faith in Christ, repent and enter the strait and narrow path through the baptism of water and of the Spirit, and keep the Lord's commandments. Indeed, through the power of the Atonement we may become peacemakers. And that is precisely what the Lord wants us to do.

To be peacemakers we need to overcome our natural impulses and stop the network of anger and contention wherever we can. But we also need to love and serve our brothers and sisters. We do this by making the teachings of the Savior come alive in our example and practice. Elder M. Russell Ballard taught this principle with a poem from Francis of Assisi:

> Once we have tasted the sweet fruit of God's peace, we are naturally inclined to share it with others. Francis of Assisi was known as the "lover of creation" who lived most of his life ministering to the poor and the needy who were around him—including the animals. The peace he found in his service energized him and made him yearn to embrace others with it. He wrote:
>
> > *Lord, make me an instrument of thy peace;*
> > *Where there is hatred, let me sow love;*
> > *Where there is injury, pardon;*
> > *Where there is doubt, faith;*
> > *Where there is despair, hope;*
> > *Where there is darkness, light;*
> > *And where there is sadness, joy.*
> > *O Divine Master, grant that I may not so much seek*
> > *To be consoled as to console;*
> > *To be understood as to understand;*
> > *To be loved as to love.*
> > *For it is in giving that we receive;*
> > *It is in pardoning that we are pardoned,*
> > *And it is in dying that we are born to eternal life.*
> > ("The Peaceable Things of the Kingdom," *Ensign*, May 2002, 89)

In our Heavenly Father's plan we learn to do away with contention and to love and serve in the first instance in our families. We love and serve through many small acts of kindness and support. There may be times when we might do something quite large and significant to be of service. But it is in the work of daily life, in a kind word, a helping hand, a note of encouragement, a word of counsel, and much else that we make peace. And we learn to do these things in our families with people whom we see every day and whom we know intimately. As I have reflected on this principle, images of family life have flooded into my mind:

• A young mother waking up in the middle of the night to the cry of a baby boy in pain from colic. Walking the floor with the baby for a long time until he finally falls asleep. The scene repeated over and over again, with different babies, over many years.

• A young couple sitting on the floor in the bedroom, each holding and feeding one of the twin baby girls. All this taking place, once again, in the middle of the night, many, many times.

• A young child struggling in school, discouraged, frustrated, getting patient attention and pure love from a busy mother under a lot of stress.

• A scared, crying boy held by his dad while the doctor stitches up a nasty cut in the boy's forehead.

• A ten-year-old girl getting up in the middle of the night to help her mother with the twins because Dad is out of town.

• A fifteen-year-old boy singing up a storm in a concert by his band, and publicly dedicating his favorite song to his seventeen-year-old sister sitting in the audience.

• Mom and Dad and many siblings sitting and standing, clapping and cheering, sometimes coaching children in the family at countless basketball, baseball, football, softball, soccer, and hockey games—not to mention enduring hours and hours of swim meets.

• Helping with homework, answering questions, offering

encouragement, pointing out that homework needs to be done, reading essays, making sure the homework gets done.

• Eagle projects, camping trips in all seasons of the year, service projects, rides here and there and everywhere, chorus concerts, band-o-rama, music lessons, recitals, talks in church, jobs around the house and in the yard.

• Waiting up late for teenagers to come home. Watching out the window wondering where they are, hoping they are safe. More waiting and watching. Hugging them when they arrive, inquiring about their activities, reminding them of the concept of curfew and the importance of calling if they are going to be late.

• Consoling and lifting up a child who did not get picked for the team; another whose project did not win first place; another whose essay came back with a lot of red marks; another whose puppy died; another who has been snubbed by friends.

• A righteous brother laying his hands on the head of his younger sister to give her a blessing of healing and comfort just hours after she was diagnosed with cancer. All the brothers and sisters and Mom and Dad fasting and praying for her.

All of those images capture glimpses of family life in which we learn to be peacemakers by putting love into action through service. Not all of those activities or all of family life is full of peace. There are times of disagreement, and times when someone in the family may get upset with another family member, and times when they let each other know about it. When Dad comes home to find that his seven-year-old son and his friends have dug a three-by-four-foot hole in the backyard lawn ("we were trying to make a swimming pool"), his natural reaction may be to get angry. But under the direction of the Spirit (and with some practice!) he can learn to discipline and correct with love instead of anger. With repentance and tutoring by the Spirit, he will learn that he is raising boys, not grass. He will see in the seven-year-old the mighty elder in Israel his son will become, an elder whose faith and testimony and sense of responsibility will set him apart in the work of the Lord. And he will put the hole in the lawn in its rightful perspective and help his son do the same.

I know from my own experience that being a peacemaker in our families and in the world is hard. We are, after all, talking about a "*mighty* change of heart." I also know, however, that nothing is too hard for the Lord. I know from my own experience that the times of service, the times of putting love into action, will be far more prevalent, far more powerful, and indeed the dominant pattern of interaction in our families if we follow the counsel of the prophets by doing three simple things: (1) praying together as a family every day, morning and night; (2) reading the scriptures together, especially the Book of Mormon, every day; and (3) holding family home evening every week. I know that if we do these things, the promises of the prophets will come true: The Lord will bless our families with his Spirit, we will learn to stop the network of anger and contention, we will serve and love the members of our family, and those experiences will build our capacity to be peacemakers in everything we do.

Moreover, when we couple our commitment to be peacemakers with the full power of the doctrine of Christ—faith in Jesus Christ, repentance, obedience—the Lord will sanctify our efforts to love, and he will bless us with the pure love of Christ. Not only will we feel his love, but we will love others as he loves them. Mormon underscored the combination of our own effort and the work of the Spirit in obtaining the pure love of Christ. Speaking to "you that are of the church, that are the peaceable followers of Christ," he said:

> Wherefore, my beloved brethren, pray unto the Father
> with all the energy of heart, that ye may be filled with this
> love, which he hath bestowed upon all who are true followers

of his Son, Jesus Christ; that ye may become the sons of God; that when he shall appear we shall be like him, for we shall see him as he is; that we may have this hope; that we may be purified even as he is pure. Amen. (Moroni 7:48)

The pure love of Christ is "bestowed" on us, but only after we seek it and become "true followers" of the Savior.

The blessing of divine love is not something that happens to us all at once, nor, when it does happen, is it a part of us once and for all time. To love as Jesus loves is something that we must develop through our faithfulness, our obedience, our efforts to confront and overcome our weaknesses and sins. The promises are sure, but we must seek them, and having found them, we must endure in diligence. Elder Russell M. Nelson underscored the developmental nature of this process and the close connection between love and obedience:

> Jesus asked us to love one another as He has loved us. Is that possible? Can our love for others really approach divine love? Yes it can! The pure love of Christ is granted to all who seek and qualify for it. Such love includes service and requires obedience.
>
> Compliance with divine law requires faith—the pivotal point of mortality's testing and trials. At the same time, faith proves our love for God. The more committed we become to patterning our lives after His, the purer and more divine our love becomes. ("Divine Love," *Ensign*, February 2003, 25)

All of this means that we can become peacemakers. We can learn to love as Jesus loves. We can stop the network of anger and contention. We can serve with love in our families, in our communities, in the world. Through the atonement of Christ, through the doctrine of Christ, we can, in fact, establish relationships of peace with our brothers and sisters.

Peace with Ourselves

The third relationship we can enrich by applying the gospel of peace is with ourselves. Here, too, the principles of the gospel have the power to establish peace. Indeed, we cannot obtain peace with God, or peace with our brothers and sisters, unless we establish peace with ourselves. Jesus taught this principle when he responded to the wicked lawyer's question about the greatest commandment in the law with these immortal words: "Thou shalt love the Lord thy God with all thy heart, and with all thy soul, and with all thy mind. This is the first and great commandment. And the second is like unto it, Thou shalt love thy neighbour as thyself. On these two commandments hang all the law and the prophets" (Matthew 22:37–40).

The Savior commands us to love God with heart, soul, and mind, and to love our neighbor with the same commitment. If we love in this way, we will keep the commandments of the Lord and enjoy the gifts of the Spirit, including the peace that only the gospel brings. But the Savior also commands us here to love ourselves. Indeed, love of self is the standard against which we are to gauge our love for our neighbor. Since love of neighbor and self is to be "like unto" our love of God, it must also be with heart, soul, and mind. This must mean that if we are to find the deep peace that serves in the armor of God, we must come to love and be at peace with ourselves.

These three dimensions of ourselves—heart, soul, mind—may serve as a framework for understanding what it means to be at peace with ourselves. Although they are closely related, the distinction among them highlights important aspects of our search for peace.

In that search we must surely be careful not to fall into pride, or arrogance, or personal conceit. That is not what the Savior had in mind. But his words are clear: the deep peace of the gospel comes as we learn who we are and as we come to love ourselves, just as we love our neighbors and our Heavenly Father. And that love and that peace must come with our hearts, our souls, and our minds.

To understand establishing peace with ourselves it is useful to imagine the absence of peace in the mind, the soul, and the heart. We can then see how the gospel can help us obtain peace. Consider first the mind. It is common to speak of "peace of mind," and common to experience its absence. When our minds are unsettled, when we are not at peace there, it usually stems from events around us that cause concern, anxiety, and stress. We may have an assignment at work that we do not know how to handle. We may have a child who has wandered from the strait and narrow path. We may have lost a job and must find another. We may have hopes or dreams that are unrealized.

We may experience a thousand different things that rob our minds of peace. At their root, however, is a gap between our expectations of what our lives ought to be and what we think is going to happen. We are unsettled over the wayward child because we have an expectation of what that child should become, and we project the child's current behavior forward and see a gap, a failed expectation. And, of course, we see ourselves failing in our responsibility, and we pull all of that back to the present and feel unsettled and anxious in our minds. Like the network of anger and contention in our relationships with others, there is a cascade of fear caused by external events that, if unchecked, can rob us of peace of mind.

What happens to us in our external environment is real. But how we react depends on our perspective. Not everything that happens must rob us of peace of mind. The gospel can help us stop the cascade of fear. I learned this lesson long ago from a true story about a mountain climber:

Jeff had planned to climb in the Himalaya Mountains for many years. He had worked and trained and made all the arrangements. The morning after he arrived in Nepal, he went to the airport to take a short flight up to the base camp where the climbing would begin. The flight, however, had been cancelled because of weather. He went the next day, and the next, and the next with the same result: cancelled. In fact, the weather was bad for almost two weeks. On the last day that Jeff could travel to the base camp he went to the airport with high hopes, but to no avail. Desperate to make the climb, he asked the airline agent if there was any other way to get to the base camp. She told him that a bus that went up to the base camp was scheduled to leave from the city center at noon. He had twenty minutes to make it. Jeff rushed back and arrived at the city center just as the taillights of the bus disappeared in the distance. He had missed the last connection to the base camp for that climbing season. As he sat on the sidewalk, he could not believe all of his planning had been totally frustrated. And to miss the bus by two minutes was almost too much to bear. How would he explain this to all those people who had sacrificed to put him on the climb? He probably would never have this chance again. Jeff was the picture of dejection and sorrow. The next morning, however, his perspective changed completely. He learned that the bus he missed had slid off the icy mountain road and plunged several hundred feet down a ravine. Everyone aboard had been killed. Jeff was shocked. He no longer worried at all about not climbing the mountain. He was grateful to be alive and to be going home to his loved ones.

The gospel of Jesus Christ can change our perspective on what happens to us just as firmly and as powerfully as that accident changed Jeff's view of missing the bus and the climb. If you know that you are a child of God, that you lived with him before you came to this earth, that you were valiant in the heavens, and that you are here to gain the experiences of mortality and learn to be obedient and faithful, you will see the turmoil and trials of life differently. If you know that Jesus Christ descended below all things, that he has all power over all things, and that you can obtain that power to help you through anything that happens, you will face those trials with hope, and you will stop the cascade of fear. If you have faith in Christ, if you are true to the covenants you have made, you can access the powers of heaven to strengthen and sustain you in the difficult hour. If you trust in the Lord and in his chosen servants, you have access to the power and authority of the priesthood, and you can receive blessings under its direction. If you love as Jesus loves—including yourself—you can experience peace of mind even in the face of serious problems.

All of this means that, no matter what happens, you are not alone. There is meaning and purpose in your circumstances, and the blessings of heaven will come. This does not mean that the gospel will eliminate trials, or that events around you won't be cause for concern. It simply means that you can see them for what they really are—part of mortal life and the great plan of your Heavenly Father, part of your education as a disciple of Christ. It also does not mean that everything will be easy. Think of the Prophet Joseph Smith in Liberty Jail. Surely that was hard! Surely he suffered! Surely he was tested! But the promise the Lord made to Joseph is the same promise he makes to you:

> My son, peace be unto thy soul; thine adversity and
> thine afflictions shall be but a small moment; and then, if

thou endure it well, God shall exalt thee on high. (D&C 121:7–8)

Know thou, my son, that all these things shall give thee experience, and shall be for thy good. The Son of Man hath descended below them all. Art thou greater than he? (D&C 122:7–8)

With that perspective, with that faith, with all the blessings of the gospel, you can see things that happen to you in their true light. You can feel the love of the Savior for you. You can look to the future with hope. Peace of mind, therefore, is strongly affected by the peace in your soul, or peace of conscience. Elder Richard G. Scott defined peace of conscience and its connection to our peace of mind this way:

God wants each of His children to enjoy the transcendent blessing of peace of conscience. A tranquil conscience invites freedom from anguish, sorrow, guilt, shame, and self-condemnation. It provides a foundation for happiness. . . .

Peace of conscience is the essential ingredient to your peace of mind. Without peace of conscience, you can have no real peace of mind. Peace of conscience relates to your inner self and is controlled by what you personally do. Peace of conscience can come only from God through a righteous, obedient life. ("Peace of Conscience and Peace of Mind," *Ensign,* November 2004, 15)

Each of us is blessed with the light of Christ. The scriptures teach us that through the light of Christ each of us has the capacity to know right from wrong. Each of us has a conscience. In order to understand the light of Christ and our conscience, and the peace of the gospel, I have found, of all things, my garage door to be a useful metaphor. My garage door has a power mechanism that opens or closes the door when I activate the motor by pushing a button. To protect against injury, there is a safety device that cuts off power if anything is standing in the path of the door. The device works by shining a beam of infrared light across the width of the door. A photoreceptor cell receives the beam. As long as the receptor cell can see the beam, the electric motor will work. But if the beam is interrupted, the motor and the door stop.

Here is the analogy. We come to earth from heaven where we lived with our Heavenly Father and where we were taught the plan of salvation and chose to follow the Savior. This is our true identity, our true nature, and our true self. We bring with us all of that experience in our spirits, but in order to make this life a time of real testing we cannot remember all that we know. Except for one thing: the Lord lets us remember just enough to know right from wrong. It is as if we are given a "light receptor" whose cells are sensitive to the light of Christ. That light strikes the cells and activates our spiritual safety circuit, or our capacity to discern right from wrong—our conscience. When we do what is right, the light shines, the cells receive that light, and our conscience is at peace. In a sense, our soul is in harmony with who we really are and who we really should be. When we contemplate doing something wrong, the system senses that the light is about to be disrupted and we receive warning signals that we are about to make a mistake. When we actually do something wrong, the light is disrupted to some extent, the cells are dimmed, and we hear about it from our conscience. Elder Scott suggests that "the ability to have an unsettled conscience is a gift of God to help you succeed in this mortal life" ("Peace of Conscience," 15).

The key to peace of conscience is to keep the commandments of the Lord, and to repent and return to the light if we sin. Moreover, if we persist in keeping the commandments our capacity to discern the light increases. Our spiritual sensitivity grows and we deepen the sense of peace that comes as a gift of the Spirit. Indeed, the promise of the Lord is that as we endure in faith and obedience it is as if our "light receptor" expands until our whole soul is filled with light. A soul that is full of light is a soul filled with love. It is a soul at peace.

When we are at peace in our souls, when we have that love and that light with us, we are able to achieve peace of mind in the face of whatever comes our way. And we may also find peace in our hearts. If the metaphor of the heart captures our innermost desires, our deepest drives and emotional commitments, and our capacity for love, to have an unsettled heart is to be deeply conflicted, to be at war with ourselves. In part this may come from sin, in part from the cascade of fear triggered by external events. If our hearts are not at peace, we surely will not have peace of mind or peace of conscience. Unless we repent and seek the blessings of the Spirit, unless we gain a gospel perspective on our situation, such inner conflict and fear of failure can degenerate into self-condemnation, self-loathing, and a deep loss of love of self, and of peace.

The great prophet Nephi, the son of Lehi, gives us a glimpse both of that inner conflict and of the way to achieve peace in our hearts. Shortly after their father died, Nephi's brothers "were angry with [him] because of the admonitions of the Lord" (2 Nephi 4:13). Their anger was so intense that "they did seek to take away [his] life" (2 Nephi 5:2). We do not know the details of what happened, but Nephi must have felt anger toward his brothers and discouragement at his situation. He must have experienced conflict between the impulses of the natural man and his commitment to the Lord, because he writes about turmoil in his heart with words of anguish:

> Nevertheless, notwithstanding the great goodness of the
> Lord, in showing me his great and marvelous works, my

heart exclaimeth: O wretched man that I am! Yea, my heart
sorroweth because of my flesh; my soul grieveth because of
my iniquities. . . . why should my heart weep . . . ? Yea, why
should I give way to temptations that the evil one have place
in my heart to destroy my peace and afflict my soul? Why
am I angry because of mine enemy? Awake, my soul! No
longer droop in sin. Rejoice, O my heart, and give place no
more for the enemy of my soul. Do not anger again because
of mine enemies. Do not slacken my strength because of
mine afflictions. (2 Nephi 4:17, 26–29)

Nephi feels the weakness of the flesh—his pride, his anger, his
natural response to strike out and thus trust in the arm of flesh. He
sees iniquity in his attitude and his behavior, and he recognizes the
danger before him. His anger has given the "enemy of [his] soul" an
opening to tempt him and to destroy his peace by giving that evil
one "place in [his] heart."

But in the very moment of anguish, Nephi sees clearly what he
must do: cry unto the Lord, rejoice in the Lord, trust in the Lord.
Instead of following the natural man and giving full vent to his anger
against his brothers, Nephi cries out for the redeeming, healing
power of the Lord:

O Lord, will thou redeem my soul? Wilt thou deliver me
out of the hands of mine enemies? . . . May the gates of hell
be shut continually before me, because that my heart is broken and my spirit is contrite! O Lord, wilt thou not shut the
gates of thy righteousness before me, that I may walk in the
path of the low valley, that I may be strict in the plain road!
O Lord, wilt thou encircle me around in the robe of thy

righteousness! . . . O Lord, I have trusted in thee and I will trust in thee forever. (2 Nephi 4:31–34)

The external danger facing Nephi was real. His brothers sought to destroy him and his family. But there was an inner danger as well. Nephi teaches us here that confidence in the future, peace in our hearts, and eternal deliverance from what we face are to be found along the strait and narrow path.

What Nephi sought does not come from a heart that is full of fear and anger, a spirit that is caught up in self-righteousness and pride, and a trust in the arm of flesh. What he sought—confidence, peace, hope, deliverance—comes through the Savior to those who come unto him with a broken heart and a contrite spirit, who enter into the strait and narrow path, the "path of the low valley." All this comes to those who keep the commandments, who are true to their covenants, who are "strict in the plain road." All this comes to those who trust in the Lord.

When we trust in the Lord and walk the plain road in the low valley, we bring to pass in our lives the doctrine of Christ. On that road we walk with God, and we may enjoy all the blessings of the Spirit, including the pure love of Christ. And because of that great gift we may enjoy peace in our hearts. As Mormon taught long ago, "perfect love casteth out all fear" (Moroni 8:16). There is, therefore, a great symmetry, a great unity in the way to achieve peace of mind, of soul, and of heart. Jesus Christ is the way. In the doctrine of Christ, in his atonement, is the great key to the peace the gospel brings. Here is the key to establishing relationships of peace with our Heavenly Father, with our brothers and sisters, and with ourselves. Here is the key to peace of mind, of conscience, of heart. Through the atonement of the Savior we can become peacemakers, and we can close up to the evil one any room to tempt us or to destroy that peace with sin, or with anger, or with pride, or with fear. When the Savior said, "In me ye might have peace" (John 16:33), he gave us the key to the preparation of the gospel of peace, the great foundation and sure footing of the armor of God.

CHAPTER 9

THE SHIELD OF FAITH

One early evening Sue and I drove west on Route 2 just outside of Boston. This highway climbs one of the highest hills in the Boston metropolitan area. As we drove up the long ascent, we saw on our left the Boston Temple standing at the very top of the hill. The sun had set by that time, and the outside lights bathed the temple in a soft glow. Approaching the temple from the front, we could see the beautiful stained glass in the windows, the steeple reaching to the sky, and the angel Moroni holding forth at the very top. It was a sight both striking and beautiful. I felt a great sense of gratitude come over me, gratitude for the tender mercies of the Lord, for an inspired prophet, for the faith of many, many Latter-day Saints, for the miracle that is the Boston Temple. It is a feeling I always have when I approach that temple, in part because we lived there for many years without the temple, and in part because I know firsthand what it took to make the temple a reality. It truly is a miracle of faith.

This chapter is about the shield of faith in the armor of God. I know of no better introduction to this wonderful topic than the story of the Boston Temple. Its story not only illustrates the power of faith but also shows how the Lord works miracles when his children exercise faith. The story begins in 1978 with a search for land to build a new chapel in the Belmont area. Kent Bowen, the bishop in charge of the search committee, asked one of his counselors, Steve Wheelwright, to identify all of the possible sites in Belmont. Steve found seventeen acres of land for sale that seemed ideal for a chapel. The land was owned by Ruth Rappoli, whose late husband had acquired the land many years before. He and his wife had always believed that the site was perfect for a church. When Steve first visited with Mrs. Rappoli about the possibility of the LDS Church buying the land, she asked, "Will you build a temple like the beautiful one you have in Washington, D.C.?"

The Church acquired the land, and plans were made to build a chapel. The original plans called for the chapel to be placed at the center of the site, but the landscape architect, a member of the local ward, felt impressed to protect the prominent hill area by locating the chapel in the farthest southwest corner of the property. Supported by local Church leaders, the architect felt strongly that the chapel should go there so that the rest of the site might be large enough to someday support a temple. The Church's building department approved the new location. That decision put the chapel as close to the neighboring houses as the zoning regulations would allow, and there was strong protest in the town. Eventually the Church received permission to build the chapel and its parking lots, but not before many difficult hearings. The chapel conformed to all the zoning codes, so there was no basis for the town to deny a building permit. However, they refused to grant permission for a parking lot. It was not until the Church brought suit in state court that the town relented and approved the parking lots. Eventually the chapel was opened, but not before arsonists burned a great deal of it to the ground, forcing the new Belmont Ward to spend a year meeting in various churches around town while the chapel was rebuilt.

We moved into the new chapel in 1985. Members of the ward talked often, and prayed often, about the possibility of a temple on the ten acres of land next to the chapel. The undeveloped site was a large, forested, granite outcropping, and the most prominent hill in the western suburbs of Boston. It seemed a perfect place for a temple. A few years later when the Church announced there would be a temple in Hartford, Connecticut (about ninety miles from Boston), our dream of a temple on Belmont Hill seemed a more distant prospect. But the Lord had more immediate plans. In October of 1995, ten years after the Belmont Ward moved into the new chapel, President Hinckley announced that a temple would be built in Boston. The site of the new temple would be the ten acres of Mrs. Rappoli's hill. In April of 1995 President Hinckley had visited the site and had recorded in his journal what happened in that visit:

> As I stood there I had an electric feeling that this is the place, that the Lord inspired its acquisition and its retention. Very few seemed to know anything about it. . . . I think I know why I have had such a very difficult time determining the situation concerning Hartford. I have prayed about it. I have come three or four times. I have studied maps and tables of membership. With all of this I have not had a strong confirmation. I felt a confirmation as I stood in Belmont on this property this afternoon. This is the place for a House of the Lord in the New England area. (Sheri L. Dew, *Go Forward with Faith: The Biography of Gordon B. Hinckley* [Deseret Book, 1996], 530)

The decision announced in October of 1995 began a long and difficult process to get the temple approved by the Belmont zoning board of appeals. At every step of the way we experienced serious opposition. Because the site was large, the temple could be placed so that it conformed to all zoning rules except for the height of the steeple. That put us before the zoning board, and they chose to examine and hold hearings on the entire project. There were a dozen public hearings held over seven months. Though we had some courageous souls in town who offered support, there was intense and widespread opposition to the temple. We felt we had the law on our side, but there was always the prospect of a protracted legal battle if the zoning board did not approve the temple. Moreover, the legal framework (called the Dover Amendment) in Massachusetts law that protected church construction from local zoning was under attack in the state courts. There was a real possibility that the courts might act to support the town if the zoning board denied permission to build. And there was always the worry that a spirit of contention and opposition would affect the standing of the Church in Belmont and throughout the Boston area. There were many times during those months that members of the Church in the New England area fasted and prayed to the Lord for help and guidance. It was a time in which our faith was tested. But we knew that the Lord had spoken through his prophet and that with our faith the Lord could work a miracle on Belmont Hill.

And that is what he did. The zoning board approved the original design of the temple in late 1996 on a 4–1 vote. After the approval President Hinckley decided to reduce the size of the temple (size had been one of the major concerns of the opposition) and to change its design (the original had been modeled after the Salt Lake Temple) to make it more compatible with traditional New England church architecture. These changes were a masterstroke. Many in the town greeted them with approval, and after yet more hearings the zoning board approved the new design unanimously. We experienced the prophet's decision as a great blessing of the Lord. It changed fundamentally the way most people in the town saw the temple and the Church. We rejoiced in the inspiration of a living prophet.

But that was not the end of opposition. A group of neighbors sued the Church and the town in state court over the height of the steeple. Though the Church decided to go ahead with construction of the temple, there followed many months of legal arguments, public scrutiny of the construction, and uncertainty about the outcome of the court case. We were shocked when the judge handed down a decision against the Church. Finding that the steeple had no religious purpose, the judge ruled that it was not protected under the Dover Amendment and that the zoning board had acted inappropriately in approving it. The Church appealed the decision to the State Supreme Court, but the lower court decision meant that the temple would not have a steeple in time for the dedication.

As the appeal worked its way through the court system, design and construction of the temple moved forward toward the planned open house and dedication in the fall of 2000. Although there were many problems during the design and construction, there were many little miracles that solved them. Indeed, there was a great spirit on the temple site throughout construction. Some examples:

• When the individual doing the site plan (a member of the Church) began work on the location of the temple, a feeling of darkness came over him. He could not think and was not able to develop any coherent ideas. He struggled for days, finally deciding that he would have to bow out of the assignment. At that very moment his bishop sent a message to the ward asking all the members of the ward to fast and pray on that coming Sunday for those working on the temple. The following Monday as he sat down to work, a marvelous spirit came over him and, almost as if someone took control of his hand, he drew the site plan and placed the temple exactly where it is located today.

• A construction worker fell many, many feet from scaffolding but suffered only minor bruises.

• Problems in installation and delays in the delivery of stained-glass windows and the exterior granite seemed sure to delay the project, but did not.

• Just before the open house was to start, the carpet for the celestial room arrived with a major problem, but there was unexpectedly exactly enough extra length in the carpet to allow for a quick solution.

There are many other examples of small miracles paving the way for the completion of the temple. Of course, many people worked very hard and prayed very hard to build that temple. But there is no doubt that the powers of heaven were at work.

The open house took place in the late summer of 2000. This, too, was a remarkable experience. Up until that time the Church had conducted only silent tours of temples during open houses. Only General Authorities were allowed to explain the ordinances and the doctrine while conducting a tour. With the Boston Temple, the Church made a change and allowed the tour guides to speak and teach during their tours. I had the great blessing of serving as a tour guide during the open house of the Boston Temple. More than 75,000 people attended the open house. I took many groups through and had opportunity to explain the marvelous blessings of the temple and bear testimony of the power of the temple in our lives.

Many people worked long hours, and many small miracles occurred to make the open house a success. Virtually the day before the open house began, the Area President decided it would be good to provide lemonade and cookies to participants after completing a tour. This would give tour guides and workers a chance to mingle with participants and to provide literature and further explanation and fellowship. Providing something like 200,000 cookies and enough lemonade for 75,000 people was an enormous project. During this time Sue became one of the "cookie ladies," helping to organize the procurement and distribution of all those cookies. And it worked! The cookies and lemonade were a tremendous success, enjoyed by the participants and creating a time for great discussions and fellowship. It took a lot of hard work and the help of heaven, but it was an inspired decision.

President Hinckley dedicated the temple on October 1, 2000. Several months later the State Supreme Court handed down a decision on the steeple, written by the Chief Justice, Margaret Marshall. Justice Marshall repudiated the argument of the lower court judge and reinstated the zoning board's decision. The steeple was added to the temple about a year after its dedication. Thus, after twenty-one years of zoning board hearings, legal battles in state court, arson, more hearings, more legal battles, a complex and difficult construction, and, finally, a case that went all the way to the Massachusetts Supreme Court, the Boston Temple was complete. It stands today on Belmont Hill, a majestic, beautiful testimony to the eternal purposes of the Lord and the power of faith.

The story of the Boston Temple illustrates the power of Paul's counsel: "Above all, taking the shield of faith, wherewith ye shall be able to quench all the fiery darts of the wicked" (Ephesians 6:16). In this chapter I want to look closely at what it means to "put on" faith in Jesus Christ, and how faith in the Savior serves as a shield.

Faith in Jesus Christ

When we lived with our Heavenly Father before we came to this earth, we knew him and heard his voice and experienced his presence. We heard his plan for us and saw our elder brother, Jesus Christ, chosen to be our Savior. Lucifer, a son of the morning, offered a different plan and sought to draw us away from the plan of the Father. Lucifer became an enemy to God and launched a battle for our allegiance and our souls. In the great ensuing war in heaven we had to make a choice, and in making that choice we had to exercise faith—faith in our Father, faith in Jesus Christ. We had to act on the understanding we had of the Father's plan. We had to have faith in the promise that Jesus would redeem us from sin and pain and weakness, even though we had not experienced any of that and could not see the future the Father described. Even then, the Father had given us agency to choose, and even then, even in his presence, we had to trust in the Savior's word. We had to act on the basis of what we knew, and what we believed, and in whom we trusted.

That same challenge is ours today. It is a challenge of which the prophets through the ages have spoken. Three of them—Paul, Alma the Younger, and Moroni—have given us particularly powerful discourses on faith. These discourses share common themes that will help us understand what it means to have faith in Jesus Christ, and how we obtain it. Consider first the central passage in each of these great sermons:

Paul writing to the Hebrews: "Now faith is the substance [assurance, basis] of things hoped for, the evidence [proof] of things not seen" (Hebrews 11:1).

Alma speaking to the poor among the Zoramites: "And now as I said concerning faith—faith is not to have a perfect knowledge of things; therefore if ye have faith ye hope for things which are not seen, which are true" (Alma 32:21).

Moroni writing to us in Ether: "And now, I, Moroni, would speak somewhat concerning these things; I would show unto the world that faith is things which are hoped for and not seen;

wherefore, dispute not because ye see not, for ye receive no witness until after the trial of your faith" (Ether 12:6).

Four words capture the central idea in these passages: *hope, things, not seen.* Though they apply to any object of faith, our purpose here is to understand faith in the Lord Jesus Christ. It is that faith that the Prophet Joseph Smith named the first principle of the gospel, and it is that faith that serves as the shield in the armor of God. So, how do these four words apply to the Savior?

Consider first the word *things.* What are the "things" connected to the Savior in which one might invest hope? They are all that Jesus has done, does now, and will do to bring about the great plan of salvation for us: he loves, redeems, heals, comforts, forgives, protects, defends, creates, blesses, changes, transforms, leads, directs, reveals, sustains, builds, prepares, teaches, judges, advocates, mediates, shepherds, commands, suffers, overcomes, rises from the dead, has all power over all things. All these "things" take on special and eternal meaning because of who Jesus is. As President Ezra Taft Benson so eloquently taught many years ago, Jesus Christ is the object of our faith because he is: the Lord God Omnipotent, the Son of God, the Firstborn, the Only Begotten Son, The Redeemer, the Lawgiver, the Resurrection and the Life, the great Exemplar, the Bread of Life, the Prince of Peace, the Good Shepherd, our Advocate with the Father, the Master (see "Jesus Christ: Our Savior and Redeemer," *Ensign,* November 1983, 6–8).

Who Jesus is and what Jesus does are the "substance of things hoped for," "that are true," "and not seen."

In what sense are the things that Jesus does "not seen"? Sometimes what Jesus does lies in the future, and we cannot yet experience it with the five senses of the natural man. Suppose a prophet of God says to us, "If you will repent and ask God for forgiveness, he will forgive you, and through the power of the atonement of Jesus

Christ you can be made clean and whole." We cannot see the forgiveness or the healing, cleansing power of the Atonement with our natural eyes, nor can we feel or taste or smell or hear it. It lies in the future. But there is more. Even if we act on the counsel of the prophet and experience forgiveness and the cleansing power of the Atonement, the process through which the Savior brings all that to pass will remain "not seen" with our natural eyes.

What then of hope? Consider again the example of repentance. When we follow the counsel of the prophets to repent even though we cannot see what they promise, we hope for a state of the world that is different from the one we currently experience. We may be burdened with guilt and shame; we may feel distress and anguish at the suffering we have caused. In the promise of the Atonement lies the possibility of a different reality, a better world where that guilt and shame will be gone, where we no longer feel distress and anguish but stand forgiven of the Lord, clean and pure, with a heart, mind, and soul that is at peace. It is that better world that is the object of our hope. Though we cannot see that future world with our natural eyes, we can envision it through hope. Indeed, to hope for that world is to see that future in our minds with confidence.

All three of the discourses on faith from Paul, Alma, and Moroni make clear the important role of vision in hope, and thus, faith. Speaking of the ancient patriarchs Enoch, Noah, and Abraham, Paul wrote: "These all died in faith, not having received the promises, but having seen them afar off, and were persuaded of them, and embraced them, and confessed that they were strangers and pilgrims on the earth" (Hebrews 11:13). Alma taught that like a little seedling, the word of God must be nourished in our hearts or it will wither: "And thus, if ye will not nourish the word, looking forward with an eye of faith to the fruit thereof, ye can never pluck of the fruit of the tree of life" (Alma 32:40). In a similar way, Moroni spoke of the faith of the brother of Jared (and others) in this way: "And there were many whose faith was so exceedingly strong, even before Christ came, who could not be kept from within the veil, but truly saw with their eyes the things which they had beheld with an eye of faith, and they were glad" (Ether 12:19). In the light of these passages we see that to hope for the things of Christ that are not seen, that are true—that is, to have faith in Jesus Christ—is to envision the reality of the Savior. It is to see with our spiritual eyes who he is, what he does, and the principles upon which he acts. It is to trust in what we envision so that we may take action to follow him.

Here then are the "things" of Christ, "not seen," for which we hope. Here is faith in the Lord Jesus Christ. Here is the faith that connects us, through our actions, to the world of our hopes. Return again to the example of repentance. As we contemplate acting on the promise of the prophets, we can see with the eye of faith the Savior in the garden of Gethsemane and on the cross of Calvary. We can see his arms reaching out to us, inviting us to come unto him. We can envision the power of the Savior acting and working on us to heal and cleanse and redeem. We can see the reality of the Atonement in our lives. We can see ourselves forgiven, whole, and at peace. We envision all of this, and having that faith and that hope and that trust, we act. We exercise our faith, acting on what we have envisioned and on our understanding of the promises we have been given. We follow the counsel of the prophets, and we repent.

As we do so, we experience the reality of our hope. It may not come immediately. There may be a time of testing and probing. But the reality of forgiveness will come. When it comes, the Spirit bears witness to us that what we have seen and done is true: Jesus is the Christ, he is all that the prophets have said he is, he has power to heal and to redeem, and we can partake of that power. The promises are true. And so our confidence increases, our hope is more sure, we see more clearly, and our faith in Jesus Christ grows stronger.

Obtaining Faith in Jesus Christ

How does one obtain such faith in Jesus Christ? Paul taught, "Faith cometh by hearing, and hearing by the word of God" (Romans 10:17).

We can hear the word of God through the scriptures, through living prophets, and through personal revelation. As Nephi taught, "When a man speaketh by the power of the Holy Ghost the power of the Holy Ghost carrieth it unto the hearts of the children of men" (2 Nephi 33:1). When we really hear—that is, when we listen with the Spirit, with a heart that is open and prepared—the Holy Ghost will testify to us that the words of the prophets are true. This is how we hear of Jesus Christ, how we learn of his gospel, how we come to know who he is and what he does.

This is the first step on the road to faith. We must hear the word of God from his authorized servants. But in hearing, we must let those words into our hearts. Alma's great sermon on faith teaches this principle through the metaphor of planting a seed:

> Now, we will compare the word unto a seed. Now, if ye give place, that a seed may be planted in your heart, behold, if it be a true seed, or a good seed, if ye do not cast it out by your unbelief, that ye will resist the Spirit of the Lord, behold, it will begin to swell within your breasts; and when you feel these swelling motions, ye will begin to say within yourselves—It must needs be that this is a good seed, or that the word is good, for it beginneth to enlarge my soul; yea, it beginneth to enlighten my understanding, yea, it beginneth to be delicious to me. (Alma 32:28)

Speaking to those who had forgotten all they ever knew of Christ and therefore had little faith in him, Alma prescribes the starting point for a plan to obtain faith in Jesus Christ: Hear the gospel of Jesus Christ, give place in your heart for its message, let the Spirit of the Lord work in your heart. There is more here than just listening to the word. In Alma's words, we must "awake and arouse [our] faculties" (Alma 32:27) and hear the gospel without rejecting it out of hand. We must consider the possibility that it is true and let that possibility work in our hearts. In effect, Alma counsels us to envision the truth of the gospel in our lives. As we do so, he promises us that the Spirit of the Lord will teach us so that our understanding will increase. As we ponder what we have heard, as we try to see what it means for us, the Spirit will guide us into new insights as the light of the gospel begins to illuminate our understanding.

The metaphor of the seed is very important here. Just as planting in fertile soil opens up the seed and unleashes the new life it carries within itself, so giving place to the word of God so that the Spirit may work in our hearts unleashes new life within us. And it becomes "delicious" because we are spirit children of the Father, we have heard the word before, we have known the joy of following Christ, and the Spirit begins to awaken those feelings within our hearts. As Alma taught, when we give place in our hearts for the gospel of Christ, new, spiritual life grows within us because the word is true.

But Alma cautions us that this is just the beginning. Though these wonderful feelings confirm that the word is good, though we see in ways we have not seen before, though our minds and our spirits have begun to expand, the seed is but a sprout. The promise is that the seed will grow into a tree and bear fruit. We have increased our faith in Jesus Christ, but Alma makes it clear that there is much more to be done: "As the tree beginneth to grow, ye will say: Let us nourish it with great care, that it may get root, that it may grow up, and bring forth fruit unto us. And now behold, if ye nourish it with much care it will get root, and grow up, and bring forth fruit" (Alma 32:37).

What does it mean to nourish the word of God sprouting in our hearts? What does it mean for the sprout to take root? The answer lies in understanding what made the seed grow in the first place. When the gospel of Jesus Christ first gets place in our hearts, we envision the truth and its promises, and we feel the confirmation of the Spirit. We know that the seed is good, but we have not yet tasted of the promises. To realize those promises and to experience all that the Savior has prepared for us, we must continue to hear the word, exercise our faith, and do what the Savior invites us to do. Having more of the word of God adds to the strength and depth of the original seed. Repentance cultivates the soil of the heart, that the doctrine of Christ may get root. Prayer establishes communication with heaven and opens our hearts to the nurturing influence of the Holy Ghost. Obedience makes the word of Christ real in us, including the redeeming power of the Atonement. Thus, obedience is the means through which the word takes root. As the gospel takes root, and as the Holy Ghost works in our hearts, we experience again spiritual and personal growth. In the words of Alma, the gospel word enlarges the soul, enlightens the understanding, and becomes delicious to us.

This nurturing cycle of hearing, praying, repenting, and obeying takes place throughout our lives. As it does, our knowledge of the gospel increases, and so does our faith in Jesus Christ. Our faith grows as our confidence in him grows, as our trust in his redeeming power grows, as our spiritual capacity to be like him grows. Yet, as Moroni teaches us in his masterful sermon in Ether 12, the confirming witness of the Holy Ghost may not come right away. There may be a time of testing and trial before we have that sweet, powerful witness to the truth of what we have done. Recall Moroni's words:

"Wherefore, dispute not because ye see not, for ye receive no witness until after the trial of your faith" (Ether 12:6).

The word *trial* here has two related meanings. The first is to exercise or to "try out" faith by following the word and doing what the Lord wants us to do. With this meaning, Moroni's words remind us of the words of the Savior, "If any man will do his will, he shall know of the doctrine, whether it be of God, or whether I speak of myself" (John 7:17). We receive a witness of the truth only after exercising faith and doing the will of the Lord.

The second meaning of *trial* is to test or to try our faith through experience. When our faith is tried in this sense, we must surely exercise our faith and do what the Lord asks us to do, but we may experience opposition or suffer difficult circumstances as we do it. It is in the opposition or the difficulties that our faith in Jesus Christ is put to the test: Will we do what is asked even when it is hard, even when the promised blessings are far off, even when we receive no witness?

An experience Sue and I had many years ago illustrates the way trials of faith work. In the fall of 1988 I was called to serve as the bishop of the Cambridge Ward in our stake. The Cambridge Ward covered a large part of the metropolitan Boston area and consisted of many young married couples going to school, a few older families, some older single adults, and many less-active members. We did not live in the ward, and Sue and I decided that it would be best if our children stayed engaged in our home ward in Belmont. Although Sue often came to sacrament meeting in the Cambridge ward, keeping the kids in the Belmont Ward meant in practice that Sue and the children attended church in Belmont.

When the stake president talked to us about this new calling, Sue and I knew that it would be hard, but we also had faith that the Lord would bless us and help us to make it work. In retrospect, we can see that we had no idea how hard it was going to be. The years have dimmed the memories somewhat, but we must have thought that the blessings (and the witness) would come immediately—our children would cooperate, we would be blessed with new capacity to handle a more complex life, problems would be solved, things would work well. That is not what happened. I certainly felt the mantle of the calling and was blessed with wonderful counselors, and with revelation and inspiration through the Spirit on many, many occasions. But I did not anticipate how difficult the problems would be, nor the extent to which they would absorb my attention and time. I became immersed in the calling.

That immersion came at a time when our children were experiencing many new challenges in their lives. We had one just entering high school, two in middle school, two in elementary school, and two preschoolers at home. Just at the moment when our family began to experience the reality of having full-blown teenagers in the household, the dad was all of a sudden not there as much (and sometimes not at all). Even when I *was* at home, I was often so preoccupied with some difficult problem that it was as if I were not there. On top of the travel and the time away from home in my job and the new demands of being the bishop of a complex ward and the family going to church without me, my immersion in bishoping often made Sue feel like she was raising seven children without a husband.

All through this time we followed the counsel of the prophets and read the scriptures together as a family, held family home evenings, and always had family prayers. As I look back on those years now, I can see that the Lord was blessing and watching over us, but what we experienced at the time did not feel like a blessing. We were looking for relief, and we got more opportunities to grow. The children, for example, did not cooperate by becoming a source of peace and tranquility. For Sue, it seemed to get harder and harder to get the family up and ready for church on Sundays, and even harder to get them to behave themselves in sacrament meeting. All sorts of new dimensions of adolescence presented themselves: a child who would repeatedly disappear after school with no phone call; a child who had great trouble getting up for seminary; a child hanging out with kids who did not share our values (to put it mildly); a child confused and depressed by the emotions of early adolescence; many calls from guidance counselors about misbehavior at school; tension and conflict between siblings. I got involved in many of these situations, but much of the frontline response fell to Sue. We talked and prayed together about all of this, but there were times when she was angry and bitter at what seemed like an overwhelming burden.

It would be nice to write that I saw all of this at the time and rose to the occasion with skillful parenting, along with strong support for and partnership with Sue. But the truth is that I perceived it only dimly at the time. I reacted and responded, but not always with great skill. Sue and I talked often, but often I simply was not there. And, as time went on, we discovered that we were sometimes not on the same page when it came to what to do. All of this added up to a very challenging and difficult period in our lives.

But—and this is the important point—we never gave up. We never stopped doing what we were supposed to do. Both Sue and I tried to serve as best we knew how in our callings in the Church. We prayed together every morning and night. We attended the temple. We paid our tithing. We did our home and visiting teaching. We taught our children the gospel of Jesus Christ in family home evening, and we tried to be good parents.

In short, we exercised our faith in Jesus Christ. And that faith was tested and tried. The Lord did not remove problems from our path, but he did help us work through them. All through this period we had important spiritual experiences. It was a hard time, but we knew we were not alone. And as time went on, Moroni's promise in Ether 12 became a reality in our lives. When Moroni wrote, "ye receive no witness until after the trial of your faith," he implied the promise: "After the trial of your faith, if you are true and faithful, you shall receive a witness of the Spirit, and your faith will be confirmed." I know that this promise is true because I have experienced it. Moreover, I know from this and many other experiences that the promises the Lord makes to those who serve him also are true. There is no doubt in my mind, no doubt in Sue's mind, that the Lord blessed us and our children for the service we rendered during those difficult years I served as bishop. Through the blessings of the Spirit our faith in Jesus Christ is far stronger today, and our capacity to serve far greater because of those experiences.

Faith in Action

Faith in Jesus Christ comes from hearing the word of God. It grows in the nurturing cycle of hearing, praying, repenting, obeying and seeking the Spirit of the Lord. It is tempered and strengthened in adversity. In all of this, righteous action is at the heart of faith in Jesus Christ. We must act to obtain it, to nurture it, to strengthen it. Moreover, the very purpose of our faith in the Savior is righteous action: to follow him, to trust in him so that we might act under the inspiration of the Spirit to do his work. When we so act, faith in Jesus Christ becomes a principle of power—his power. Elder Dallin H. Oaks taught this principle with a caution against thinking that the power is ours. The starting point is to recognize that our faith is in Jesus Christ and his power:

> If we think we have faith, we should ask, faith in whom or faith in what? For some, faith is nothing more than faith in themselves. That is only self-confidence or

self-centeredness. Others have faith in faith, which is something like relying on the power of positive thinking or betting on the proposition that we can get what we want by manipulating the powers within us.

The first principle of the gospel is faith in the Lord Jesus Christ. Without this faith, the prophet Mormon said, we "are not fit to be numbered among the people of his church." (Moroni 7:39)

With our faith clearly focused on the Savior, we must also learn that it really is his power through which our faith has effect. Elder Oaks goes on in his talk to describe the implications of relying on the power of the Lord:

> When we try to develop faith in the Lord Jesus Christ rather than merely cultivating faith as an abstract principle of power, we understand the meaning of the Savior's words: "If ye will have faith in me ye shall have power to do whatsoever thing is expedient in me" (Moro. 7:33).
>
> Similarly, the Savior taught the Nephites that they must always pray to the Father in his name, adding: "And whatsoever ye shall ask the Father in my name, which is right, believing that ye shall receive, behold it shall be given unto you" (3 Ne. 18:20).
>
> Here the Savior reminds us that faith, no matter how strong it is, cannot produce a result contrary to the will of him whose power it is. ("Faith in the Lord Jesus Christ," *Ensign*, May 1994, 99–100)

Notice how the Lord connects the power of faith in him to action that is "expedient in me," and "which is right." When we act with faith in Jesus Christ, under his direction, according to his will, trusting in him, we have access to his power. And with that power we can accomplish whatever it is that the Lord would have us do. This is not only true of us and the action that we undertake, but Moroni argues that this essential role of faith in the Savior applies to the Savior himself: "If there be no faith among the children of men God can do no miracle among them" (Ether 12:12). An understanding of this remarkable fact will help us understand how faith in Jesus Christ opens to us the powers of heaven.

When the Savior visited the Nephites following his resurrection, he brought them great blessings. In a series of wondrous miracles the Lord healed the sick, blessed the little children, opened the heavens, called down angels to surround the children "in the midst of fire," and prayed with words "so great and marvelous" that they "cannot be written, neither can they be uttered by man" (3 Nephi 19:34). After all this, the Savior taught the power of faith with these words: "So great faith have I never seen among all the Jews; wherefore, I could not show unto them so great miracles, because of their unbelief. Verily I say unto you, there are none of them that have seen so great things as ye have seen; neither have they heard so great things as ye have heard" (3 Nephi 19:35–36).

There are at least two things worth noting about this statement of the Savior. First, because he had raised the dead, walked on water, healed the sick, changed water to wine, and stilled the tempest during his earthly ministry, the miracles he did among the Nephites must have been truly astonishing beyond all understanding. Second, it is at first glance puzzling why the Savior's ability to do such miracles would be limited by the faith of his followers. How can it be that he who created the heavens and the earth, who had all power over all things, could not exercise that power on behalf of his disciples unless they had faith in him? I believe that the reason this is so lies in three closely related principles of the gospel:

Blessings and the Laws of Heaven

The miracles the Savior did among the Nephites were a blessing to them. This is true of all the "workings of the Lord"—they are his intervention on behalf of those who have faith and who exercise it in doing the Lord's work. Like all blessings, the Lord's intervention is predicated on our fulfilling the law on which the blessing is based (see D&C 130:20–21). To the extent there is unbelief, to that extent we do not fulfill the law, and thus do not receive the blessings of the Lord's intervention.

Humility and the Savior's Grace

As Paul and Moroni taught, many of the miracles we have in the scriptural record are instances of the Lord working through his servants to accomplish his purposes. If we are in a state of unbelief, the Lord cannot work through us. Unbelief clouds the spirit and guides behavior and action and attitude away from the light. In that state, the natural man has sway, and pride and trust in the arm of flesh are the rule. Without humility we do not have access to the Savior's grace, so that our weaknesses do not become strengths. We cannot serve as instruments in the Lord's hands, both because our "hearts are far from him" and because we are not capable. In a state of unbelief, we are not worthy of the miracles Jesus can do.

Agency and the Plan of Salvation

Miracles occur to bring to pass the Lord's work, and to bless those whose faith qualifies them for his grace. But Jesus will not force anyone to believe in him or to follow him. That was Satan's plan. Heavenly Father's plan, the great plan of salvation, requires that we exercise our own free will to follow the Savior. Each of us is given the light of Christ, and as we act in faith on the Savior to do his will, we receive more and more light, more and more of the powers of heaven. In the plan of salvation, faith precedes the miracle. If it were not so, if Jesus were to work mighty miracles on us before we had faith, the power of those miracles could so overwhelm our agency that we would have no choice. Someday every knee will bow, and every tongue confess that Jesus is the Christ, whether they want to or not. But in the day of our probation, we must choose to walk by faith in the strait and narrow path that leads to life and salvation. Only in that path, only after the trial of our faith, do we experience the miraculous power of the Savior.

These three principles not only explain why the Savior could do no miracles until after his people had faith in him, but they also help us to understand how we gain access to the power of heaven as we exercise our faith in Jesus Christ. The key word is *exercise*. We need to put our faith into action by keeping the commandments, following the light of Christ within us, and heeding the promptings of the Holy Ghost. As we do so, the plan of salvation has effect in us because we open the door to the Savior. Furthermore, we must humble ourselves before the Lord, cast off the natural tendency to pride and arrogance, trust in the power of the Savior, and seek his grace. As we do so, he will show unto us our weaknesses, and if we trust in him, he will make weak things become strong. We will then be capable instruments in his hands. And we will be blessed with power from on high—in the Lord's way, on the Lord's timing—because we will have fulfilled the laws of heaven. Faith in Jesus Christ is the first principle of the gospel, and for all of these reasons, it is a principle of power.

Faith As a Shield

Faith in Jesus Christ is the shield in the armor of God. I have found it useful to think of the shield of faith as a web of principle and promise with Christ at its center. When we have faith in Jesus Christ, we envision in our minds and in our hearts who he is and what he has done, does now, and will do in the future. With the eye of faith and hope we see the role of Jesus in the plan of salvation, his capacity for redemption and salvation, his power over all things, his relationship to the earth and all its elements, our relationship to him, and his relationship to everyone around us. We have faith in Jesus Christ as the Redeemer, the Prince of Peace, the one whose love for us knows no bounds, who has descended below all things that he might have power to sanctify, to redeem, and to save. What we see with our eye of faith is the only one in whom we might trust and hope for salvation, he who is the Light and the Life of the world.

All of this we see and hold in our minds and hearts when we have faith in Jesus Christ. Each aspect of his being and character, each principle on which he acts, each promise that connects him to us, is like a node in a network or web, with a connector linking the principle or promise to the Savior. The nodes in the web are also interconnected to one another. With the image of a web in mind, imagine the Savior at the center, with connectors radiating out from him to nodes of principle and promise. Each node may also be connected directly to other nodes, thus forming a web of connections linking the principles and promises to each other and to the Savior. The connectors are defined by our understanding of the principles and the promises and their relationship to Christ. As we hear the word of God about a principle, and as we act on it, we receive light and truth through the Spirit, our understanding increases, our trust in that principle deepens, and the connector grows brighter and stronger. This process is Alma's nurturing cycle—by putting our faith to work, by acting on what we hope for with all prayer and diligence, we receive a witness of the Spirit (of course, on the Lord's timetable, and in his way), and our web of faith grows stronger.

The Lord's commandment to pay tithing illustrates the web of faith. I begin with basic principles that children learn in Primary:

• Jesus has commanded us to pay tithing: "Bring ye all the tithes into the storehouse" (Malachi 3:10).

• The earth is the Lord's.

• This is his work; this is his church.

• My tithe, no matter how small, is acceptable to the Lord.

• The Lord will bless me if I obey this commandment.

• I love the Lord and his work, and want to do my part.

With respect to the commandment of tithing, these principles are nodes in our web of faith. They are connected to the Savior and interconnected to each other and to other principles of the gospel: Jesus is the Creator; God speaks through prophets; obedience brings forth the blessings of heaven; the gospel of Jesus Christ has been restored to the earth; The Church of Jesus Christ of Latter-day Saints is the Lord's church. With that faith, we act. We pay our tithing year in and year out. And Moroni's promise becomes a reality—we receive a witness of the Spirit that the principle of tithing, indeed, the whole web of principle and promise connected to it, is true. Thus, in this principle of tithing, our faith is strengthened and the web grows brighter and stronger.

The web of faith is, thus, not static. It grows and changes as we walk the strait and narrow path. Moreover, not only does the nurturing cycle strengthen our understanding and trust in the principles we already know, but we learn new principles and gain new insights that add to our web of faith. We gain new nodes and new connections and interconnections. This very process of growth is itself based on faith in Jesus Christ—we search the scriptures in faith that the Lord speaks to us through them; we listen to the prophets in faith that the Spirit of the Lord works through them to bring us his word; we seek understanding through prayer, exercising faith that we may receive personal revelation.

As an example, consider once again the law of tithing. To the basic principles already mentioned we might add these two:

• Tithing is a preparatory commandment: By paying our tithing we prepare ourselves to live the law of consecration.

• In addition to tithing, we should follow the counsel of the prophets and give generously of our means to fast offerings, and in other donations help to build the kingdom of God on the earth.

These two principles deepen our understanding of the law of tithing. They establish new nodes in our web of faith, and new connections to the Savior (the nature of his commandments; how he works in our lives) and to other principles of the gospel (consecration, revelation through prophets, the Church as the kingdom of God). Thus, as we add to our web of faith, it grows more dense, more robust. As we live these principles, the connectors grow in number and in strength.

But they also grow brighter. The nodes of the web of faith are true principles. They are connected to Jesus Christ, the light of the world. The light of Christ is the light of truth, and it flows through the connectors and illuminates the web of faith. Obedience to the commandments of the Lord puts us in tune with the Holy Ghost, and we receive more light. The web of faith glows more brightly, and the shield of faith becomes what Paul described in his epistle to the Romans—the armor of light: "The night is far spent, the day is at hand; let us therefore cast off the works of darkness, and let us put on the armour of light" (Romans 13:12; see also 1 Thessalonians 5:4–5).

When we put on the shield of faith as Paul admonished us, we put on protection against the forces of darkness. Indeed, it is the bright, shining, web of faith in Jesus Christ that "quench[es] all the fiery darts of the wicked" (Ephesians 6:16). This great promise of the protective power of faith is important because we are engaged in a great struggle against evil. Paul reminds us that we are engaged in a battle against the "rulers of the darkness of this world," and in that battle, the adversary and those he uses ("the wicked") will hurl against us "fiery darts." Whether they be subtle and devious temptations, or the designs of evil men, or apostasy, or ridicule, or sophistry, or false doctrine, or betrayal, or physical abuse, or sin masquerading as goodness, or loss of property, or sickness, or conspiracy, or whatever they may be, the shield of faith in Jesus Christ stands as a bulwark against them. The bright, shining, burning shield of faith will quench them—render them harmless, without lasting effect.

There is no better illustration of the way the shield of faith works than the experiences of the Prophet Joseph Smith. Two of these experiences stand out. The first occurred in 1828 when the Prophet gave Martin Harris the first 116 pages of the Book of Mormon translation. Martin lost the manuscript, and the Lord chastised the Prophet with strong words. In his words we find important insights into the shield of faith:

> Although a man may have many revelations, and have power to do many mighty works, yet if he boasts in his own strength, and sets at naught the counsels of God, and follows after the dictates of his own will and carnal desires, he must fall. . . . For, behold, you should not have feared man more than God. Although men set at naught the counsels of God, and despise his words—yet you should have been faithful; and he would have extended his arm and supported you against all the fiery darts of the adversary; and he would have been with you in every time of trouble. (D&C 3:4, 7–8)

To be faithful is to act with faith in Jesus Christ and trust in him. It is to deploy the shield of faith against the fiery darts, to have confidence that the Lord will be there "in every time of trouble." It is to keep the commandments, even in the face of real threats and dire circumstances, with faith in the power of the Savior. If we do not act in faith, but set aside the counsel of God, and rely on our own understanding and our own strength, the web of faith will grow dim. To be a shield, the web of faith must be activated by obedience, by the Spirit, by the light of Christ.

A second experience took place in Liberty Jail. After six months in awful conditions, apart from his wife and family, unable to assist his brothers and sisters against the mobs in Missouri, the Prophet received a revelation from the Lord about the "fiery darts" of the wicked and the powers of heaven. We have this revelation as the 122nd section of the Doctrine and Covenants. It is a wonderful description of the power of the shield of faith.

The Lord begins the revelation by reassuring the prophet that his trouble will be "but for a small moment" and then his voice will sound in the "midst of thine enemies" more terrible "than the fierce lion, because of thy righteousness; and thy God shall stand by thee forever and ever" (D&C 122:4). The Lord then lays out for the Prophet many examples of the kinds of tribulation that he has been called upon, and may be yet called upon, to endure. The list is daunting: false brethren, robbers, false accusations, forced capture, torn away from family by the sword, thrown into prison, cast into the pit, in the hands of murderers, sentenced to death, cast into the deep, forces of nature arrayed as an enemy, the very jaws of hell gaping open. In the face of all of this the Lord counsels the Prophet to trust in him:

> Know thou, my son, that all these things shall give thee
> experience, and shall be for thy good. The Son of Man hath
> descended below them all. Art thou greater than he?

Therefore, hold on thy way, and the priesthood shall remain with thee; for their bounds are set, they cannot pass. Thy days are known, and thy years shall not be numbered less; therefore, fear not what man can do, for God shall be with you forever and ever. (D&C 122:7–9)

We do not sit in Liberty Jail, nor do wicked men wielding swords and guns tear us from our families. We are not cast into the pit or hauled into shameful legal proceedings by false accusations. Evil men who once called us brother do not attack us, nor are we hunted and disparaged and slandered on every side. These are not our challenges. But we do face temptation and wickedness and the forces of evil. Some of us must face the ancient evils of debilitating hunger, poverty, sickness, murder, terror, and war that rage across the earth. We face the lure of the world in all its seductive power—physical pleasures of every kind, material wealth, power, the honors of men. We face strong temptation to put ourselves first and seek our own well-being and ignore those less fortunate than us. Evil and designing men have found new ways to thrill and surprise and delight our senses and lead us into addictions that are every bit as much a prison as Liberty Jail. New technologies like the Internet that can be a source of great righteousness (e.g., family history) are used by the forces of evil to wreak great havoc on individuals and families (e.g., pornography). Indeed, we face the effects of all sorts of new technologies that help to create the frenetic pace of modern life that distracts us away from that which is quiet, and peaceful, and good. The pressure of peers, and of the society in which we live, can be intense and dangerous. We face a society in which divorce, abortion, and adultery are regarded as liberating, healthy, and normal. It is a society whose scholars, writers, and commentators often see the family as an antiquated tradition, or worse, as an instrument of oppression.

On top of all of these modern forms of wickedness and evil, the very same forces that sought to tear down the Prophet Joseph and to destroy the Church are still at work in our day. If anything, they have grown more subtle, more sophisticated, more insidious. In popular books, in academic journals, in news magazines, in the newspapers, in movies, we face attacks on the gospel of Jesus Christ, on the restoration of his Church, on the prophets and apostles who walk the earth today, on the Savior himself. Some of these attacks are just that—direct and conscious attempts to destroy. But many come clothed in the language and idiom of disinterested scholarship, personal confession, praise for good works, tolerance, and even acceptance. But for all that subtlety and apparent goodwill, their effect is to deny the truth and serve the "rulers of the darkness of this world."

These "fiery darts of the adversary" do not affect all of us in the same way. Some of us are more at risk for one than the other. But we all face temptation of some kind, and we all must do battle against the forces of evil if we are to prevail. In this battle the shield of faith in Jesus Christ is critical. Paul uses the words "above all" to describe its importance. A shield that is strong repels the darts of wickedness so that they cannot penetrate to the heart and wreak spiritual damage. Whether they come as temptations to sin, as attacks on the truth, or in some other way, the shield of faith exposes them for what they are—false, wicked, evil. With the eye of faith, we see and recognize a dart of the wicked that will lead to nothing but sorrow and destruction of that which is right and good. Moreover, our faith in Jesus Christ provides the power to overcome the evil we face. Having seen the dart for what it is, we reject it and call upon the Lord for help in delivering us from its effects. As we exercise our faith in him, we receive strength and support. The promise to the Prophet Joseph is also a promise to us: "God shall be with [us] forever and ever" (D&C 122:9).

That support and strength are there even when we succumb to temptation, or give place in our minds for the clever arguments and sophistry of men, or let anger or discouragements lead us astray. Our web of faith may have areas of weakness where the adversary focuses his darts of wickedness. Because we are weak, those darts may bruise us. But the web of faith still protects and defends if we repent with faith and turn away from wickedness. Indeed, it is precisely our faith in the Savior that gives us the strength to overcome the weaknesses, problems, and sin in our lives.

The key for us, as it was for the Prophet Joseph, lies in the Lord's admonition to "hold on thy way." To "hold on thy way" is to exercise faith, to stay on or return to the strait and narrow path, to heed the counsel of the Lord and carry out all that he has for us to do. President Gordon B. Hinckley has emphasized these principles in our day:

> If we will pursue a steady course in the implementation of our religion in our own lives, we shall advance the cause more effectively than by any other means.
>
> There may be those who may seek to tempt us away. There may be those who will try to bait us. We may be disparaged. We may be belittled. We may be inveighed against. We may be caricatured before the world. . . .
>
> There may be times of discouragement and deep concern. There certainly will be days of decision in the lives of each of us. . . .
>
> Without contention, without argument, without offense, let us pursue a steady course, moving forward to build the kingdom of God. If there is trouble, let us face it calmly. Let us overcome evil with good. ("Pursue the Steady Course," *Ensign,* January 2005, 5–7)

If we are to hold on our way and pursue a steady course, we must set Christ at the center of the web of faith and trust in his redeeming, saving power. We must see with the eye of faith that Jesus Christ has all power over all things, and that through that power we may overcome whatever comes our way. We must, therefore, put on the shield of faith—the bright, shining, burning web of faith that quenches the fiery darts of the wicked. In this, as in every element of the armor of God, we shall stand and prevail if we are "strong in the Lord, and in the power of his might" (Ephesians 6:10).

CHAPTER 10

THE HELMET OF SALVATION

I will never forget the phone call Sue and I received on a Friday night in January of 2001. On the other end of the line was Lloyd Baird, our stake president. President Baird told us that our son Michael had to come home from his mission. This would have been a shock under any circumstances, but Michael had been on his mission for only two days. He was in the Missionary Training Center to prepare for his mission to British Columbia. President Baird told us that there were things in Michael's life that he had not resolved before he left. Later we learned that Michael had felt the Spirit very strongly in the MTC and knew that he had to repent. He went to the president of the MTC and told the president what he had done. From that conversation and others, it became clear that Michael needed to go through the process of repentance before he would be worthy to serve a mission. And so Michael had to come home.

Sue and I were naturally worried and sad. We spoke to Michael briefly that night, trying to offer our love and encouragement, and learned of his travel arrangements. Our hearts were heavy as we drove to the airport the next afternoon to meet Michael's flight from Salt Lake City. He was the last person off of the airplane. As we watched him walk down the jetway and enter the terminal we saw a very sad young man—but there was no darkness in him. There was pain and disappointment, but also a spirit of repentance. As we hugged him and walked down the hallway, I felt strongly that Michael was on the right path.

Though in those first few hours after President Baird's call Sue and I did not think we were about to have one of the most wonderful experiences of our lives, that is what happened. And it happened because the Atonement and the great plan of redemption became a living reality in the life of our son. Over the next nine months Michael went through the difficult but sweet process of repentance. He knew that the Lord had forgiven him, but he also knew that he needed to experience the mighty change of heart of which the scriptures speak. He needed to deepen his faith and his understanding of the gospel. He needed to be fully worthy to return to the house of the Lord, and he needed to be fully prepared to return to the mission field, there to serve the Lord with all his heart.

And so, he went to work. He read and studied the scriptures. He prayed often, seeking the Lord's blessing. He sought to be of service and to be active in his ward. During this time Michael lived at home. He would often come into our bedroom at night and talk to us about his efforts. The path was not easy. He got discouraged at times. When he did, he would come into our room and ask for a blessing. I gave Michael many blessings during those months, and I knew through the Spirit that Michael was changing, that the Atonement was working in his life.

And so it went, day after day, night after night for a long time. Sue and I were witness to the miracle of forgiveness, to the miracle of the atonement of Jesus Christ in the life of our precious son. The Savior reached out and took hold of that young man and changed him from the inside out. During those months Michael met often with the bishop of our ward, Mark Ott. Bishop Ott was a great blessing to Michael. He counseled with him, encouraged him, and loved him. And he held Michael to high standards of daily prayer, scripture study, and service. One day he asked Michael to give Sister Naomi Cranney a ride to and from church. Sister Cranney was ninety-seven years old. And so every week when she was able to come Michael would arrive at her home, help her down the steps into the car, drive her to church, help her get to the chapel, and sit with her during sacrament meeting. He would then take her home at the end of church. Sister Cranney had a wonderful spirit about her, and she grew to love Michael dearly. Over many weeks Michael was blessed to come to know and serve a great Latter-day Saint.

After many weeks and months, and many interviews with his bishop and his stake president, the day came for Michael's interview with a General Authority. That interview would determine whether Michael would be able to return to the mission field at that time, or whether additional time at home would be needed. The General Authority assigned to interview Michael was Elder Spencer Condie. He arranged to meet Michael in Pittsburgh. I will never forget the day that Michael came home from that interview. I picked him up at the airport. The contrast between Michael's arrival from Pittsburgh and his arrival from Salt Lake City nine months earlier was sharp and sweet. On the day he came home from Pittsburgh he was just about the first person off of that airplane. As he came down the jetway, he was radiant! The Spirit of the Lord shone brightly in his eyes. He had a big smile on his face, and I knew that he had had a wonderful experience with Elder Condie. Not long after the interview Michael received his call to serve in British Columbia, the same mission as his original call.

And so, Michael returned to the temple, and to the mission field. His mission was not easy, but he served faithfully and well. When Michael left the second time for the MTC, he was on fire. His testimony of the gospel burned within him, and he was fully prepared to serve the Lord. Throughout his mission he had many opportunities to bear testimony and to serve the Lord. His knowledge of the gospel deepened, and his understanding of the Atonement increased. What began that week in January of 2001 continued through his time in British Columbia. And it continues today. He has come to know the Savior in a deep and powerful way through his own experience. He has been true to his covenants, he has proclaimed the gospel and helped many others to feel the power of the Atonement in their lives, and he has made the power of the Atonement a reality in his life.

Michael experienced forgiveness and a remission of his sins. He experienced the refining fire of the Holy Ghost. He experienced the pure love of Jesus Christ. His experience is a living testimony of the truth of Amulek's promise to the Zoramites: "Yea, I would that ye would come forth and harden not your hearts any longer; for behold, now is the time and the day of your salvation; and therefore, if ye will repent and harden not your hearts, immediately shall the great plan of redemption be brought about unto you" (Alma 34:31).

This is the spirit in which Paul admonishes us to put on the "helmet of salvation" as part of the armor of God. Though our ultimate salvation is beyond the grave, it is clear, from Amulek and from Paul and from many other prophets, that we may experience redemption and salvation here in mortality. In this chapter I explore the meaning of salvation here and now in our earthly lives, and the process through which we might obtain it, with special emphasis on the role of the Church of Jesus Christ. Our Heavenly Father has given us a plan, a process, and a path that lead to salvation. Every part of the plan, every element of the process, every step along the path centers on the Lord Jesus Christ and his atonement. He is the Way. As Peter proclaimed: "There is none other name under heaven given among men, whereby we must be saved" (Acts 4:12). To accomplish that purpose the Lord has established his church and placed in it the doctrines, ordinances, covenants, and plan of salvation. Thus, we will find the helmet of salvation only in the Church of Jesus Christ.

The Need for Salvation

Down through the ages, beginning in the great Council in Heaven, our Heavenly Father has taught us about salvation. Standing with our Father in the heavenly realm we learned about the purpose of our time on earth, why salvation was necessary, how it would come about, and what it would mean for us. We learned about the need for a Savior, one who would go to earth and suffer for all of us, and overcome everything that might stand in the way of our progression and our destiny as children of God. That destiny—to "dwell in the presence of God and his Christ forever and ever" (D&C 76:62), to enjoy the life that our Heavenly Father enjoys and receive "of his fulness, and of his glory" (D&C 76:56)—is "the greatest of all the gifts of God" (D&C 14:7).

In the Council in Heaven and through the prophets in this life our Heavenly Father has taught us about all those things from which we must be saved if we are to return home to live with him in the eternities. Following are the principal, interrelated barriers that must be overcome. (See Dallin H. Oaks, "Have You Been Saved?" *Ensign,* May 1998, 55–57, for a discussion of the different dimensions of salvation.)

Death

In order to fulfill our destiny we must obtain a physical body. But that body—because of the Fall—is mortal and must die. Through death we pass from this mortal life to the world of spirits, leaving our body behind. Without being reunited with our body we cannot experience a fulness of joy or progress eternally (see D&C 93:33–34). We must be saved from death to achieve our destiny.

Sin and Its Consequences

Mortality is essential, but fraught with danger. This is a probationary state, a time of testing (see Alma 42:4). As little children we are "alive in Christ"—alive to the Spirit and protected by God from temptation and the devil (see D&C 29:46–47; Moroni 8:8, 12). But once we reach the age of accountability we no longer have that protection unconditionally. In effect, we become like Adam and Eve just after the Fall: Without further action on our part, we are separated spiritually from God. Alma calls this temporal and spiritual separation being "cut off from the presence of the Lord" (Alma 42:9). In this state we are all subject to temptation, we are all free to choose, we are all weak.

From the moment his evil plan was rejected by Heavenly Father, Satan has tried to gain control over us, to bind us down and make us "miserable like unto himself" (2 Nephi 2:27). His purpose, therefore, is not just to keep us from reaching our destiny but to grasp us in his "awful chains" (2 Nephi 28:22), the "chains of hell" (Alma 12:11), and to "reign over [us] in his own kingdom" (2 Nephi 2:29). Though we have the light of Christ and the commandments of God, we all transgress the laws of God. We are all sinners. No unclean thing, no one whose life is stained by sin and wickedness, may enter the kingdom of God (see 1 Nephi 15:34). We cannot return home and experience eternal life unclean. We cannot return home if we are bound by the chains of hell. To get home, we must be saved from our sins and their consequences.

The Natural Man

We are all children of God, and have within us the potential to become like him. Indeed, to achieve our eternal destiny we must become like him. And yet, we are all weak; we all make mistakes; we all act in error. Furthermore, we all lack knowledge. We come to earth with a veil over our memories, obscuring our knowledge of Heavenly Father and Jesus Christ and of all that we learned when we lived with them. Thus, we are weak, mistake prone, and ignorant. But there is more. We are all subject to natural drives, appetites, and passions. Satan and his followers play upon our drives and passions in order to tempt us to follow them into works of darkness. If we give in to those temptations and let those appetites and passions have complete control over what we do, if we give unbridled rule to our innate drives to defend ourselves and to acquire things, if we become full of pride and arrogance and exercise unrighteous dominion (D&C 121:37), we give full expression to what King Benjamin called "the natural man" (Mosiah 3:19). We cannot return home if we are not saved from the potential "natural man" in all of us. As King Benjamin taught, we must "[put] off the natural man" and become a "saint through the atonement of Christ the Lord."

In that process, knowledge is crucial. The Prophet Joseph Smith taught, "It is impossible for a man to be saved in ignorance" (D&C 131:6). We must gain knowledge, first and foremost, of God and the things of God. Jesus said, "And this is life eternal, that they might know thee the only true God, and Jesus Christ, whom thou hast sent" (John 17:3). To know our Heavenly Father, to know the Savior, to know the gospel and all that it encompasses, we must be saved from our ignorance. We even must be saved from our mistakes and weaknesses. Not all of the consequences of our weaknesses, or our mistakes, are sins. But they prevent us from becoming like God. We have the capacity to learn and to grow, but the task is great, and we are all inadequate. Unless we are saved from our inadequacies and our mistakes, we cannot obtain eternal life.

Adversity

In order to fulfill the plan of salvation, we are born into a fallen and corrupt world full of weeds and thorns, sickness and pain, natural disasters and disasters made by men. It is a world where the devil and his angels and conspiring men may bring great evil and wickedness upon us, where even the mistakes and errors and foolishness of men may wreak havoc in our lives. All of us experience adversity in many forms throughout our lives. Adversity comes with mortality and is part of our probation here on earth. It is part of the plan. We are not saved from adversity. But if that adversity were to be so powerful as to overwhelm our agency, if it were so devastating as to exceed our capacity to endure, it would make our probation an empty charade. The plan of salvation would be frustrated, and we could not obtain eternal life. Though adversity is our lot in this life, we must be protected and saved from its overwhelming eternal consequences.

The Nature of Salvation

When we learned about death, sin, the natural man, and adversity in the Council in Heaven, it would have been clear to us, as it was to our Heavenly Father, that without divine help we could not be saved. The barriers are too high, and our capacity too limited. In his great plan of salvation, therefore, Heavenly Father provided for a Savior, and chose our elder brother, his Firstborn Son, even the Lord Jesus Christ, to be the Redeemer. From the perspective of the Council in Heaven, several aspects of the plan of salvation must have struck us with significant force. First, the Atonement would give the

Savior power over death, sin, hell, the devil, indeed, everything. He would descend below all things that he might have power over all things. This meant that salvation—our salvation—would be in and through him. The great, overriding, all-encompassing truth of the plan of salvation was divinely clear: Jesus Christ would be our Savior. Through his atonement he would be "mighty to save" (2 Nephi 31:19). Imagine the joy we felt when we heard Jesus say, "Here am I, send me" (Abraham 3:27), and we realized that the plan would work.

The Savior is the first and most important aspect of the plan of salvation. A second is that our time on earth is a time of testing, a time of probation. What we do in that time has eternal consequences. The power of that idea is expressed in the third Article of Faith: "We believe that through the Atonement of Christ, all mankind may be saved, by obedience to the laws and ordinances of the Gospel."

There are many barriers to eternal life, and, thus, many dimensions of salvation. Each is essential, but each confers only a part of all that must occur for us to achieve eternal life. Some dimensions come to us unconditionally as a free gift from the Savior. All of us will overcome death through the resurrection, and none of us will be punished because of the fall of Adam and Eve. All of us will return to God to be judged of our own works. Some dimensions of salvation, however, depend on what we do. This is true of salvation from sin, from hell, from spiritual separation from God, from ignorance, from the natural man, and from our weaknesses and mistakes. The word *may* in the third Article of Faith is important here. For while it is eternally true that we cannot overcome any of these barriers by ourselves, and thus must depend on the grace of Jesus Christ in all of them, it is just as eternally true that our salvation depends on what we do. As Nephi said, "For we labor diligently to write, to persuade our children, and also our brethren, to believe in Christ, and to be reconciled to God; for we know that it is by grace that we are saved, after all we can do" (2 Nephi 25:23).

Thus, the test of mortality is to see whether we will believe in Christ, exercise faith in him, and obey the laws and ordinances of the gospel.

There is a third aspect of the plan of salvation that must have brought us great comfort when we heard it in the Council in Heaven. It is that salvation is a process. It is, indeed, a personal development process. Everything our Father does, everything the Savior does, points to the great end and purpose of their work: immortality and eternal life. Thus, ultimate, final salvation happens beyond the grave, beyond the resurrection, beyond the day of judgment.

But in Heavenly Father's plan we do not have to wait until then to experience the power of the Atonement and thus, the blessings of the plan of salvation. The plain fact is that many dimensions of salvation begin in mortality. Moreover, in the plan we make covenants with God to do the things that will lead to our ultimate salvation. We receive in return the promise of God that if we are true and faithful to our covenants, we will receive eternal life. This has enormous power and significance. It means we are not cut off until the end. We can gain access to heaven, to its powers, and to the love and mercy of our Savior, Jesus Christ, here in mortality.

King Benjamin taught this marvelous principle to his people as recorded in Mosiah chapter 4. After learning about the plan of salvation, the power of the Atonement through the Lord Jesus Christ, and the awful fate that awaits those whose works are evil and who do not repent, the people of King Benjamin cried out: "O have mercy, and apply the atoning blood of Christ that we may receive forgiveness of our sins, and our hearts may be purified; for we believe in Jesus Christ, the Son of God, who created heaven and earth, and all things; who shall come down among the children of men" (Mosiah 4:2).

The scripture records that immediately after they had spoken those words, "the Spirit of the Lord came upon them, and they were filled with joy, having received a remission of their sins" (Mosiah 4:3). The Spirit testified of the truth of King Benjamin's words, brought the people "to a knowledge of the goodness of God, and his matchless power" (Mosiah 4:6), and "wrought a mighty change in [their] hearts" (Mosiah 5:2). This is a powerful example of the truth of Amulek's promise of the immediacy of redemption and salvation: "immediately shall the great plan of redemption be brought about unto you" (Alma 34:31).

The people of King Benjamin rejoiced in the Spirit they felt and the knowledge they received of redemption and salvation from the barriers to eternal life. Yet it is important to reflect on what salvation meant to them at the time of King Benjamin's address. Consider each of the barriers to salvation one by one:

Death: The people remained mortal, but they had faith in the Savior's (and thus their own) resurrection.

Sin: They received a remission of their sins through faith in the Savior and his atonement, through repentance and their commitment to righteousness and obedience. They received the Spirit of the Lord, and the Spirit bore witness to them that they had been forgiven and stood clean before God. Having received the Holy Ghost in their lives, the people of King Benjamin were no longer dead to the things of righteousness, nor separated spiritually from God. Indeed, they were "spiritually begotten" through Christ's atonement and became "his sons, and his daughters" (Mosiah 5:7). They remained physically separated from God, but enjoyed the presence of deity through the Holy Ghost. Moreover, they felt the love of God for them immediately and powerfully. Thus, they were saved from their sins, and would remain so conditional on their obedience and faithfulness in the future.

Natural Man: With the mighty change of heart they experienced, the people lost the "disposition to do evil" (Mosiah 5:2) and "put off the natural man" (Mosiah 3:19). They were on their way to becoming saints, "through the atonement of Christ" (Mosiah 3:19), but much remained for them to do and to become. Both the words of King Benjamin and the Spirit of the Lord had given them knowledge of God and his goodness. They had learned much about the plan of salvation, and the light of the gospel had dispelled the darkness of unbelief. Yet, their knowledge was not full or perfect as it might become. Though they had felt the joy of redemption, the full power of the Atonement was yet to work in their lives. They had faith in the Savior, but the experience of becoming like him awaited them in the future.

Adversity: These people had known war and the adversity of mortal life. But they had experienced the power of the Atonement, and the Spirit (and King Benjamin) bore witness to them of the Savior's power over all things. Though adversity awaited them in the future, they knew that its bounds were set, and that through their faith they could obtain all they needed to prevail in the kingdom of God.

In powerful and important ways the people of King Benjamin experienced some of the dimensions of salvation immediately upon their repentance, based on their commitment to serve the Lord and be obedient to his commandments. Ultimate salvation remained conditional on their righteousness and their willingness to do the will of the Lord in all things throughout their lives. However, there is one additional blessing of the plan of salvation they received that changed everything about their lives. Because of what they learned, and because of what they felt, they received the blessing of hope. Not only had they felt the joy and comfort and power of the Atonement through the Holy Ghost, but they had received a divine witness that such power could be with them to sustain them and help them to do all they had to do to return home to Heavenly Father. They could hope for a continuation in this life of the joy and redemption they had felt. And they could hope for the eventual and ultimate power of the Savior to redeem them completely in all the dimensions necessary to secure eternal life. Thus, they could look forward to the future with what Moroni called "a more excellent hope" (Ether 12:32).

That hope changed their perspective on the future—"we . . . have great views of that which is to come" (Mosiah 5:3)—and reinforced the importance of faithful obedience. As King Benjamin explained, those who "[receive] salvation, through the atonement" (Mosiah 4:7) must "put [their] trust in the Lord and be diligent in keeping his commandments, and continue in the faith even unto the end of [their lives]" (Mosiah 4:6). If they would do these things, they would merit a remarkable promise of blessings of salvation in this life: "And behold, I say unto you that if ye do this ye shall always rejoice, and be filled with the love of God, and always retain a remission of your sins; and ye shall grow in the knowledge of the glory of him that created you, or in the knowledge of that which is just and true" (Mosiah 4:12).

Each element of the promise reflects the central role of the atonement of Jesus Christ in the plan of salvation. The people of King Benjamin rejoiced as the Spirit bore witness to them that through Christ they could go home, they were not lost forever. When the angel announced the Savior's birth to the shepherds he brought "good tidings of great joy" (Luke 2:10). Well does our hymn proclaim "Rejoice! The Lord is King." If the people of King Benjamin were true and faithful, that joy would be with them forever.

Coupled to joy was the promise of the love of God. The phrase "filled with the love of God" is rich with meaning. In the first instance it means that they would feel God's love for them in full measure. They would be "filled" with that love. But it also means that they would experience a great outpouring of love *for* God. Thus, they would satisfy the first and great commandment to love God with all of their heart, might, mind, and strength. But they would also satisfy the second great commandment, since they would be filled with charity, the pure love of Christ. This love of God in all its meanings is a gift of the Spirit and follows obedience to the commandments of the Lord. Indeed, as Mormon taught, this love is "bestowed upon all who are true followers of his Son, Jesus Christ" (Moroni 7:48).

To be "filled with the love of God," to rejoice in the "more excellent hope" of eternal life, one must stand clean before God—one must receive a remission of sins. This, too, comes through the power of the atonement of Christ. The people of King Benjamin knew the Lord had forgiven them because the Spirit of the Lord had come upon them and witnessed to them of the Lord's forgiveness. But this forgiveness would be at risk, subject to the ongoing probation of mortal life. If they were true and faithful, King Benjamin promised them that they would retain a remission of their sins. Moreover, that lifelong process of faithful obedience would be a learning experience in which they would grow "in the knowledge of the glory of him that created you" (Mosiah 4:12). Thus, not only would they feel the perfect love of the Savior for them, but through the Holy Ghost they would grow in the knowledge of truth and righteousness and all things pertaining to the kingdom of God.

These are our promises as well. This truly is salvation, our salvation, through the Lord Jesus Christ—hope in a glorious resurrection into eternal life, a remission of our sins through the mercy and power of the Savior, a new heart filled with the love of God to sustain us in the journey to become like our Father, the powers of heaven available through the ministry of the Holy Ghost to comfort, protect, witness, and teach. This is salvation through Christ, and it is the helmet in the armor of God.

The Gate, the Path, and the Caravan

What must we do to put on the helmet of salvation? And having put it on, how do we keep it on forever? Down through the ages the prophets have sought to teach us about the process of salvation in the metaphor of the gate and the path. As with the people of King Benjamin, the beginning of salvation for us is recognition of our need for salvation. Next comes faith in Jesus Christ and in his power to redeem. Then we must act—we must repent of our sins, enter the waters of baptism, and receive the gift of the Holy Ghost. The Savior himself has shown us the way. Here is Nephi's classic description of the gate to the path of salvation:

> Wherefore, my beloved brethren, I know that if ye shall follow the Son, with full purpose of heart, acting no hypocrisy and no deception before God, but with real intent, repenting of your sins, witnessing unto the Father that ye are willing to take upon you the name of Christ, by baptism— yea, by following your Lord and your Savior down into the water, according to his word, behold, then shall ye receive the Holy Ghost; yea, then cometh the baptism of fire and of the Holy Ghost; and then can ye speak with the tongue of angels, and shout praises unto the Holy One of Israel. . . . Wherefore, do the things which I have told you I have seen that your Lord and your Redeemer should do; for, for this cause have they been shown unto me, that ye might know the gate by which ye should enter. For the gate by which ye should enter is repentance and baptism by water; and then

cometh a remission of your sins by fire and by the Holy
Ghost. (2 Nephi 31:13, 17)

This is the gate to the path that leads to eternal life. The path is
strait and narrow, but it is sure and true. If we follow the path, we
follow the Savior. It is his path. He is the Way. It is essential to enter
the gate, but mere baptism is not enough. As Nephi said, we "must
press forward with a steadfastness in Christ" with hope and faith and
"endure to the end" (2 Nephi 31:20). The path, therefore, is not easy.
Nephi had seen this firsthand. When he wrote those words he was
close to the end of his life. He spoke with the voice of wisdom born
of experience. In an important sense Nephi's life journey had been a
metaphor for the challenge and promise of the strait and narrow
path. The way had been hard, but the Lord had blessed and protected Nephi and his family according to their faithfulness.
Disobedience, however, had brought problems and sorrow.

In addition to his life experience with the path, Nephi had
received revelation from God about the strait and narrow path. He
had seen in vision his father Lehi's dream of the tree of life, one of
the most powerful depictions of the strait and narrow path in all of
scripture. (Lehi's dream is recorded in 1 Nephi chapter 8.) In the
dream Lehi saw that the strait and narrow path led to a remarkable
tree whose fruit was "desirable to make one happy" (1 Nephi 8:10).
The tree represented the love of God. The fruit of the love of God
"is the most desirable above all things" (1 Nephi 11:22). Indeed, Lehi
testified that the fruit of the tree "filled my soul with exceedingly
great joy" (1 Nephi 8:12). This language in Nephi's description of
the tree and the fruit recalls what we have read in King Benjamin's
address—it is the language of the plan of salvation, the language of
redemption through the Lord and Savior Jesus Christ. Indeed, in his
vision Nephi saw that the advent of the Savior on the earth is the

"condescension of God" (1 Nephi 11:16), the manifestation of that perfect love that motivated both our Heavenly Father and his Son to put the plan of salvation into action. The Savior is the source of the joy and peace of redemption and the hope of salvation. And all of this love and this joy, we may experience here in mortality if we follow the strait and narrow path. That is the message of the dream and the vision.

Both Lehi and Nephi saw that many people ("numberless concourses") sought to reach the path, that they might obtain the tree and the fruit. But the path was difficult. Lehi saw "mists of darkness" that obscured the path and caused confusion and misdirection. Nephi later learned that this represented "the temptations of the devil, which blindeth the eyes, and hardeneth the hearts of the children of men, and leadeth them away into broad roads, that they perish and are lost" (1 Nephi 12:17). From this we learn not only that the strait and narrow path passes through "mists of darkness," but that there are other paths, other roads close at hand. Moreover, because they represent temptation, these are no regular mists. These mists not only obscure and confuse, they misdirect and lead people astray into paths that are not strait and narrow. The wrong roads are "broad," and presumably easy to see and to navigate. They are also right there to see and follow, even if one is on the strait and narrow path. One might imagine these broad roads crossing the strait and narrow path, creating many crossroads and many choices. The broad roads may even run along with the strait and narrow path for some way. (After all, the devil is the father of lies and a master of disguise.) The strait and narrow path does not exist in isolation. There are many travelers and many roads.

Fortunately, there is the iron rod, the word of God, sure and strong, running along the strait and narrow path. In the dream Lehi sees that those who grasped the rod and held on could make it through the mists of darkness, avoid all of those other roads, and reach the tree of life. But even then the time of testing and probation was not finished. The tree and the fruit and all that they represent— redemption, the love of God, joy and rejoicing, peace, and salvation—are part of the journey of mortality, not ultimate salvation. Thus, Lehi saw that even after partaking of the fruit of the tree, some people fell away. They tasted of the fruit and experienced its joys, but then "cast their eyes about as if they were ashamed" (1 Nephi 8:25). What had caught their attention was the "great and spacious building," filled with many, many people who mocked and scorned those who walked the strait and narrow path. The building was imposing in its height ("high above the earth"), and in its scale and splendor. It was filled with people of all kinds, dressed in clothes of great beauty. This building represents the "vain imaginations and the pride of the children of men" (1 Nephi 12:18). It was (and is!) apparently quite attractive even to those who had followed the strait and narrow path to the tree of life. Feeling the scorn of those in the building, and hearing the ridicule and seeing the worldly splendor that was there, they "fell away into forbidden paths and were lost" (1 Nephi 8:28). Here again we find more paths vying for attention. The Lord forbids these paths, but they are, again, right there, ready to be taken even after one has partaken of the fruit. But, alas, they are not true paths, and lead only to destruction. Like the broad roads, the forbidden paths are a counterfeit, and their promises are hollow.

The iron rod that runs along the strait and narrow path is a powerful metaphor. It teaches true principles and focuses our attention on that which matters most in obtaining salvation: holding fast to the word of God, faith in Jesus Christ, hope in his atonement, obedience to his commandments, pressing forward no matter what. Without in any way diminishing its power and importance, I would like to marry Nephi's metaphor of the iron rod to another image

and rivers to cross. But the implication is the same: If we hold fast to the iron rod, if we stay with the caravan ("maintain [our] position"), we shall obtain salvation.

Combined in this way, the metaphors of the iron rod and the caravan bring The Church of Jesus Christ of Latter-day Saints to the center of our search for salvation. I think there are three aspects of the Church that help us in powerful ways not only to reach the tree of life but to partake of the fruit forever. The first is that prophets of God lead the caravan. We have the word of God in the scriptures, to be sure, but we also have living prophets through whom God reveals his direction and counsel and will for us. Those who stand at the head of the Church, those we sustain as prophets, seers, and revelators, act on behalf of the Savior for the whole Church and the whole world. It is the Lord's caravan, and he speaks through the President of the Church to guide and direct its progress. Moreover, the prophet holds all the priesthood keys, authority, and power required to move the caravan forward on the course the Lord has set.

This great principle of revelation and priesthood authority establishes an overriding fact about the caravan: It is always on the strait and narrow path. This has enormous significance for our search for salvation. Those who join the caravan are, of course, blessed with the gift of the Holy Ghost. Each member may receive personal revelation to help in making decisions along the path, and even about the paths to walk. Indeed, such personal revelation is essential to our salvation. However, we know that the Lord will never reveal something to us contrary to revelations he gives the prophet. We have, then, a sure guide to salvation. If we come to points in our lives where the way ahead is not clear, where the mists of darkness obscure the path, where competing paths clamor for attention, where we feel weak or discouraged, we may pray and seek direction of the Spirit, and we may look to the direction of the caravan and follow the Brethren. The caravan always moves forward on the strait and narrow path.

Leadership by prophets called of God is the first important aspect of the Church's role in our search for salvation. The second is the structure of daily gospel living. Life in the Church is highly structured. It begins with covenants we make with God. Those covenants are commitments we make to live our lives in accordance with the commandments of God. These covenants and the ordinances in which we make them—in baptism, in the priesthood, in the temple—create a framework for our daily lives. That framework begins with the life of the family. Personal and family prayer, study of the scriptures, adherence to the Word of Wisdom and to the law of chastity, the payment of tithes and offerings, keeping the Sabbath day holy, temple attendance, family duties, working together, learning "even by study and also by faith" (D&C 88:118), service in and out of the family, wholesome recreation—these are the stuff and substance of life in the family, the basic unit of the caravan. As we organize our lives around these fundamental activities, we create a structure of righteousness that guides, protects, and supports us in our journey on the strait and narrow path. Along the way, we receive the companionship of the Holy Ghost, our faith in Jesus Christ increases, we fulfill the conditions as King Benjamin taught, and we reap the promises of salvation in the caravan of the Lord.

And then there are callings and meetings. Members of the Church have been commanded to meet together often, to teach one another, to inspire, to solve problems, to direct the affairs of the kingdom. These, too, give a structure of righteousness to our lives. We meet in family council, we meet in quorums, we meet in Relief Society, we meet in Primary and in Sunday School, we meet in bishoprics, we meet in sacrament meeting, we meet in firesides, we meet in high council, we meet in presidency meetings, we meet in youth conferences and in Young Men and Young Women classes, we meet in general conference. In every meeting there is prayer, opening an opportunity to learn and to be taught of the Spirit. We prepare and teach and go to all these meetings because we have been called to the work. Those callings are part of the framework of righteousness in the caravan of the Lord. Through our callings the Lord uses us in his work, teaches us through our experience, and helps us to grow in faith through service to our brothers and sisters. Callings and the meetings that go with them help us to stay in the caravan and on the strait and narrow path.

Covenants and ordinances, commandments and callings are closely related to the third aspect of the Church that has a powerful effect on our search for salvation: the community of Zion. In the caravan we do not travel alone. We travel in families, in wards, in stakes, in the communities of Zion. The caravan, the Church, is Zion, as Moses said of the Saints in Enoch's day: "And the Lord called his people ZION, because they were of one heart and one mind, and dwelt in righteousness; and there was no poor among them" (Moses 7:18). Thus, in the Church we are bound together in mutual commitments to love and serve one another. This means that when any of our number begin to waver in their faith, or succumb to temptation, or drift away from the caravan, we go after them. Family members are always the first line of love and support. But in the Lord's church there are "captains of tens and captains of hundreds"—bishops, Relief Society presidents, quorum presidents, home teachers, visiting teachers, youth leaders—who reach out and seek to bring back into the caravan those who have wandered. This reaching out is a sacred commitment, organized and directed by the Lord through his chosen servants.

We also reach out to those who are not members of the caravan, who are seeking the truth and long for the peace and joy and salvation to be found in the kingdom of God. An important part of walking the strait and narrow path in the caravan of the Lord is the covenant we make to share the gospel with those who do not have it. All of us are called of God to be witnesses for him. The Lord also sends out his missionaries to seek out those who are wandering in strange roads, those who are pressing forward to find the true path, those whom the Lord has prepared. Indeed, in this reaching out to those not yet part of the community of Zion, and to those who have fallen away, the Lord's Church gives us opportunity to do the Lord's work. We cannot do that work unless we are firmly in the caravan, pressing forward on the strait and narrow path. Thus, learning to reach out to others is a central part of building the community of Zion and pressing forward on the path to salvation.

My family and I have been greatly blessed by the leadership of prophets of God, by the structure of righteousness in the covenants and commandments, and by the Zion community in The Church of Jesus Christ of Latter-day Saints. A good example of these blessings and of the power of the caravan is the experience of my oldest son, Bryce. This is the story of a long journey to salvation with many ups and downs that began when Bryce was in high school.

When Bryce entered high school in 1988, he had a history of strong activity in the Church. That pattern continued throughout his high school years. He attended seminary, advanced in the priesthood, held leadership positions in his quorums, was a home teacher, and was involved in the activities of the Church. At home he participated in family home evenings, in daily family prayer and scripture study, and in the life of the family. At school he got good grades, played on the high school basketball and baseball teams, and had good friends. But in those years we began to worry about changes in Bryce's attitudes and behavior that we later (much later, as it turned out) learned were the early symptoms of depression. In his senior year, he began to drift away from the Church and the commandments, especially the Word of Wisdom. He began to miss church meetings on Sundays and had a hard time getting up for seminary during the week. By the spring of 1992 Bryce had begun to give in to peer pressure to drink. Thus began a long slide into the depths of depression, inactivity in the Church, and alcoholism.

Over the next eight years there was a great battle in Bryce's life between the forces of darkness, illness, and addiction on one side and the light of the gospel, the strength of the Church, the love of his family and friends, and the power of the atonement of Jesus Christ on the other. It took several years before the doctors who treated Bryce found the right medication to treat the depression and mood swings. Alcohol became Bryce's way to avoid depression, and he became addicted to it. The alcohol, of course, did not solve the depression, but its grip on Bryce became very, very strong. With the alcoholism and the mood swings, it is not surprising, looking back, that Bryce's behavior, especially his performance in school, was erratic at best. He was in and out of five different colleges during this time, trying to find a situation in which he could succeed. For a young man with great talent and high expectations for himself, the failure he experienced was extremely discouraging. This, too, fed his depression and his dependence on alcohol in a dark, deadly, downward spiral. Although he had some periods in those years when he did not drink and was active in the Church, the pattern of depression-drinking-more depression-more drinking took hold of Bryce's life. He became an alcoholic.

That was the dark side of Bryce's life in those long years. But the forces of righteousness were not idle. Indeed, there were four powerful experiences that brought light and hope, and eventually the power of salvation, into Bryce's life. In each one, the Lord worked through his trusted servants to touch Bryce's life and help him find the courage and the strength to come back into the caravan. And, as we shall see, the Lord also used Bryce to bless the lives of others. In this way, Bryce came to know the power of the Atonement in his own life and in the lives of those he served. These are the four experiences:

1. Toward the end of his first year in college, Bryce received several letters from friends and Church leaders, including his stake president, Mitt Romney, who was also our home teacher. Each person who wrote bore testimony of the truthfulness of the gospel and encouraged Bryce to attend church and stay close to his Heavenly Father. The power of those letters was magnified in his mind because they all arrived in the same week.

2. In the spring of 1993 Bryce came home and met with President Romney to talk about his life, to describe his problems, and to confess some of his sins. The upshot was that Bryce returned to Church, felt once again the Spirit of the Lord, and made the decision to go on a mission. However, as the Spirit touched his heart, Bryce realized he needed a much longer period of repentance and would need to wait to go on a mission. He began the process of repentance but did not sustain the effort. The destructive pattern returned.

3. In the midst of a subsequent cycle of depression and drinking, I challenged Bryce to read the Book of Mormon and pray about it to find out for himself whether it was true or not. Bryce not only accepted the challenge but also told one of his friends, Mark Schmitt, about it. That conversation led to missionary discussions in our home. Bryce continued to struggle with his own problems, but his testimony grew. On several occasions he was instrumental in helping Mark grow in faith and understanding of the gospel. Mark joined the Church, served a mission in Uruguay, married in the temple, and served in the bishopric in his ward. Mark's conversion was an important step in Bryce's return to the strait and narrow path.

4. Following yet another period of depression and inactivity in the Church, Bryce returned home and one day asked me to give him

a blessing. In the blessing he received a promise that if he would repent and return to the Church, the Lord would bless him, and he would find his eternal companion. Bryce began to attend church and accepted a calling in his singles ward as family home evening group leader. That is where he met Stephanie Ashby and where their relationship began. Stephanie had a wonderful influence on Bryce. He began to work with his bishop to be worthy to go to the temple. Through many weeks and months of study, prayer, and keeping the commandments, he grew in his testimony. Bryce and Stephanie prepared together, and in September of 1996 they were married in the Salt Lake Temple.

These four experiences (and many others I have not mentioned) helped Bryce return to the strait and narrow path. But even after marriage in the temple his return was not complete. Marriage and activity in the Church (and the right medication) had a wonderful effect on Bryce, but he had not yet addressed his addiction to alcohol. The urge to drink was always present. Though there were times when he slipped in the first years of marriage, by the time children started to come (Spenser was the first in 1998) Bryce had given up alcohol and was, as he later described it, "white-knuckling" his way through the terrible urge to drink. His activity and callings in the Church and his continued prayer and study of the gospel were great blessings to him in his battle. He was assigned to home teach a man who was a drug addict. Through that experience he learned about addiction, and about the Addiction Recovery Program in the Church, led in our stake by George and Marci McPhee.

Bryce knew George, and knew that he had struggled with alcohol. A short time later Bryce saw George in the temple and told him that he wanted to come to the program because he thought he might be an addict. Bryce entered the Church's Addiction Recovery Program and in that process discovered the power of the Atonement.

George and Marci helped Bryce understand the Savior and how the Atonement works. He had to confront his addiction, his responsibility for his behavior, and his utter dependence on the redeeming power of Jesus Christ. As he exercised his growing faith in the Lord, as he repented of his sins and sought the Savior's mercy and help, Bryce experienced a "mighty change of heart." Gradually, the desire to drink diminished, and through the Savior his capacity to resist increased. Bryce became a committed disciple of Jesus Christ, firmly on the strait and narrow path, solidly in the caravan of the Lord.

When I look back on the long years of Bryce's journey to faith and redemption, the role of the Church looms large. Each of the dimensions of the caravan I have emphasized in this chapter—prophetic leadership; the structure of righteousness in covenants, commandments, and organization; and the community of Zion—played an important role in Bryce's journey. Of course, Sue and I prayed night and day for Bryce and we exercised faith in the Savior on his behalf. And as with Alma the Elder, Heavenly Father heard our prayers and answered them by sending not one angel, but many—a wonderful home teacher and stake president, good and faithful friends not afraid to bear testimony, missionaries who were true messengers of the gospel, a lifelong friend whose own conversion, faith, and testimony provided a great inspiration, strong quorum presidents and bishops who offered assignments and callings and wise counsel, an eternal companion whose gentle spirit and eternal commitment were life-giving, a fellow alcoholic whose righteousness and strength brought Bryce face-to-face with his addiction and his Savior. All of these people connected with Bryce through the Church. Through his Church and through his trusted servants the Lord Jesus Christ touched Bryce's heart and brought him back. The caravan of the Lord truly was a caravan of salvation for our son.

Having committed himself to walk the strait and narrow path in the caravan of the Lord, Bryce is now in a position to help many other people. And he has, and he does. The light of the gospel that shines in him is a beacon to others, helping them find their way. I can see that light in the eyes of our little grandchildren who are growing up in a home of faith. For them, salvation is a daily experience. I have seen it in the many young people Bryce has touched in his callings in the youth programs of the Church. Because of his experiences, he has a gift from God to touch the hearts of young people who struggle with temptation. Bryce has the capacity to connect with those who have wandered from the caravan because he knows their experience. Bryce has the journey of a lifetime ahead of him, and ultimately, his salvation depends on his faithfulness. But he knows the Savior, and he knows the joy of forgiveness and the power of the Atonement. As he pushes forward in the caravan of the Lord, he will have many opportunities to help others partake of the blessings of salvation.

The salvation that is in the plan of happiness of the Father is a great protection against evil, a source of strength in the battle against the forces of darkness. I believe that this is what Paul had in mind when he made salvation part of the armor of God—to have the atonement of the Savior become a reality in our lives, to experience the pure love of Christ, to receive deep in our souls the forgiveness that comes only through Jesus Christ, to have a bright, shining hope of eternal life, to grow in knowledge of him and our Father, to enjoy—and rejoice in—the companionship of the Holy Ghost. Well did Paul make such salvation the helmet, the crown and head of the armor of God. With the pure love of Christ in our souls, with our feet firmly on the strait and narrow path, with our hands on the iron rod, and with our hearts and souls committed to the caravan of the Lord, we are ready to "stand against the wiles of the devil" and to "wrestle . . . against the rulers of the darkness of this world" (Ephesians 6:11–12).

CHAPTER 11

THE SWORD OF THE SPIRIT: THE WORD OF GOD

In August of 2000, I received a calling in the Church that has changed my life. The calling came in the woods of New Hampshire. Our family had been on vacation, and on our way home we stopped by to visit with our stake president and his family in their home at Loon Mountain. While everyone else was eating pizza and watermelon, the president pulled me aside and called me to serve as a counselor in what was then the stake mission presidency. (Stake missions were dissolved in early 2002, and responsibility for missionary work was given to the wards and the bishops. At that time I was called to serve as the high councilor responsible for missionary work in the Cambridge Stake.) There in New Hampshire amidst the bustle and tumult of a summer afternoon the Lord called me on my second mission.

The call was not a surprise. For a long time I had felt the need to do more missionary work than I had been doing. I had served a mission in Germany between 1968 and 1970, and had had many missionary experiences since then. But there came a time when the thought, "you need to do more," impressed itself on my mind. In fact, it was almost as if I had a little angel sitting on my shoulder whispering in my ear: "There is more to be done; you need to do more." I began to look for opportunities to share the gospel—and I found them. More people began to ask me about the Church, and I had more discussions about what we believed. But still the angel on my shoulder persisted. When President Baird issued the call to me, I knew there was much more that I needed to do and that this was the Lord's way to help me do it.

After I had been sustained, the stake president set me apart as a missionary in the Cambridge Massachusetts Stake of Zion. My calling was not an administrative calling, although I had some of those responsibilities. My calling was to be personally engaged in the great work of proclaiming the gospel—to find the honest in heart, to bear witness of Jesus Christ, the restoration of the gospel, the Book of Mormon, and the great blessings of the plan of salvation. It was a calling to invite, to share, to teach, and to fellowship. In the time I served in that calling I came to understand much more deeply than ever before what it means to be a witness of God, and to teach the word of God by the power of the Spirit. Because of these experiences I feel that I know what Paul meant when he completed the armor of God with the word of God: "Wherefore, take unto you the whole armour of God. . . . Stand therefore, . . . and take . . . the sword of the Spirit, which is the word of God" (Ephesians 6:13, 14, 17).

In this chapter I want to use missionary work as a lens through which to see and understand the word of God as the sword of the Spirit. The word of God is powerful in many other contexts, but missionary work illustrates the basic issues we face in putting the word of God into our lives and using it in the battle against evil. The following experience sets the stage.

In January of 2005 I made a trip to New York City to visit with several alumni of the Harvard Business School. I made such trips many times during a year and the routine was almost always the same: a car service to the airport in Boston, flight to LaGuardia Airport, a car service into the city and around to appointments all day, back to LaGuardia, another flight to Boston, and a car service home. Since my calling as a missionary I had made it a practice to talk about the Church with the people I met on these trips. On that particular trip a man named Javier, who would be my driver for the day, met me at LaGuardia Airport. As we drove into the city, I asked him where he was from. That led to a long explanation of his background. He explained that he was born in Ecuador, that he had Inca and Indian ancestors, and that he had been in the United States for more than twenty years. In between appointments during the morning I learned more about his family and his interests, and I shared with him some of my background, including my service as a missionary for the Church. Javier told me he had seen missionaries before with their name tags and white shirts. We talked for a little while about religion, and in that conversation he told me that he loved to read and that he loved history. As he said that, I saw an opportunity to introduce him to the Book of Mormon.

I told Javier that I had a book that I thought he might enjoy. I pulled a copy of the Book of Mormon out of my briefcase and gave it to him. I explained the origins of the book, and its purpose. During the rest of the day Javier read the introductory material while he waited for me. At the end of the day we had an opportunity to talk between my last appointment and the drop-off at my hotel. This was my chance to teach Javier the word of the God, the marvelous message that God is our Heavenly Father, that down through the ages he has spoken to his children through prophets, that he sent his Son Jesus Christ to be our Savior and Redeemer, to teach and minister, and to establish the Church of Jesus Christ. I taught Javier that the Church was taken from the earth because of wickedness and apostasy, and that it has been restored in our day through the Prophet Joseph Smith. I bore him my testimony that the heavens are open, that God speaks again through prophets, that the Book of Mormon is a second witness of Jesus Christ, and that we can know the truth if we pray and ask God. (This is the first lesson that missionaries teach investigators. For a full discussion of these principles see *Preach My Gospel: A Guide to Missionary Service* [The Church of Jesus Christ of Latter-day Saints, 2004], 45–54.)

Javier was quiet for a moment, and then he told me that he knew there was something missing in his life. It was not about money or material things, but about God. He was looking for that something, and was grateful to hear what I believed. The next day, when he drove me to the airport, I asked him if he would like to host the missionaries in his home. He said he would, and I got his address and phone number and told him that I would have the missionaries get in touch with him. Through our mission president in Boston I contacted the missionaries in New York and gave them all the information I had. They told me that Javier lived close to a chapel and that a brother from Ecuador had just been baptized in the last few months.

I did not hear from the missionaries after that phone call, but I continued to think and pray about Javier. Two months later I again traveled to New York. As I got ready for the trip I thought about meeting people on the planes and in the cars, and I committed myself to speak to them. In my prayers I asked Heavenly Father to put people in my path that he had prepared and, as I had done for the last four and a half years, I promised him that I would speak to them. I wondered if I might see Javier, and I had an impression that I might. When I got off the plane and walked into the baggage claim area to meet my driver, who should be standing there with my name on a card but Javier! I had been going to New York on trips just like that one several times a year for almost ten years, and I had never had the same driver on two straight trips. I had rarely even seen the same driver twice. The odds of me getting Javier on the very next trip just by chance were extremely low. But there he was.

Javier told me that he had spoken with the missionaries but that he had been working two jobs and had not yet made it to church. I asked him about the Book of Mormon, and he reached across the front seat and pulled the copy I had given him out of his bag. He told me that he had been reading it and enjoying it. We reviewed the principles we had discussed the last time, and talked about what he had been reading in the Book of Mormon. As we talked, I received the impression that I needed to teach Javier how to pray. I asked him about prayer, and he told me that the missionaries had encouraged him to pray, but that he did not have the courage to tell them that he did not know how. Javier thought that to pray to God he needed to learn a set prayer, and he did not know any prayers to say. Here again was an opportunity to share with Javier the word of God. I taught him about prayer, about Heavenly Father, about gratitude, about asking for blessings and for help, and about Jesus Christ as our Advocate with the Father.

Javier thanked me for helping him. He told me that he was continuing to search for what was missing in his life. He wanted to find out if what I had been teaching him was it. His problem reminded him of Lehi's dream in the Book of Mormon. He wanted to taste of the fruit of the tree, and he wanted his family to partake. I followed another prompting and encouraged Javier to go home that very night and gather his children and his wife around him and say a prayer to God for them. I promised him that if he would do that, there would come into his home a sweet spirit, and he and they would come to know that what I had told him was true. Before we parted company

I told Javier that I believed that God had sent me to see him that day, to teach him to pray and to help him in his journey. There was no doubt in my mind then, and there is no doubt in my mind now, that I was on the Lord's errand and that God was watching over Javier.

Javier's story continues to unfold, but in his experience thus far we can see the power of the word of God—the power to instruct, to comfort, to guide, to inspire, to change hearts, to convert. In this chapter I want to probe more deeply what the word of God is, how we obtain it, and how we use it as the sword of the Spirit. Our starting point is to understand the several meanings attached to the phrase *the word of God.*

What Is the Word of God?

The phrase *the word of God* appears numerous times in the scriptures in different contexts and with a small number of different, but closely related, meanings. In the context of missionary work, a very common meaning is: the gospel of Jesus Christ. In the Acts of the Apostles, for example, Luke writes that Philip (one of the seven presidents of the Quorums of the Seventy in his day) went to Samaria and "preached Christ unto them," healed the sick, taught the people "the things concerning the kingdom of God, and the name of Jesus Christ," and "baptized both men and women" (Acts 8:5, 12). Luke then notes the reaction of the Apostles to this news:

> Now when the apostles which were at Jerusalem heard that Samaria had received the word of God, they sent unto them Peter and John: who, when they were come down, prayed for them, that they might receive the Holy Ghost: (For as yet he was fallen upon none of them; only they were baptized in the name of the Lord Jesus.) Then laid they their

hands on them, and they received the Holy Ghost. (Acts 8:14–17)

What Philip had preached to the Samaritans was the gospel of Jesus Christ—faith in Jesus Christ, the Son of God, the Savior and Redeemer, who had come among men, worked mighty miracles, taught the way to eternal life, suffered for sins, was killed, and rose the third day. Philip also taught repentance, baptism by immersion for the remission of sins, and the gift of the Holy Ghost. All of that—all the principles, the doctrine, all the covenants and commandments, all the ordinances that define the gospel of Jesus Christ—the apostles called "the word of God."

The idea that the word of God is the gospel of Jesus Christ explains why Luke would write later in Acts that "the word of God grew and multiplied" (Acts 12:24), meaning that the missionaries of the day had taken the gospel to more and more people. We find this same meaning in the descriptions of the great missionary labors of Alma, Amulek, and the sons of Mosiah in the Book of Mormon. There we learn that "Alma went and began to declare the word of God unto the church which was established in the valley of Gideon" (Alma 6:8). Later, in the aftermath of war, "Alma and Amulek [did] go forth, and also many more who had been chosen for the work, to preach the word throughout all the land" (Alma 16:15). Summarizing the work of Alma and Amulek, Mormon wrote that "the word of God [was] preached in its purity in all the land" (Alma 16:21).

The sons of Mosiah likewise had great success in proclaiming the gospel of Jesus Christ—the word of God—among the Lamanites. Mormon described the impact of the proclamation of the king of the Lamanites to all his people that "they should not lay their hands on Ammon, or Aaron, or Omner, or Himni, nor either of their brethren who should go forth preaching the word of God, in whatsoever place they should be, in any part of their land" (Alma 23:1). Here, once again, the "word" is the gospel, and the intent of the king's proclamation was that the sons of Mosiah "might go forth and preach the word according to their desires . . . that the word of God might have no obstruction" (Alma 23:3). And, indeed, Aaron and his brethren took the message of the gospel "from city to city, and from one house of worship to another," establishing the church and setting apart priests and teachers "to preach and to teach the word of God among them" (Alma 23:4).

A second, closely related meaning of the *word of God* is the scriptures. In the eighth Article of Faith the Prophet Joseph Smith declared, "We believe the Bible to be the word of God as far as it is translated correctly; we also believe the Book of Mormon to be the word of God." As a record of God's work among his children, the scriptures tell us what God and his Son, Jesus Christ, have said to different people, including prophets, at different times. Some of those words teach doctrine, some are prophecies of things to come, some are commandments, some define the laws of heaven and of earth. Words of this kind, words that God has spoken for all mankind, are like a framework, an architecture of salvation. They are like an exquisite, marvelous building—framed together, constructed, and finished—within which all of God's children are born, grow and develop, are tested and tried, and will be judged and rewarded. Taken together, the doctrines, the commandments, the prophecies, and the laws of God that define that framework are the word of God. In the first section of the Doctrine and Covenants the Lord spoke about his word in just this way:

> What I the Lord have spoken, I have spoken, and I excuse not myself; and though the heavens and the earth pass away, my word shall not pass away, but shall all be fulfilled,

whether by mine own voice or by the voice of my servants, it is the same. (D&C 1:38)

As the framework of salvation, the word of God is the standard against which we will be judged. It is the sure guide, the iron rod that helps us stay on the strait and narrow path through the mists of temptation. Used in this way, the word of God defines the righteous structure of our lives, giving us protection and direction. That is why the Lord speaks of "establishing" his word. When he sent the sons of Mosiah off on their mission he said, "Go forth among the Lamanites, thy brethren, and establish my word" (Alma 17:11). Their mission was to preach the gospel and lay a firm foundation for the structure of righteousness—the word of God—among the Lamanites.

It is in this sense of an eternal framework that the word of God "shall not pass away." But the scriptures (and the framework) also contain prophecies and promises that "shall all be fulfilled." These, too, are established. Indeed, when God makes a covenant with his children, he makes to them eternal promises. He says, in effect, "I give you my word." Thus, the scriptures are the record of the promises of God and of God's covenant people. The Bible contains the Old Testament, or a witness or testimony of the promises given to God's covenant people before the Savior's birth. It contains the New Testament, or the witness and testimony of the promises given by Jesus Christ in the covenants of his gospel made possible by his atonement. The Book of Mormon is another testament of Jesus Christ, a witness and testimony of his atonement and the promises of salvation through him. The Doctrine and Covenants is a witness and testimony of the restoration of the gospel of Jesus Christ in its fulness, with all the promises of the new and everlasting covenant. All of these scriptures are the word of God.

When we read the scriptures, we read a record of God's work

with his children. The scriptures are a record of God in action. Through the stories, the prophecies, and the revelations, we can see who God is, what he does, and what principles govern his relationship to us. Moreover, we learn what he wants us to do. The scriptures are God's message for us. Every time we open them and read them it is as if God says to us, "May I have a word with you?" God speaks to us through the scriptures because the scriptures have been given to us through his power and according to his will. They are sacred and holy, and the words in them—words divinely spoken and divinely written—are mediated and transmitted by the Holy Ghost.

When we read the scriptures under the direction and influence of the Holy Ghost, we can hear the voice of the Lord and can, therefore, know his words. The miracle of the scriptures is that they literally can be the word of God to us. This is also what happens when we hear the living prophets of God speak under the direction of the Holy Ghost. When the members of the First Presidency and the Quorum of the Twelve speak through the power of the Holy Ghost, the Lord has told us that their words "shall be scripture, shall be the will of the Lord, shall be the mind of the Lord, shall be the word of the Lord, shall be the voice of the Lord, and the power of God unto salvation" (D&C 68:4). When the Lord's anointed speak through the Spirit, they stand where Jesus would stand, they speak in his name, they say what he would say if he were here, and what they speak is the word of the Lord. Truly, the ancient, the modern, and the living scriptures literally are the word of God.

An experience that one of my grandchildren had illustrates the great power of the word of God as spoken by an Apostle of the Lord under the direction of the Holy Ghost. In the fall of 2004 my son Bryce was sitting in his living room watching general conference. The speaker was Elder Henry B. Eyring. As Elder Eyring began to speak, Bryce's fifteen-month-old son, Parker, toddled into the living room.

Parker had recently learned to walk, and he was reveling in his new-found mobility. He was in constant motion. But on this day as he walked into the living room he looked up at the television, saw Elder Eyring, and sat down on the floor. Normally, Parker's attention span is about twenty seconds. But he sat and listened to Elder Eyring speak for much longer. Bryce noticed him there and expected him to get up and wander away, but Parker did not move. In fact, it was clear that he was listening intently to what Elder Eyring said. Elder Eyring spoke about priesthood keys, priesthood power, and faith. In his talk he told this story:

> In a chapel far from Salt Lake City, in a place where a member of the Quorum of the Twelve rarely goes, a father approached me. He led his young son by the hand. As they reached me, he looked down at the boy, called him by name, and said, nodding his head towards me, "This is an Apostle." I could tell by the sound of the father's voice that he was hoping his son would feel more than that he was meeting a dignified visitor. He hoped that his son would feel a conviction that priesthood keys were on the earth in the Lord's Church. His son will need that conviction again and again. He will need it when he opens a letter from some future prophet he has never seen calling him to a mission. He will need it when he buries a child or a wife or a parent. He will need it for courage to follow direction to serve. He will need it for the comfort that comes from trusting a sealing power that binds forever. ("Faith and Keys," *Ensign,* November 2004, 26)

The young son needed exactly what my little grandson needs, and that is what he received. I know through the witness of the Spirit to me that little Parker Clark, fifteen months old, heard the voice of the Lord through Elder Eyring that Saturday afternoon. In fact, he sat on that floor until Elder Eyring was about halfway through his talk. Parker then stood up, looked at his dad, turned and pointed to Elder Eyring on the television, and then walked over and crawled up on his dad's lap. He sat on Bryce's lap watching and listening to Elder Eyring with the same intensity until Elder Eyring had finished his talk. Bryce recounts that the Spirit was very strong in that living room. Bryce was a witness to, and a participant in, a miracle. After Elder Eyring finished his talk, Parker climbed down from Bryce's lap and resumed his travels around the house (and I do not think he has stopped since). But in those moments when Elder Eyring spoke under the direction of the Holy Ghost, the Lord spoke through him to the soul of that little boy. And the promise of the Lord is that he can speak to each of us with just that power every time we read the scriptures, and every time we listen to the prophets of God.

As the "word of God," the gospel of Jesus Christ and the scriptures are closely related to the third meaning of that phrase: personal revelation. One of the greatest blessings of the restoration of the gospel is the gift of the Holy Ghost and the opportunity to receive personal revelation. Revelation from God is important for everyone, but it has particular salience for missionaries. Personal revelation comes in many ways and has many purposes. But for missionary work, whether it comes to strengthen testimony, or to instruct, or to inspire, or to guide, or to constrain, or to comfort, or to confirm, the overriding objective of personal revelation is to put the missionary in a position to do the Lord's work. Personal revelation is the means through which the Lord qualifies his missionaries for the work. The work is his, but he works through his missionaries to accomplish his purposes. He does so by communicating with them. He gives them his word.

Two experiences illustrate the role that personal revelation plays in missionary work. The first took place in Germany while I was serving a full-time mission. My companion and I were teaching a young woman named Christa Cascarelli. It was clear to us when we started to teach her that the Lord had prepared Christa to hear the gospel. She was a close friend of one of the sisters in the branch where we served, and we taught her with the member family. Our first discussion with Christa had gone well and we returned one evening for the second discussion, which in those days focused on the Book of Mormon. As we began to teach, we could tell that Christa was concerned and had many questions, not only about the Book of Mormon but also about prophets and about the Restoration. We decided to depart from the prepared lesson and to address her questions and concerns.

In that moment my companion and I experienced the Lord's promise: "Speak the thoughts that I shall put into your hearts, and you shall not be confounded before men; For it shall be given you in the very hour, yea, in the very moment, what ye shall say" (D&C 100:5–6). We felt the power of the Holy Ghost come into that living room, and we were given what the Lord wanted Christa to hear. What my companion and I taught her that day was not what we had planned. We spoke under the direction of the Spirit. I know we taught her about the Restoration and the Book of Mormon, but to this day I do not remember the words we said. But I remember vividly what I felt, and I remember what Christa felt as the Holy Ghost bore witness to her that what we said was true. Soon thereafter Christa joined the Church, later married another member of the branch, and has gone on to raise a wonderful family in the Church.

The second experience happened many years later, after I had been called to serve in missionary work in the Cambridge Stake. One evening I was in my office at home preparing to go on a trip to New

York. I knew I might have the opportunity to speak to someone about the Church on the plane ride, so I grabbed a few pass-along cards and put them in my briefcase. I usually carry a copy of the Book of Mormon with me, but I knew I had given one away and did not have another in my briefcase. I thought about taking a copy of the Book of Mormon, but reasoned that the plane ride was so short I probably would not have time to explain the book and give it away. I decided not to put a copy of the Book of Mormon in my briefcase. The next morning as I was on my way out the door of my office, I had the distinct impression that I had made a mistake. I did not hear a voice, but the message of the Spirit was very clear: "Take the Book of Mormon with you." I followed that prompting and put the book in my briefcase.

As I got on the plane that morning, I wondered whom I would meet. I was surprised to find that one of the people sitting in my row was Alice Crawford, who worked in our development office at school. Alice had been assigned to go with me on some of the appointments I had that day. When I saw her sitting in the window seat of my row (I was on the aisle) I wondered if she was the one I needed to talk to. We did not have a chance to talk on the way down, but on the way back to Boston at the end of the day the opportunity came. I was looking for a moment in our conversation when I might be able to talk with Alice about the Church when she turned to me and asked me if I paid tithing. The question came up in a conversation we were having about philanthropy. I said that I did. She told me that she was supposed to pay tithing too, but had grown disenchanted with her church. I asked her what she knew about The Church of Jesus Christ of Latter-day Saints. That question led to a conversation in which I was able to explain what we believe about our Heavenly Father, about prophets, about the Savior, and about the restoration of his gospel and his Church.

Alice listened intently and then asked, "What is this I have heard about the Book of Mormon? What is that?" I explained what the Book of Mormon is and its role as another testament of the Savior. I then said, "This morning as I left the house I had an impression that I should bring a copy of the Book of Mormon with me on this trip." I then reached down into my briefcase, pulled out the book, handed it to Alice, and said, "I think this is for you." Alice took the book and said, "That is spooky." I told her it was not spooky, it was just the way Heavenly Father works. Alice opened the book and read all the way back to Boston. As we began our descent into the airport she turned to me and said, "You and I are going to have to have more discussions about this book." I explained missionaries and lessons and agreed that there were more discussions about the Book of Mormon and the gospel in her future. And that is what happened. Her journey of discovery and faith was not easy, but she persevered, gained a testimony of the gospel, and joined the Church in October of 2004.

In both of these experiences personal revelation was the means through which the Lord accomplished his work. Yet the other dimensions of the word of God were also at work. Just as it was in ancient times, so in these modern missionary experiences the word of God came to Heavenly Father's children through personal revelation, through the scriptures, and through the gospel of Jesus Christ. But if we look a little closer, we can also see the fourth meaning of the *word of God:* the Lord Jesus Christ. The Savior himself is the Word of God. Jesus said, "I am the way, the truth, and the life: no man cometh unto the Father, but by me" (John 14:6). God our Father sent his Son into the world to bring about the plan of salvation. In his perfect life, in his being and character, in his teachings and ministry, and in his atonement and resurrection, Jesus showed us how to return home to our Heavenly Father, and he made that return possible. He defined the strait and narrow path that leads us to heaven. Moreover, what he taught through word and deed he received from the Father. He said, "The words that I speak unto you I speak not of myself: but the Father that dwelleth in me, he doeth the works" (John 14:10). He himself is the message of salvation and redemption that our Heavenly Father has prepared for us.

But there is more. Jesus encompasses all other meanings of "the word of God" in his life and ministry. The gospel of Jesus Christ is just that: It is the message of hope, the good news of his birth, his life, his atonement and resurrection. When we teach the first principles and ordinances of that gospel, we first teach faith in the Lord Jesus Christ. Everything else flows from that faith in who he is, what he did, and what he can do for us. The scriptures likewise are centered on Jesus Christ, and the centrality of Christ is also evident in personal revelation, as the light of Christ is one of the means through which the Holy Ghost ministers to us and reveals the word of God to us.

In all of these ways Jesus Christ is the Word of God. All that the Father would have us know comes through the Son. This is why God the Father said to the Prophet Joseph Smith, *This is My Beloved Son. Hear Him!* (Joseph Smith–History 1:17). It is why the Father said to the Nephites gathered at the temple in Bountiful, "Behold my Beloved Son, in whom I am well pleased, in whom I have glorified my name—hear ye him" (3 Nephi 11:7). The Son reveals the Father, and speaks the words of the Father, unto us. His life is the good news God wants us to hear. He reveals the word of God to us through the prophets and the scriptures. Through his light the Holy Ghost teaches us the word of God and brings to our remembrance all that our Father wants us to know. Jesus is in very deed the Word of God. Thus, when Paul speaks in Ephesians about taking "the sword of the Spirit, which is the word of God," he is admonishing us to put on

Jesus Christ and all that he reveals to us through the scriptures, the prophets, and the Holy Ghost.

Obtaining the Word of God

In the early days of the Restoration, the Lord gave his new missionaries instructions that serve us well today. Speaking to Hyrum Smith about his assignment to preach the gospel, the Lord said, "Seek not to declare my word, but first seek to obtain my word, and then shall your tongue be loosed; then, if you desire, you shall have my Spirit and my word, yea, the power of God unto the convincing of men" (D&C 11:21). This was counsel not just about patience but about priority and focus. Hyrum was to "obtain" the word of God. If we apply all the meanings of *the word of God* to this instruction, Hyrum's mission was clear: gain a testimony of Jesus Christ; understand the gospel, including the scriptures and the doctrines and principles of salvation; hearken to the words of the prophets; and receive personal revelation through the Holy Ghost.

What the Lord had in mind for Hyrum and for all of His missionaries is much deeper than awareness or familiarity. His instruction to "seek" and "obtain," applied to testimony, doctrine, and revelation, conveys a sense of depth, of possession born of effort and endeavor. Mormon captured well the power of this divine injunction to seek and to obtain the word of God with this description of the sons of Mosiah:

> They had waxed strong in the knowledge of the truth; for they were men of a sound understanding and they had searched the scriptures diligently, that they might know the word of God. But this is not all; they had given themselves to much prayer, and fasting; therefore they had the spirit of prophecy, and the spirit of revelation, and when they taught,

they taught with power and authority of God. (Alma 17:2–3)

The sons of Mosiah had sought the word of God, and they had obtained it in just the way the Lord outlined for Hyrum and for each of us. In fact, Mormon's description of what they did provides a pattern for missionaries (and all) who desire to obtain the word of God:

Make and keep sacred covenants

The sons of Mosiah had been set apart by their father to preach the gospel to the Lamanites. They had made covenants with the Lord to keep his commandments and to do his will. When Alma met them fourteen years later, they had been true to the covenants they had made. They were committed to the Lord and to his work.

Search the scriptures and the words of the prophets

The sons of Mosiah had searched the scriptures diligently. This means that they had not only read them but also pondered them. They had likely compared passages and discussed their reading with one another, puzzling over the meaning of what they read, and looking and looking until they found new insight. As they read and pondered, they began to see and understand more fully and completely. That is why they were men of sound understanding. That is why they waxed strong in the knowledge of the truth.

Fast and pray

The sons of Mosiah did more than study and think about what they read. They sought the guidance of the Spirit through prayer. They went further and prepared themselves to receive the ministry of the Spirit by fasting. In fact, Mormon tells us that they not only did this a lot, but that when they did it, they "gave themselves" to the task. They made a concerted effort to humble themselves before the Lord, an effort of the whole soul to find out the word of God. Because they did this, they received the spirit of prophecy and of revelation, and when they taught, they taught with power and authority of God.

Obtaining the word of God requires the combined effort of mind and heart. It must engage all the faculties of learning that our Heavenly Father has given us. That means we must use our powers to read, to hear, to reason, to ponder, to speak, and to listen. The word of God must get into our minds through reading and studying, through listening and discussing. It must get processed in the mind and organized and stored there, ready to be accessed, prepared, and communicated in whatever circumstance we need to use it. But that is only part of what we can do. Our Heavenly Father has also given us powers of the Spirit through which we can learn. Through the light of Christ, and through the ministry of the Holy Ghost, we can feel the word of God in our souls and in our hearts. This spiritual learning reinforces, augments, and deepens what we read and study and hear. Reason and revelation work together to give us the word of God with power and authority.

President Boyd K. Packer taught us about the process of spiritual learning through revelation:

> The Holy Ghost speaks with a voice that you *feel* more than you *hear*. It is described as a "still small voice." And while we speak of "listening" to the whisperings of the Spirit, most often one describes a spiritual prompting by saying, "I had a feeling . . . "
>
> Revelation comes as words we *feel* more than *hear*. Nephi told his wayward brothers, who were visited by an angel, "Ye were past *feeling*, that ye could not *feel* his words."
>
> The scriptures are full of such expressions as "The veil

was taken from our minds, and the eyes of our understanding were opened," or "I will tell you in your mind and in your heart," or "I did enlighten thy mind," or "Speak the thoughts that I shall put into your hearts." There are hundreds of verses which teach of revelation. ("Personal Revelation: The Gift, the Test, and the Promise," *Ensign*, November 1994, 60)

In the principles taught by President Packer, and in the experience of the sons of Mosiah, there is an important, vital connection between the body and the spirit, between the mind and the heart. What we feel with the Spirit does indeed enlighten our minds. If we are to access what we have felt, so that we may use it, the word of God that comes to us spiritually through the ministry of the Holy Ghost and through the light of Christ must get into our physical memories and be stored and organized and connected to other things that we have learned and know. Even though the words and ideas from the Lord do not come through the usual channels (seeing, hearing), we need to embrace them. The body needs to be the servant of the spirit in order for us to receive the word of God in all its power.

This same principle is at work when the word of the Lord comes to us through the physical channels. When the angel visited Laman and Lemuel outside Jerusalem while they were in search of the brass plates, the words the angel spoke created sound waves that hit their eardrums and were transmitted along the auditory nerve to their brains. They heard the words physically, but they were "past feeling" and did not feel the words in their hearts. The Spirit did not augment and enrich and deepen what they heard, and thus, they did not truly understand what the angel said. If we are to "obtain" the word of God, we must hear and feel what the Lord says. We must use all the capacity to learn in our minds and in our hearts.

Two examples of this important principle appear in the book of Third Nephi in the Book of Mormon. In the first, a group of people was gathered around the temple in the land of Bountiful some time after the great destruction that occurred at the Savior's death. As they talked among themselves, they heard a voice "as if it came out of heaven" (3 Nephi 11:3). They heard the voice, but they did not understand what it said. Though they did not understand it, they felt the voice because it made them "quake; yea, it did pierce them to the very soul, and did cause their hearts to burn" (3 Nephi 11:3). Here is an example in which the spirit feels the words, even causing a physical experience (the frame quakes, the heart burns), and yet the mind does not comprehend what is being said. The voice spoke again, and again they heard it but did not understand it. But the third time they heard the voice they "did open their ears to hear it; and their eyes were towards the sound thereof; and they did look steadfastly towards heaven, from whence the sound came" (3 Nephi 11:5).

When Mormon says that they opened their ears the third time, he implies that they became spiritually and physically in tune. Before that, it appears that even though they heard the sound of a voice, and even though their spirits had felt the words of God (for it was God the Father speaking), they had not joined the spirit and the body to understand what God said. Perhaps because they had not expected words from heaven, the prevailing patterns in their minds so occupied their attention that they did not process the sounds of the voice as words. In addition, the voice of God was quiet; Mormon describes it as "small." Perhaps their minds were full of other thoughts and other sounds, so that the quiet, small voice was hard to understand. Moreover, at the first sound of the voice, they "cast their eyes round about" (3 Nephi 11:3). Perhaps their first response was to look at the usual sources of voicelike sounds—other people. It was only when they concentrated and focused their minds on the voice of God, only when they turned their "eyes . . . towards the sound thereof," only when they "did look steadfastly towards heaven," that their minds were in tune with their hearts and their spirits. With that congruence of body and spirit they not only heard the words and felt the voice, but understood the words and comprehended the message of God: "Behold my Beloved Son, in whom I am well pleased, in whom I have glorified my name—hear ye him" (3 Nephi 11:7).

We, too, need to concentrate our attention on the voice of God, bring our spirits and our minds into harmony and congruence, and raise our eyes to heaven, if we are to obtain the word of God. With that focus, and with that harmony, the Holy Ghost can teach us through our minds and through our hearts.

The second experience in Third Nephi gives us a glimpse of the power of that ministry and of the word of God. It took place as Jesus taught the people gathered at the temple in Bountiful following his resurrection. After he had taught them his gospel and healed the sick, he had the people bring all the little children and set them on the ground around him. He then asked everyone to kneel upon the ground. Jesus then knelt himself and prayed unto the Father. Those who were there bore this testimony in the record:

> The eye hath never seen, neither hath the ear heard, before, so great and marvelous things as we saw and heard Jesus speak unto the Father; and no tongue can speak, neither can there be written by any man, neither can the hearts of men conceive so great and marvelous things as we both saw and heard Jesus speak; and no one can conceive of the joy which filled our souls at the time we heard him pray for us into the Father. (3 Nephi 17:16–17)

Though the words that Jesus spoke could not be conceived or spoken by man, yet the people understood and felt what he said through revelation. The very same thing happened when Jesus visited them the next day. After the people had gathered, the twelve who had been chosen and given authority by the Savior taught the people and baptized them. Following their baptism, "the Holy Ghost did fall upon them, and they were filled with the Holy Ghost and with fire" (3 Nephi 19:13). As angels ministered unto them, Jesus returned. Once again he directed the people to kneel on the ground and pray. He went off a short distance from them and prayed, and the record contains the words that he prayed. In that prayer, what he said was in language that the people heard and understood and wrote down. But as he continued his prayer, he used words from a more exalted sphere. The record reports that these words were "so great and marvelous" that "tongue cannot speak" them, nor can they be written (3 Nephi 19:32, 34). The implication is that the words Jesus spoke could not be processed in the way we normally process words. It was as if they had too many dimensions and could not therefore be organized, manipulated, and transmitted through the brains, the nerves, the mouths, and the hands of mortals. Yet, with the power of the Holy Ghost, the people heard these higher-order words of the Lord, and they understood them. They did not have the language to say what Jesus said. But they understood him. Mormon underscores the miracle involved here by giving these passages a chiastic structure:

> *And tongue cannot speak the words which he prayed (a)*
> *Neither can be written by man the words which he prayed (b)*
> *And the multitude did hear and do bear record (c)*
> *And their hearts were open (d)*
> *They did understand in their hearts the words*
> *which he prayed (c)*

Nevertheless, so great and marvelous were the words
which he prayed, they cannot be written (b)
Neither can they be uttered by man (a) (3 Nephi 19:32–34)

Through their faith in the Savior and through the ministry of the Holy Ghost, these people were blessed with a great miracle. Of this experience, Jesus said, "So great faith have I never seen among all the Jews; wherefore I could not show unto them so great miracles, because of their unbelief" (3 Nephi 19:35).

Whether it comes through the scriptures, or through personal revelation, or through the voice of a living prophet, we obtain the word of God through the ministry of the Holy Ghost. The mission of the Holy Ghost is captured in the descriptions of his work we have in the scriptures—witness, bear record, teach, testify, guide, reprove, sanctify, enlighten, comfort, reveal. Jesus taught his disciples that "the Holy Ghost, whom the Father will send in my name, he shall teach you all things, and bring all things to your remembrance, whatsoever I have said unto you" (John 14:26).

Speaking of the Book of Mormon (and of the words of God in general), Moroni taught that if we go to Heavenly Father with a sincere heart, and ask him with real intent and with faith in Christ, Heavenly Father "will manifest the truth of it unto you, by the power of the Holy Ghost. And by the power of the Holy Ghost ye may know the truth of all things" (Moroni 10:4–5).

It is clear from the scriptural record that sometimes the Holy Ghost works through quite marvelous means to bring us the word of God. The miracle of Jesus' prayer is one example. But, as President Packer noted, more often—indeed, usually—the Holy Ghost works through quiet means. This is why we often speak of the "whispering of the Spirit." The "still, small voice" speaks to our hearts and enlightens our minds when we read the scriptures, or when we listen to the prophets speak. Sometimes the Spirit testifies of truth or gives us knowledge through personal revelation. Sometimes the Spirit tells us what to say. But very often the message is about some action that we should take.

The privilege to be taught and guided by the Holy Ghost is available to all members of The Church of Jesus Christ of Latter-day Saints. Each member receives the gift of the Holy Ghost, the right to have the Holy Ghost as a constant companion. It is like having a special receiver in our hearts that can be tuned to the messages of the Holy Ghost. If we keep that receiver in tune through our diligence in keeping the commandments, through our study of the scriptures, through prayer and fasting, we can have the Holy Ghost with us every hour of every day. Like the sons of Mosiah, we too will have the spirit of prophecy and of revelation, and when we teach, we too will teach with power and authority of God.

But there is one more thing we may receive from the Holy Ghost that is of special importance. Everyone who is in tune, everyone who seeks to obtain the word of God, may receive from the Holy Ghost a testimony that Jesus Christ is the Son of God, the Only Begotten of the Father, the Savior and Redeemer of the world. Paul taught that "no man can say that Jesus is the Lord, but by the Holy Ghost" (1 Corinthians 12:3). Whether it comes as sure knowledge, or as belief in the words of those who know, this testimony of Jesus is a gift from the Holy Ghost: "To some it is given by the Holy Ghost to know that Jesus Christ is the Son of God, and that he was crucified for the sins of the world. To others it is given to believe on their words, that they also might have eternal life if they continue faithful" (D&C 46:13–14).

This, then, is the true objective of all who seek to obtain the word of God. Jesus is the Word of God. All that our Father in Heaven desires to reveal, all that he wants us to know, all of it is in and through his Son. If we would have a deep knowledge of the scriptures, if we would embrace the gospel, if we would comprehend the words of the prophets, if we would receive personal revelation, we must follow the great admonition of Moroni: "And now, I would commend you to seek this Jesus of whom the prophets and apostles have written, that the grace of God the Father, and also the Lord Jesus Christ, and the Holy Ghost, which beareth record of them, may be and abide in you forever" (Ether 12:41).

Wielding the Sword of the Spirit

If we follow the Lord's admonition to Hyrum Smith and "first seek to obtain my word," we qualify to receive the very same promise that Hyrum received: "And then shall your tongue be loosed; then, if you desire, you shall have my Spirit and my word, yea, the power of God unto the convincing of men" (D&C 11:21). This is the power that Paul described as the sword of the Spirit. It is a critical element of the armor of God in the battle against the forces of darkness. It is, therefore, at the center of missionary work.

Alma's experience with the Zoramites in the Book of Mormon illustrates the importance and power of the word of God in missionary work. The Zoramites were an apostate group (Mormon calls them dissenters) that had broken away from the church and had moved into an area near to the wilderness "which . . . was full of the Lamanites" (Alma 31:3). Alma was greatly concerned about the iniquity among the Zoramites, fearing that they might strike up an alliance with the Lamanites. It appears from the record that some among the Nephites had thought about some kind of military action to compel the Zoramites to return, but Alma had a very different approach in mind. This is how Mormon describes Alma's approach to reclaiming the Zoramites: "And now, as the preaching of the word had a great tendency to lead the people to do that which was just—

yea, it had had more powerful effect upon the minds of the people than the sword, or anything else, which had happened unto them—therefore Alma thought it was expedient that they should try the virtue of the word of God" (Alma 31:5).

And so they did. Alma organized a mission to the Zoramites and took with him two of his sons, three of the sons of Mosiah, and Amulek and Zeezrom. This powerful group of missionaries preached the word of God and touched the hearts of many of the Zoramites, particularly among those who were poor. Their preaching also broke the hold that the wicked leaders of the Zoramites had over the people. Mormon writes that the word "did destroy their craft" (Alma 35:3).

The power of the word of God "unto the convincing of men" comes through the ministry of the Holy Ghost. Nephi taught this principle in his great valedictory sermon: "And now I, Nephi, cannot write all the things which were taught among my people; neither am I mighty in writing, like unto speaking; for when a man speaketh by the power of the Holy Ghost the power of the Holy Ghost carrieth it unto the hearts of the children of men" (2 Nephi 33:1).

When we do missionary work today, we do it by preaching the gospel of Jesus Christ under the direction of the Holy Ghost. That is how missionary work always has been done. We do it that way because that is the way in which Heavenly Father's children can hear and feel his voice and his word if their hearts are open and their spirits prepared. In the early days of the Restoration the Lord gave this commandment about missionary work: "And ye shall go forth in the power of my Spirit, preaching my gospel, two by two, in my name, lifting up your voices as with the sound of a trump, declaring my word like unto angels of God" (D&C 42:6).

When we receive the Holy Ghost we have the privilege of speaking with "the tongue of angels" (2 Nephi 32:2). Nephi taught,

"Angels speak by the power of the Holy Ghost; wherefore, they speak the words of Christ" (2 Nephi 32:3). Thus, when we preach the gospel in the name of Jesus Christ, and under the direction of the Holy Ghost, we draw upon heavenly power to say exactly what the angels of heaven would say if they were there—the words of Christ.

Carried by the Spirit, and spoken by true messengers, the word of God has power to dispel darkness, to evoke hope, and to touch the prepared heart. It has that power because it is light and truth. It illuminates life. It carries the doctrines of salvation to the hearts and minds of those who truly hear. It does so because it connects with something that is already there. President Packer taught this important principle in these words:

> Every man, woman, and child of every nation, creed, or color—everyone, no matter where they live or what they believe or what they do—has within them the imperishable Light of Christ. . . .
>
> It is important for a teacher or a missionary or a parent to know that the Holy Ghost can work through the Light of Christ. A teacher of gospel truths is not planting something foreign or even new into an adult or a child. Rather, the missionary or teacher is making contact with the Spirit of Christ already there. The gospel will have a familiar "ring" to them. ("The Light of Christ," *Ensign*, April 2005, 10)

The word of God is like a power source that ignites the light of Christ within the souls of those who hear. Some are so prepared that they receive a witness of the Spirit almost immediately upon hearing the word of God. Some will not listen because their hearts are hard and their ears closed. But even someone whose life is full of sin and darkness, even someone whose heart is hard, even such people have the light of Christ, however dim, within them. If they will listen, if they will hear the words of life and light and truth, the word of God spoken by the Spirit will cause the light of Christ to burn brighter within them. With more truth and more light, even those who begin far away may come to the point where the Holy Ghost may visit them and confirm to them the truth of what they have heard. In this way the word of God can vanquish the forces of evil and bring light and truth and hope and joy to the repentant soul. This is why Paul called the word of God the sword of the Spirit.

Having obtained the word of God, and knowing what it can do when preached under the direction of the Holy Ghost, what shall we do? For full-time missionaries the answer to this question is clear: Find the honest in heart and teach them the gospel of Jesus Christ; talk to all who will listen; contact them through referrals, on the street, at their doors, at church, wherever they are. But what is the answer for members of the Church who are not serving full-time missions? How should we proclaim the gospel? First, we can set an example for all who know us and see us in action. And we can, of course, respond with enthusiasm to teach with the missionaries and support them in other ways as we are asked. But, guided by the Spirit and motivated by love, there is much more we can do to find those whom the Lord has prepared, share with them the word of God, and thus help everyone with whom we speak make progress in their lives.

Over the last several years I have found the following actions to provide a powerful way to help each of us fulfill the covenant we have made at baptism "to stand as witnesses of God at all times and in all things, and in all places" (Mosiah 18:9):

• Make a personal covenant with the Lord that we will speak to those he puts in our path; prayerfully set a date by which time we will have someone for the missionaries to teach.

• Pray each day for opportunities and guidance; courageously pray about specific people, such as an acquaintance or inactive member; pray for the promptings of the Spirit and for faith to act on those promptings; make missionary work a *serious* focus of our daily prayers.

• Be prepared to invite: carry pass-along cards; have copies of the Book of Mormon available.

• Exercise our faith. Speak to those the Lord puts in our path.

• Bear testimony of our experiences. Share our stories with our families, those we serve with in our callings, and the members of our wards.

The starting point for me has been the personal covenant. This personal promise to the Lord that we will speak to those whom he has prepared renews the covenant we made at baptism. It makes explicit our commitment to share the gospel and gives expression to our faith that the Lord does indeed prepare people and can put them in our path. Praying daily for opportunities and guidance makes that covenant a defining characteristic of our lives. In that way, missionary work becomes a significant priority. If we pray every day about sharing the gospel, and every day remember what we have promised, we open our minds to the influence of the Spirit.

Elder M. Russell Ballard emphasized the importance of making missionary work a spiritual priority in his talk on setting a date:

> May I suggest a simple way in which each one of us can exercise our faith and start our personal missionary service. Write down a *date* in the near future on which you will have someone ready to be taught the gospel. Do not worry that you do not have someone already in mind. Let the Lord help you as you pray diligently for guidance. Fast and pray, seeking guidance and direction from our Heavenly Father.
>
> Many, if not all, of you will have special spiritual

experiences as the Lord inspires you. I know from my own personal and family missionary experience that the Lord will enlighten your mind. He will sharpen your vision of this work by bringing names of nonmembers to your mind that you have never before regarded as potential members of the Church. As you continue, you will be blessed to know what you should say and how you should approach each person. ("Write Down a Date," *Ensign,* November 1984, 16–17)

The practice of setting a date as Elder Ballard suggests can have the effect of an action-inspiring deadline if it is accompanied by daily prayer and reflection on missionary work. Setting a date is a powerful way of exercising faith and making our covenant with the Lord specific and tangible. It can help to make sharing the gospel a priority in our lives, an integral part of our everyday walk with the Lord. And I know from my own experience that the Lord will bless us with opportunities to share the gospel. We will meet people he has prepared.

We then confront a very basic question: What should we say to those we meet? What to say may seem straightforward to some, but I have learned that many of us have a hard time sharing the gospel because we do not know how to do it. An experience I had illustrates what I have learned about what to do. The starting point is to open the door, and then, under the direction of the Spirit, share the word of God with those who enter the door, inviting them to take the next step toward the light of truth.

My experience began on a flight to Seattle. I had prepared myself for the trip through prayer and by bringing along pass-along cards, a copy of the Book of Mormon, and Elder M. Russell Ballard's book *Our Search for Happiness.* As I boarded the plane, I discovered two people who wanted to sit together but had been separated. I agreed to switch seats with one of them and sat down next to a man I will call Tom. From many experiences, I knew that if I did not introduce myself in the first twenty seconds after sitting down I would have a hard time engaging Tom in conversation, so I spoke and introduced myself. I learned that Tom was the general manager of an environmental services company and that he lived in Alaska. Over the course of the next hour I asked Tom some questions about his work and his company; I learned a lot about environmental services and about Alaska. I also told Tom some things about myself, and in that telling made sure that Tom knew that I was a member of The Church of Jesus Christ of Latter-day Saints. The Church came up naturally in my description of where I was born, where my children were going to college, my missionary service, and so forth. I think of this as opening the door. But Tom did not pick up on any of it, and seemed uncomfortable when I mentioned something about the Church.

Since this was a six-hour flight, I knew there was plenty of time to see if Tom might be open to learning what I had to share with him. But as the time wore on, I began to think that perhaps this was one of those cases where the person is simply not interested. At about that point in the flight, the time came for dinner. In a quiet moment I decided to offer a short, silent prayer. I told Heavenly Father that I was willing to talk to Tom, but I did not know how to spark his interest. I asked for help. As we ate, we talked a bit more about Alaska (I was interested in his views about drilling for oil in the Arctic). A thought came into my mind: Tom is a pioneer—ask him about moving to Alaska. And so I did. He had moved from New Hampshire to Alaska, and I asked him what it was like to go to such a different and new place. He told me about his experience. As he talked, I had another impression: Tell him about your ancestors.

I told Tom that I had pioneers like him in my family. I then told him about my great-great-grandfathers and grandmothers, and a little about the history of the Church. I asked Tom if he had ever heard that story before. He told me that indeed, he had a friend who was LDS, and he had heard some of it before. Then I said something to him that often opens the door to sharing the gospel: I told Tom how much the Church meant to me. I said, "I love the way my Church helps me understand the purpose of life and brings me closer to God." And then a remarkable thing happened. Tom began to tell me about the help his LDS friend had given him when his son had died shortly after moving to Alaska. He described that experience of anguish and grief and then told me about a comforting, recurring dream he had in which he visited a place where people who had died live, and found that his son was there. This, of course, opened up a wonderful opportunity to teach Tom about the plan of salvation, about the Savior, the Restoration, and the Book of Mormon. I ended up giving Tom the copy of Elder Ballard's book and the Book of Mormon, and I got his contact information in Alaska and encouraged him to contact his friend.

The story does not end there. A short while after I returned home from Seattle, I read in the *Church News* that the Anchorage Alaska Temple had been renovated and would be open to the public for a period of time. I immediately e-mailed Tom and told him about the temple open house. I encouraged him to contact his friend and arrange to go to the open house. He sent me an e-mail sometime later that he had contacted his friend, had gone to the open house, and had been deeply touched by the experience. I do not know whether Tom will ever join the Church. But I do know that our meeting on the airplane was not a coincidence, and that Tom has heard the word of God. He has been touched by the Spirit and has made progress in his eternal journey.

This process of opening the door by bringing the Church into conversation, and then sharing some aspect of the gospel with those who walk through the door, is the way I have found to do the work of proclaiming the gospel in my daily life. The conversational starting point may be something about the history of the Church, or the plan of salvation, or the importance of families, or temples, or the welfare program, or the Book of Mormon, or many other aspects of the Church or the gospel. But that starting point can lead in a natural way to an opportunity to teach the word of God.

When we invite people to take some action on the path that leads to further light and truth—to read, to visit church, to learn more—the Spirit of the Lord will touch their hearts and they will be blessed with some measure of progress in their lives. Whether they accept the invitation or not is up to them. But for us, success is in the invitation. We do not know where they are in their personal journey. We may be the starting point for their journey toward serious investigation of the gospel and the Church. We may be a point on the way. Or we may be the one whose invitation leads them to meet with the missionaries, receive a testimony of the gospel, and enter the waters of baptism. No matter where they are, our invitation is a part of their journey, and it is our great blessing to be part of the Lord's work in their lives.

The last item in my list of what to do to share the gospel is to bear testimony of the experiences we have. The bearing of testimony about missionary experiences brings the Spirit of the Lord into whatever setting we are in. Whether in fast and testimony meeting, in a talk in sacrament meeting, in a family home evening lesson, in a fireside, or in a private conversation, the bearing of testimony helps to inspire and to motivate our family members and our brothers and sisters in the gospel. It helps them to learn how to wield the sword of the Spirit. It helps them develop the courage to speak the words of truth and invitation to those they meet.

Not only can the bearing of testimony help others, but it can also strengthen our faith and help us deepen our commitment to do the Lord's work. Shortly after I had the experience with Tom on the flight to Seattle, I told that story in high council meeting. The meeting took place early (6:30 A.M.) on a Saturday morning. The high council was seated in a semicircle. The stake president asked if anyone would like to share a missionary experience. I volunteered and told the story. As I got to the end, I bore my testimony of the Lord's work. I told the brethren gathered there that I knew that meeting Tom on that airplane was not a coincidence. As I said those words, the Holy Ghost bore witness to me that what I said was true. In that brief moment the Spirit confirmed in a powerful way that the Lord does indeed prepare his children to hear the gospel, that he brings them together with his trusted servants to touch the hearts of those he has prepared, igniting the light of Christ within them with the word of God. Sitting there at that early hour among my brethren of the high council I received a great blessing of the Spirit that strengthened my faith and taught me about the power of the word of God.

The message to me in that experience and in many, many others is clear: In order to put on the *whole* armor of God, including the "sword of the Spirit, which is the word of God," I must do missionary work. I must do missionary work not only by being an example but by giving voice to the things that I know to be true—a loving Heavenly Father, the gospel of salvation through the Lord Jesus Christ, the Restoration through the Prophet Joseph Smith, the Book of Mormon, eternal families, the marvelous blessings that come through membership in The Church of Jesus Christ of Latter-day Saints. I must obtain the word of God through diligent study, through fasting and prayer, and through the ministry of the Holy Ghost. I must seek to have the spirit of prophecy and the spirit of revelation, that I might teach the word of God with power and with authority. And then I must speak the words of truth and invitation to those whom the Lord puts in my path. If I do this, I know that the Lord will bless me with many opportunities to share the gospel, to wield the sword of the Spirit in the marvelous work of building the kingdom of God. And I know that if I do these things, Paul's inspiring admonition to "be strong in the Lord, and in the power of his might" will become a reality in my life.

CONCLUSION

The writing of this book began with an answer to prayer in the middle of the night. That prayer was the beginning of a journey into the scriptures and the words of the prophets. It has been a journey of discovery, reflection, reaffirmation, and commitment. Along the way, what began as a quiet, gentle, even peaceful whisper of the Spirit has become a powerful clarion call. Part of the power of that call comes from the voice of ancient prophets who saw our day with the clarity of true vision. Their voice calls us to trust in God, to exercise faith in the Lord Jesus Christ, to pray, to repent, to covenant, to obey, to listen to the Spirit, to search the scriptures, to serve, to prepare. But it has also come from modern and living prophets who not only have the clarity of true vision, as all true prophets do, but who live and experience what we live and experience. Their voice is a voice prepared for us and for our time. Their message is clear and unmistakable: This is the day and now is the time to "be strong in the Lord, and in the power of his might"; this is the day and now is the time to "put on the whole armour of God."

The Church is growing and flourishing in the world in a wonderful way. But if we could see or even just glimpse its future the way the Lord sees it, we would see that there is much, much more to be done. We would see homes and families of great strength and power in every part of the earth. We would see numerous wards and stakes of great righteousness. We would see a great host of missionaries, prepared and committed. We would see the Church as a beacon, an ensign, the bright shining light of the world. We would see that we are preparing the earth for the second coming of the Lord Jesus Christ, who will come to rule and reign in righteousness in his kingdom on the earth. We would see that The Church of Jesus Christ of Latter-day Saints is the kingdom of God on the earth, the stone spoken of by Daniel when he interpreted King Nebuchadnezzar's dream of the image of the kingdoms of the world (see Daniel 2).

This is the great, unfolding work of the Lord Almighty, foretold by ancient prophets, proclaimed by living prophets. It goes forward in our families, in our wards and branches, in our temples, in missionary work, in family history, in living the gospel, in home teaching, in caring for each other, in making the gospel of Jesus Christ a reality in our lives and in the lives of our brothers and sisters. It is the Lord's work, and it is full of joy and peace, great promises and glorious opportunities. It is the fulfillment of a prophecy made by Joseph Smith in the early days of the Church:

> The Standard of Truth has been erected; no unhallowed hand can stop the work from progressing; persecutions may rage, mobs may combine, armies may assemble, calumny may defame, but the truth of God will go forth boldly, nobly, and independent, till it has penetrated every continent, visited every clime, swept every country, and

sounded in every ear; till the purposes of God shall be accomplished, and the Great Jehovah shall say the work is done. ("The Wentworth Letter," *Ensign,* July 2002, 31)

What Joseph Smith said in 1842 truly describes the work of the Lord in our day. It also describes the great opposition the Church faced in his day and still faces in ours. This has been a theme in the words of the living prophet as well. At the very same time he has rejoiced in the growth and development of the Lord's work, President Gordon B. Hinckley has warned of the dangers we face:

> The flood of pornographic filth, the inordinate emphasis on sex and violence are not peculiar to North America. The situation is as bad in Europe and in many other areas. The whole dismal picture indicates a weakening rot seeping into the very fiber of society. . . .
>
> The tide of evil flows. Today it has become a veritable flood. ("In Opposition to Evil," *Ensign,* September 2004, 3, 6)

> The traditional family is under heavy attack. I do not know that things were worse in the times of Sodom and Gomorrah. . . . We see similar conditions today. They prevail all across the world. I think our Father must weep as He looks down upon His wayward sons and daughters. ("Standing Strong and Immovable," Worldwide Leadership Training Meeting, January 10, 2004, 20; as quoted in Richard G. Scott, "How to Live Well amid Increasing Evil," *Ensign,* May 2004, 100)

If we will listen we can hear the voice of the living prophet warning us about the forces of evil. This is the context in which Paul's admonition to put on the whole armor of God takes on its latter-day significance. As in the days of the Ephesians, we "wrestle not against flesh and blood, but . . . against the rulers of the darkness of this world" (Ephesians 6:12). As in their day, so in ours, the prophets have warned us of two particular elements of the arsenal of evil. The first are the "fiery darts of the wicked" (Ephesians 6:16), or, in the language of the Restoration, "the fiery darts of the adversary" (D&C 3:8; 1 Nephi 15:24). These are the overt, blatant attacks on things of righteousness—ridicule and scorn directed at the Church, its leaders, and its doctrines; the glorification of evil and the denigration of good in popular culture, literature, art, and the media; direct attacks in society on the family, on marriage, and on the bearing and raising of children; harassment of the Saints by governments or by angry opponents, including the destruction of property.

The second are what Paul calls the "wiles of the devil" (Ephesians 6:11). These are the indirect, subtle, devious, insidious temptations the devil uses to get hold of the hearts of the children of men. Much of this has to do with gratification of the natural man: greed, pride, laziness, a desire for recognition and power, satisfaction of sexual appetites, the achievement of wealth and status, control over other people, and the acquisition of "much learning." These forms of wickedness are cloaked in respectability or in popularity. They are presented in small increments, masked by expert packaging. They are a fulfillment of Isaiah's prophecy of our time: "Woe unto them that call evil good, and good evil; that put darkness for light, and light for darkness; that put bitter for sweet, and sweet for bitter!" (Isaiah 5:20).

We live in just such a time, when much of what we see and hear is warped and twisted and it can often seem that the forces of evil are especially powerful. And yet, that impression itself is one of the "wiles of the devil." It is true that we live in a fallen world where Satan can tempt and lure and entrap and enlist to serve his evil purposes. He is the enemy, who "soweth the tares" (the children of the wicked one) and would "choke the wheat" (the children of the kingdom) (D&C 86:3). But the power of Satan is limited. Through the Lord Jesus Christ there is protection and redemption and power to overcome all the "wiles of the devil" and all the "fiery darts of the wicked." That protection and that power is the armor of God. It is available to us all. But if we would "be strong in the Lord, and in the power of his might," we must "put on the *whole* armour of God," every bit of it, so that there are no holes, no chinks, no unguarded, unprotected places where evil may enter in.

To see the armor of God whole, and to put all of it on, we must comprehend that Christ is at the center. It is through him and in him that all the elements of the armor of God have meaning. It is in him and through him that we gain the strength and power to "stand against the wiles of the devil" and to "withstand in the evil day." It is precisely his strength and "the power of his might" that we need. We obtain it through faithful obedience to the plain and simple truths of the gospel.

By way of summary, these are the elements of the armor of God, centered in the Lord Jesus Christ; this is what we must "put on" if we are to be "strong in the Lord":

Take on the name of Christ.

At baptism we enter into a covenant with God to take upon ourselves the name of Jesus Christ. Through faith in the Savior and the power of his atonement, we repent, keep the commandments, and put off the natural man. Through the refining fire of the Spirit we lose the disposition to do evil, experience a mighty change of heart, and become Latter-day Saints. By hearkening to the voice of the Lord, we learn to do the will of the Father. The name of Jesus Christ, the only name given "whereby salvation cometh," is thus written in our hearts. This is the foundation of the armor of God.

Receive the blessings of the priesthood.

We receive the blessings of the priesthood through the oath and covenant of the priesthood. When we are true to our covenants, and magnify our callings, the Lord blesses us with the powers of heaven. Those blessings and powers come when the redemption of the Atonement works in our lives. They are available to all of God's children who are worthy to receive them and who act according to righteous principles. When Paul counsels us to "be strong in the Lord," he is counseling us to receive the blessings of the priesthood.

Go to the house of the Lord and be endowed with power from on high.

If we are to "put on the whole armour of God," we must go to the temple, the house of the Lord. When we enter the temple, we enter into the presence of the Lord and may feel his glory, Spirit, and power. Because the temple is a place of revelation, the Spirit will teach us what is of most worth to us; in that learning there is great power. The temple is a sacred place for making sacred covenants that bind us eternally to the Lord and to our families. The creation of an eternal family through the ordinances of the temple is a critical part of the "whole armour of God" and a tremendous source of divine strength and protection.

Seek truth.

We have been commanded to search after truth, to expand our knowledge of things as they are, as they were, and as they are to come. This commandment is all-encompassing. Our guiding light in the search for truth is Jesus Christ. In his roles as Creator, Light of the World, and Redeemer, Jesus *is* the truth. And he has given us the way (by study and by faith) and the means (the power of the Holy

Ghost) to know the truth of all things. As we search for truth in the Lord's way, our knowledge of the truth will grow and deepen and we will be prepared to "stand . . . , having [our] loins girt about with truth."

Put on the breastplate of righteousness.

If we are to follow the Savior's commandment to "seek . . . first the kingdom of God, and his righteousness," we must learn to obey his commandments, do the will of the Father, and become like the Savior. Our search for righteousness is a development process. As we obey despite all obstacles, the Lord shapes us. We are in his hands, shaped and perfected through his work and through the refining power of the Spirit to become like him. All along the way the atonement of Jesus Christ gives our search for righteousness meaning and purpose and power. To put on the breastplate of righteousness is to "be strong in the Lord."

Embrace the gospel of peace.

The peace of the gospel is peace of the Spirit born of the exercise of faith and obedience to the commandments of the Lord. He is the Prince of Peace. Jesus Christ is the key to establishing relationships of peace with our Heavenly Father, with our brothers and sisters, and with ourselves. He is the key to peace of mind, of conscience, of heart. Through the atonement of the Savior we can become peacemakers, and we can close up to the evil one any room to tempt us with sin, anger, pride, or fear. When the Savior said, "In me ye might have peace" (John 16:33), he gave us the key to the preparation of the gospel of peace.

Stand with the shield of faith.

The great shield in the armor of God is faith in Jesus Christ. When we act with faith in Jesus Christ, we have access to his power.

Each aspect of his being and character, each principle and promise that connects him to us, is like a node in a network with connectors linking the principles (or promises) to the Savior and to one another. As we live gospel principles the connectors grow in number, in strength, and in brightness. The light of Christ flows through the connectors and illuminates the web of faith. The shield of faith in Jesus Christ—the bright, shining, burning web of faith—quenches the fiery darts of the wicked.

Take the helmet of salvation.

Though our ultimate salvation is beyond the grave, we may experience redemption and salvation here in mortality through the atonement of Jesus Christ. To accomplish that purpose the Lord has established his church and the doctrines, ordinances, covenants, and plan of salvation. With faith in Jesus Christ and obedience to the laws and ordinances of the gospel we may experience salvation—hope in a glorious resurrection, a remission of our sins, a new heart filled with the love of God, the powers of heaven to comfort, protect, witness, and teach. Well did Paul call such salvation the helmet or crown of the armor of God.

Wield the sword of the Spirit: the word of God.

The word of God is Jesus Christ and all that he reveals to us through the scriptures, the prophets, and the Holy Ghost. We obtain the word of God and a testimony of Christ through making and keeping sacred covenants, studying diligently, and fasting and praying. The word of God is like a power source that ignites the light of Christ within the souls of those who hear it. If we covenant to speak, pray for opportunities, and work to obtain the word of God, the Lord will bless us with the opportunities to wield the sword of the Spirit in the marvelous work of building the kingdom of God.

This is the armor of God. It is what the Lord intended me to know and understand that night I prayed to him in a moment of great concern and anguish of spirit. The answer I sought is right there in the inspired words of the great Apostle: "Put on the whole armour of God." I already had a lot of it. But the message was and is so clear . . . put on *all* the armor, every bit of it. Become a *true* follower of Jesus Christ. Experience the *mighty* change of heart. Do *all* in your power to have the *constant* companionship of the Holy Ghost. *Magnify* your calling and receive the power and blessings of the priesthood in righteousness. Go to the house of the Lord *every* week. Become an ordinance worker in the temple and go in a spirit of service and of learning. Keep the commandments with *exactness* and honor. *Deepen* your faith in the Savior through fasting and prayer. *Search* the scriptures and the words of the prophets *diligently*. Search them every day. Be more kind, more thoughtful, more willing to serve. Be a peacemaker. Share the gospel. Really *share* the gospel, not just by example. Covenant with the Lord, pray every day for opportunities, and speak the words of truth and invitation in person, in humility.

All this and more came to me over the months as I sought to understand and heed the message of the Lord. That message and all that I have learned is a great blessing. It is a precious gift from my Heavenly Father. Looking back, it is clear that this gift came in what was a time of choosing, though I did not see that at the time. In an important sense, our whole lives are a time of choosing. That is what our mortal probation is all about. But the broad sweep of mortality is full of many specific times of choice. And this was one for me.

I was greatly blessed to serve for ten years as dean of the Harvard Business School. In that time I met many, many wonderful people and saw great courage and wisdom and leadership in action. Because of my position, and because of the institution I represented, I traveled to many countries and was privileged to meet with men and women of great wealth and influence and power all across the earth. Everything that the world offers to honor and reward people I saw in all its splendor and glory. I sat in the great halls (even the greatest halls) of the academic world; I saw the prizes and medals and honors that come to those the world judges to be the best and brightest stars in the firmament. I visited imposing seats of government and stunning offices of state and saw the power that society confers upon its leaders. I have been in the centers of commercial and financial power and seen wealth beyond imagination. I have seen the power of the media in action, and the lure of popularity and celebrity. In short, I have seen in full measure what the prophets have called the "honors of men."

I felt the pull of the world every day I served as dean. I knew early on that I had to be very careful not to get caught up in it. And so I prayed every day that I would always be able to see what happened to me as being a blessing of the Lord; that I would be able to see the Lord's hand in my life; that I would not lean on my own understanding, but trust in the Lord. However, in the last few years I have come to understand that for my heart to be right, I needed to make a deeper choice, a deeper commitment. I had to follow the admonition of Joshua in that great moment of decision for the children of Israel: "Choose you this day whom ye will serve . . . but as for me and my house, we will serve the Lord" (Joshua 24:15). For me, that meant putting on the whole armor of God.

And so, I chose (and I choose) the Lord. I chose to put the Lord Jesus Christ at the center of my life. I chose to put on the whole armor of God. I chose to stand—to stand up, to stand as a witness of God, to stand for truth and righteousness, to stand in holy places. I chose to be strong in the Lord and in the power of his might. And that has made all the difference.

I know the promises are true because I have experienced them.

Like Ammon in the Book of Mormon, I know that through the power of the Lord we can do all things the Lord commands us to do. I know that the power and the protection are real. The armor of God really is like armor. It is the armor of light, the sure protection against the "wiles of the devil" and the "fiery darts of the wicked." But the whole armor of God is more than protection. It also confers on us the capacity to be on the Lord's errand in building the kingdom of God in the great battle against evil in the world. When we put on the whole armor of God, we are prepared to serve him on the front lines of that battle. We become his trusted servants, and he may use us in his work in new and important ways.

The Lord taught me that principle personally and powerfully in the spring of 2005. On a stormy spring evening, I was cleaning up the dishes after dinner. Sue was listening to messages on the phone. Suddenly she said, "Kim, I think you'd better listen to this one." I listened to the message. Sue was right: The message was from President Gordon B. Hinckley's office, asking me to call. I returned the call and waited while President Hinckley came on the line. After asking me a few questions about my service at the Harvard Business School, he asked me if I would be interested in presiding over Brigham Young University–Idaho. I told him that I would. In that moment our lives changed.

We talked some more, and President Hinckley asked me to talk to Sue, to pray and think about it. The next day I called him back and told him that we would love to accept that assignment if that was what he wanted us to do. And so began a new adventure, a new chapter in our lives. In the succeeding days and weeks we had many wonderful experiences that confirmed to us the preparation the Lord had given us in the years and months leading up to President Hinckley's phone call. It is a great privilege to serve at BYU–Idaho, and I know it would not have come had I not made that commitment to put on the whole armor of God.

And so, I thank the Lord every day for his tender mercies, his reaching out for us, his love, and his watchful care. And I know with all my heart and soul that the message that came to me in that night of searching and reaching was a message from the Lord. It was a call to prepare and to choose. It was a call to serve. It is a call to all who would be engaged in the great latter-day work of the Lord. I quote it here once again in its fulness and in conclusion. May it ever sound in our hearts and in our ears in just the way that Paul intended, as a great call to faith, to righteousness, to obedience, and to wholehearted commitment to the Savior:

> Finally, my brethren, be strong in the Lord, and in the power of his might.
>
> Put on the whole armour of God, that ye may be able to stand against the wiles of the devil.
>
> For we wrestle not against flesh and blood, but against principalities, against powers, against the rulers of the darkness of this world, against spiritual wickedness in high places.
>
> Wherefore take unto you the whole armour of God, that ye may be able to withstand in the evil day, and having done all, to stand.
>
> Stand therefore, having your loins girt about with truth, and having on the breastplate of righteousness;
>
> And your feet shod with the preparation of the gospel of peace;
>
> Above all, taking the shield of faith, wherewith ye shall be able to quench all the fiery darts of the wicked.
>
> And take the helmet of salvation, and the sword of the Spirit, which is the word of God. (Ephesians 6:10–17)

INDEX